HANOI
BIOGRAPHY OF A CITY

WILLIAM S. LOGAN holds the UNESCO Chair of Cultural Heritage at Deakin University in Melbourne. He has worked as an advisor and consultant to UNESCO, AusAID and the Australian Heritage Commission, and was a member of the Australian government-funded Hanoi Planning and Development Control Project.

HANOI

BIOGRAPHY OF A CITY

WILLIAM S. LOGAN

UNIVERSITY OF WASHINGTON PRESS
SEATTLE

A UNSW Press book

Published by
University of New South Wales Press Ltd
UNSW SYDNEY NSW 2052
AUSTRALIA
www.unswpress.com.au

Published simultaneously in the United States of America by
University of Washington Press
PO Box 50096
Seattle WA 98145-5096.

Library of Congress Cataloging-in-Publication Data

Logan, William Stewart, 1942- .
   Hanoi, biography of a city / William Stewart Logan.
   p. cm.
   Includes bibliographical references and index.
   ISBN 0-295-98014-1
   1. Hanoi (Vietnam) — History. 2. Hanoi (Vietnam) —
   Description and travel. I. Title.
   DS559.93.H36 L64 2000
   959.7—dc21.   00-060704

Design Di Quick + Dana Lundmark
Print/bind Hyde Park Press, Australia
Cover illustration The Governor-General's palace
(Austral International)

CONTENTS

In memory of my parents, Norma and William Eric

TIMELINE

BC

2879–258	Hung dynasty
850–300	Dong Son culture (Late Bronze Age)
257–208	Thuc dynasty
207–111	Trieu dynasty; ends with Han conquest

AD

39	Trung Sisters lead revolt against Chinese overlords
544–602	Early Ly dynasty
939–68	Ngo dynasty
969–80	Dinh dynasty
980–1009	Early Le dynasty
1009–225	Ly dynasty; capital transferred to Thang Long
1225–1400	Tran dynasty
1400–1407	Ho dynasty
1407–27	Chinese occupation; defeated by Le Loi in 1427
1428–1527	Le dynasty
1470–71	Defeat of Champa kingdom
1527–92	Mac dynasty
1558–1772	Conflict between the Trinh and Nguyen clans
1627	Alexandre de Rhodes, French Jesuit missionary, arrives in Hanoi
1771	Tay Son Rebellion
1802	Nguyen Anh accedes to throne as Gia Long; capital shifted to Hue
1802–1945	Nguyen dynasty
1847	French vessels bombard Da Nang
1859	French forces capture Saigon
1873	Francis Garnier attempts to capture Hanoi

1874	Franco-Vietnamese treaty (Philastre Agreement) opens up Tonkin and Red River trade to the French
1882	Captain Henri Rivière reoccupies the Hanoi citadel
1883	New treaty making Tonkin a French protectorate (Harmond Convention), confirmed by Treaty of Hue (1884)
1887	Indochinese Union formally established with Hanoi as capital
1897–1902	Paul Doumer appointed Governor-General
1930	Foundation of Indochinese Communist Party by Nguyen Ai Quoc (Ho Chi Minh)
1940	French capitulation to Germany; Admiral Jean Decoux appointed Governor-General; Franco-Japanese Treaty signed
1941	Foundation of Viet Minh by Ho Chi Minh
1945	End of World War 2 in Asia and the Pacific; the August Revolution
1946–54	First Indochina War (against France)
1954–76	Democratic Republic of Vietnam, with Hanoi as capital
1955–75	Second Indochina War (against the United States and allies)
1964	Tonkin Gulf incident leads to US military intervention in Vietnam
1973	Paris Agreement (27 January)
1974	Fall/Liberation of Saigon (30 April)
1976	Reunified Socialist Republic of Vietnam proclaimed (July)
1978–79	Third Indochina War (against China)
1986	Sixth Party Congress: introduction of *doi moi* policies
1990	USSR withdraws from Vietnam
1994	End of US-led trade and investment embargo
1995	Vietnam admitted to ASEAN
1995	'Foreign social evils' campaign
1997	Asian financial crisis
2010	Hanoi's 1,000th birthday celebrations

ACKNOWLEDGMENTS

The research for this book was conducted in Hanoi, Paris, Aix-en-Provence, Moscow and at Deakin University in Melbourne. Funding was provided by the Australian Research Council, although some material was collected during the course of my involvement in Hanoi planning projects with UNESCO and AusAID.

Over the years, very many people have given me their support and to them I am deeply indebted. I particularly wish to thank those who assisted me in Hanoi: Professor Nguyen Lan and Mr Ha Van Que at the Hanoi People's Committee Chief Architect's Office; Mr Nguyen Ngoc Khoi, Dr Le Hong Ke and Dr Lai Tinh at the National Institute of Urban and Rural Planning; Mr Ngo Thieu Hieu, Mrs Dao Thi Dien, Ms Vu Thi Minh Huong and Mr Le Huy Tuan at the National Archives Centre No. 1; Mr Nguyen Truc Luyen and Mr Doan Duc Thanh, editors of *Kien Truc*, the journal of the Vietnamese Architects' Association; Professor Phan Huy Le, Head of the Department of History at Hanoi University; the historian and author Nguyen Vinh Phuc; and Hanoi architect Dr Hoang Dao Kinh.

At UNESCO, my work has been encouraged and supported by Anne Raidl, Mounir Bouchenaki, Sonia Ramzi, Hideo Noguchi and Anne-Chantal Lampe, while at AusAID (then AIDAB) Charles Andrews played an important role in developing the UNESCO Old Sector interest into the larger Hanoi Planning and Development Control Project. At the Australian Embassy in Hanoi, Graham Alliband and David Abotomey provided me with initial inspiration and assistance. Mal Horner, Susan Balderstone, Roz Hansen and Lawrie Wilson of the AusAID Hanoi Planning and Development Control Project provided information and encouragement. I am also grateful to Dr Anatoli Sokolov of the Moscow State University who assisted me in Hanoi and Moscow, and to the Russian planners, Natalia Dmitrievna Sulimova, Irena Grigorievna Zabolotskaya and Vladimir Reviakin, who allowed me to interview them about their work in Hanoi.

Many research assistants worked for me on the project in Melbourne and all of them were excellent: Ton That Luyen, Nguyen Minh Phuong, Annabel Biles, Jacinta Vines, David Grabau and Colin Long. Comments by Mr Ton That Quynh Du, now Lecturer in Vietnamese at the Australian National University, on early attempts to map out Hanoi's history were helpful. The translations from Vietnamese were done in Melbourne by Nguyen Ngoc Phach, Nguyen Binh Tri and Dinh Luong; those from Russian are by Rae Mathew, Eliezer Paltiel and Anatoli Sokolov, while those from French are my own.

Except where indicated in the captions, I have taken all of the photographs. I would like to acknowledge the editor of the *Nhan Dan* newspaper in Hanoi, my colleague Ian Adie who graciously provided me with several photographs, and the editors of the journal *Europe-Asia Studies* for allowing me to re-work my article 'Russians on the Red River: The Soviet impact on Hanoi's townscape' for Chapter 6 of this book. The Bibliothèque nationale de France, Musée Guimet, Centre des Archives d'Outre-Mer and Centre Militaire d'Information et de Documentation sur l'Outre-Mer (CMIDOM) in France also gave permission for the use of illustrative materials from their collections.

My family patiently put up with my many trips away from home gathering material for the book. Denise has now accompanied me on several visits and has come to share my enthusiasm for Hanoi and Vietnam. As is usual in book acknowledgments, I end by taking upon myself all blame for errors of omission and commission.

Aerial view of the Van Mieu,
c. 1935, looking towards the
Governor-General's palace and
West Lake. (Musée Guimet,
Paris. ©PHOTO R.M.N.)

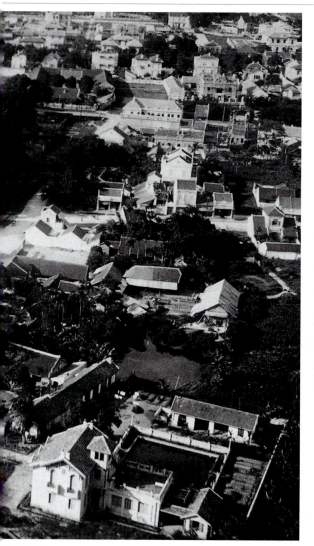

A landscape is a cultural image, a pictorial way of representing, structuring or symbolising surroundings. This is not to say that landscapes are immaterial. They may be represented in a variety of materials and on many surfaces — in paint on canvas, in writing on paper, in earth, stone, water and vegetation on the ground.

Denis Cosgrove and Stephen Daniels (eds), *The Iconography of Landscape* (Cambridge University Press, Cambridge, 1988), p. 1

Hang Chieu Street, the
major east–west axis
through the Ancient
Quarter, 1994.

The presence of the past persistently interferes with the promise of the future. There are no dreams in isolation; all are in reflection and reaction, in a swirling confusion of past existence. This accumulation, on the land and in the mind, causes irreconcilable confusion in the order of things. In the progression of realities the physical presence of so many pasts denies the operation of any simple struggle of opposite, and all attempts at synthesis seem to increase the fragmentation.

Alan Balfour, *Berlin: The Politics of Order, 1737–1989*
(Rizzoli, New York, 1990), p. 249

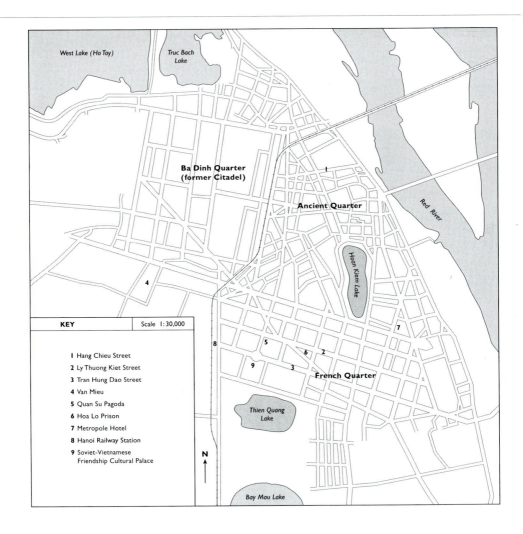

West Lake (Ho Tay)

Truc Bach Lake

Ba Dinh Quarter (former Citadel)

Ancient Quarter

1

Red River

Hoan Kiem Lake

4

7

KEY | Scale 1:30,000

8

5

6 2

9

3

French Quarter

Thien Quang Lake

1 Hang Chieu Street
2 Ly Thuong Kiet Street
3 Tran Hung Dao Street
4 Van Mieu
5 Quan Su Pagoda
6 Hoa Lo Prison
7 Metropole Hotel
8 Hanoi Railway Station
9 Soviet-Vietnamese
  Friendship Cultural Palace

N
↑

Bay Mau Lake

Chapter 1
Ideology, memory and heritage significance

During the Vietnam War, Hanoi was seen as the embodiment of Vietnamese opposition to American might. Over the past decade the war image has gradually been replaced by a new fascination – with the peaceful images of the city's cultural landscape. This goes far beyond an interest in ancient monuments as isolated objects to visit and admire. In fact, by universal standards, Hanoi does not have any great individual monuments. What seems to attract visitors is the distinctive sense of place that this city possesses. Visitors quickly become entranced by the cultural landscape in its entirety – the whole mix of human activities, systems of meaning and symbolic forms within the physical setting of the city. The cultural landscape juxtaposes reminders of the past with the rapid new developments that have been occurring since Vietnam was reopened to the West under the *doi moi* (renovation) policies introduced at Hanoi's Sixth Communist Party Congress in 1986.

Major claims have been made about Hanoi's unique qualities as a city – and there have been a number of recent interventions aimed at protecting these qualities while at the same time helping it to build new infrastructure and achieve higher standards of living for its inhabitants. The municipal planners in the Hanoi People's Committee Chief Architect's Office have developed a *Hanoi Master Plan 2010* that has, as one of its aims, the protection of Hanoi's historic buildings and precincts. In August 1993, and again in June 1999, they prepared sets of regulations for the city's Ancient Quarter. International agencies have also played an important role. The Regional Council of Île-de-France signed a cooperative agreement with Hanoi in 1989 leading to training, economic development and town planning. The Australian government aid agency, AusAID, carried out a Hanoi Planning and Development Control Project in 1994–97. Since 1990, international organisations, especially the United Nations Educational Scientific and Cultural Organisation (UNESCO), have conducted studies, held conferences and made statements about the need to protect the city's cultural heritage. Although the first UNESCO project in 1990 failed to lead to a major international campaign to protect Hanoi's heritage,[1] it remains important as the first 'expert' recognition of the world significance of that heritage – a recognition that continues to be cited by conservationists, both Vietnamese and foreign.

Private organisations and individuals have also been involved. In the early 1990s a group of Australian businessmen operating in Vietnam set up the Friends of Hanoi Architectural Trust, which for a while seemed set upon good works and, indeed, restored a small pagoda in the Ancient Quarter. The Amis du Patrimoine Architectural du Vietnam (Friends of the Architectural Heritage of Vietnam), inspired by the Vietnam-born but then Paris-based architect Cuong Le, had more directly professional interests. Academics, too, from French, German, Dutch, Canadian, Japanese and Australian universities – myself included – have conducted surveys and delved into the colonial archives in Hanoi, Paris and Aix-en-Provence seeking to describe the particular qualities of the city and their origins.

Yet, more than ten years after *doi moi* and despite all this work, modern high-rise buildings have appeared above the traditional roof-line and tree-tops of old Hanoi and little actual protection of the heritage seems to have been achieved. Some scepticism of the motives of the bilateral aid donors is a healthy check against utopian expectations. Certainly, the French government was quite open about its underlying aim of maintaining '*la francophonie*'. The Regional Council of Île-de-France, for instance, sent books and language course materials for present and future leaders.[2] Historic restoration work was a significant part of the lead-up to the major Francophonie conference in Hanoi in November 1998. Like many Western governments, the Australian Hawke and Keating Labor governments (1983–96) tended to link aid and trade.[3] One might also question the cargo cult mentality of some Vietnamese recipients of international aid who have welcomed the computers, motor vehicles and study tours that were part of the aid package but appear to have largely ignored the recommendations of the aid projects.

What does it take to convince a government to implement and seriously enforce cultural policies that include protection of the built heritage? Is it more difficult to win this battle in developing countries, where, as even the staunchest of conservationists acknowledge, the highest priority for government action must go to improving the people's living conditions? These issues resurface throughout this book. But niggling doubts about national and international interventions do not negate the very real fascination that the Vietnamese and foreigners have with Hanoi's cultural heritage. At the most fundamental level, this book seeks to explain what lies at the basis of this fascination and to identify what the threats are to Hanoi's rare heritage. It shows how easy it is for a city to lose its uniqueness and attractiveness, and underlines the need to find policy and planning approaches that balance development and heritage protection.

Hanoi: Contextual and created space

Hanoi has a special (although not visually spectacular) physical setting or 'contextual space'. As a result of the initiative and ingenuity of the people living in that setting, this contextual space became a 'created space' with its own specific dynamic. Another task of this book is to uncover the formative processes, both as they operated historically and as they continue to operate today. Penelope Woolf saw the analysis of Parisian architecture – particularly the Garnier Opera House – as a window on to the period of the French Second Empire when it was constructed; so, too, the analysis of an urban landscape tells us much about the processes of development of the society that constructed that city.[4]

Hanoi occupies part of the Red River flood plain, about 100 kilometres from the Gulf of Tonkin delta. The city lies below the wet season river level, and only a series of man-made dykes prevents it from being inundated and destroyed. The many lakes scattered throughout the city are a reminder that the site was once little more than a swamp. Even today, Hanoi is a physically compact city, contained by the Red River in the north and east, and surrounded by paddy fields on the other sides. It is highly focused on the central area around Hoan Kiem Lake. Much of Hanoi's 'sense of place' derives from the marriage of water and town, the survival of vegetation among the hard built surfaces, and the monsoonal climatic effects that produce the usual hot tropical wet summers but also the unusual, misty grey winters.

The city began with the construction of a royal citadel in AD 1010, the capital of the Dai Viet kingdom covering the Red River delta region. Between it and the river, a market town grew up at the confluence of the To Lich River. Much of the impetus for urban development came from the Chinese traders unloading wares from their junks into their depots on shore. This market town now goes by various names, the Hanoians calling it the Pho Co (Ancient City), while foreigners refer to it either as the 'Ancient Quarter' or, to note the important role of trade and crafts guilds in feudal times, the 'Area of the Thirty-Six Commercial Streets'. The street pattern and temples largely date from the fifteenth century, but most of today's shop-houses were constructed much later, in the colonial period.

During the French colonial era (1883–1954) the city came to comprise five main quarters. The Citadel area acquired a monumental character due to Hanoi's role as political capital of the French Indochinese Union. After 1954 it became known as the Ba Dinh Quarter and was home to the government of independent Vietnam. The Ancient Quarter had become a thriving commercial area occupied by Vietnamese and Chinese. Around and to the south of Hoan Kiem Lake were two areas settled by and largely for the French colonial residents or the Vietnamese elites that collaborated with them – the French (or Western) Quarter and the newer Bay Mau Quarter. The fifth quarter at this time was the Truc Bach Extension to the north-west of the Ancient Quarter. In this book these are referred to collectively as the Old Sector. Sprawling suburbs grew up after World War 2 at a time when Hanoi came under the influence of Soviet bloc countries, especially the Union of Soviet Socialist Republics (USSR). These suburbs are for the most part uniform and uninspiring, and their residents look to the Old Sector for shopping, entertainment and recreation, as well as communal inspiration.

From about half a million in the 1950s, the population has climbed to around three million today. Reflecting the highly focused character of the city, over half a million people move in and out of the Ancient Quarter daily and the street life in that area is a dazzle of colour, smells and sounds. Hanoi has been a boom town during most of the 1990s, its upward trend only coming to a halt with the Asian financial crisis from July 1997. The boom can be traced back to the shift away from economic socialisation that began in the late 1970s, and especially to the introduction of the *doi moi* policies in 1986. Economic liberalisation and modernisation have led to redevelopment pressures that are without precedent in the city's history. The annual growth in Hanoi's gross domestic product is estimated to have been slightly over 11 per cent in 1991–94, rising to 14 per cent in 1996–98. The city is now a jostle of modern cars, taxis, motorcycles, supermarkets and karaoke bars alongside traditional elements such as temples, flower-sellers on bicycles, and pigs driven through the streets to market in the early hours of the morning.

The redevelopment pressures generated by this economic growth present a serious threat to Hanoi's environmental quality according to some of the city's politicians and planners. There is no doubt that the rapid growth represents a challenge – and a stressful situation for decision-makers. The public policy setting in which Hanoi planners work is complicated, inefficient and largely ineffective, and yet the planners are held personally responsible for the physical changes occurring in the city. One consequence is that the city's architectural and planning heritage, which was left mostly intact by American bombs during the Vietnam War and through the lack of commercial redevelopment pressures in the socialist era after 1954, is now in a state of siege.

Hanoi in 1990: Imagined and 'real'

Clearly these changes threaten the collective memory of events and physical settings that Hanoi's population share. Many Hanoi residents feel frustrated that the decades of struggle against the capitalist enemy have come to this. The changes also undercut the mental images people have formed of Hanoi, whether they are residents, or foreigners who visited in the period before this growth began. Already the city is radically different from the time – January 1990 – when I set out on a first visit to Hanoi, capital of the Socialist Republic of Vietnam. I was on a 'mission' for UNESCO, the purpose of the visit being to assist the local planners to prepare a strategy to attract international financial and technical support for the protection of the Old Sector. Although this was before the impact of *doi moi* on the cultural landscape started to be felt, the Vietnamese expected that normalisation of relations with the Western world, especially the United States, would lead to capitalist investment and urban redevelopment. Some Vietnamese planners were keen to put mechanisms in place to protect the heritage before such investment commenced. This was a brief window of opportunity when it might have been possible to make the most of the stagnation of the socialist regime, and to have avoided the loss of the traditional and colonial ambience occurring in other Asian cities that had passed directly from colonialism into capitalist independence. Unfortunately, that window closed quickly without the opportunity being taken.

Few Westerners at that time had a clear mental picture of Hanoi and its cultural heritage. This was in spite of the fact that the city's political masters had engaged first France and then, between 1955 and 1975, the United States and its allies in wars that were among the most intensely covered by the print and electronic media in history. At the time of my first visit, my own vision of Hanoi was of a city largely destroyed by the Vietnam War (1955–75)[5] or by the earlier war against the French (1946–54). Colleagues shared my puzzlement that UNESCO should be showing such interest in Hanoi. A preliminary library search had provided few clues, there being almost no details of Hanoi's urban environment in print in English and little more in French. To my surprise, far from being a city destroyed, I found it still substantially intact – an enchanting city much of which dated from the nineteenth and early twentieth centuries but with a scatter of ancient pagodas and temples often more than 800 years old.

How could the collective Western memory of the Vietnam War and its impact on the cities and towns of Tonkin, the northern third of Vietnam, be so far from the mark? War-time propaganda and media biases had evidently distorted the image of the city, just as one's personal experience

Hang Dao Street, the
major north–south
axis through the
Ancient Quarter, 1991.

of the war – as a member of the military forces sent to Vietnam or, more safely, as a pro- or anti-Ho Chi Minh demonstrator back home – continues to colour attitudes to developments in Vietnam today. What 'really' existed in Hanoi in 1990? For the residents of Hanoi, the usual key factors determining how the individual experiences and remembers the world, such as age, gender, race, ethnicity and occupational category, are augmented by Party membership and length of residence in the city. But most saw Hanoi as the cradle of their civilisation, their capital city and home. Most knew little else, apart from villages and provincial towns they may have visited; few had travelled outside the country, except for those who had been to other socialist countries for education and training. Hanoi was, therefore, an exciting combination of heritage, political monuments, and place of work and recreation.

By contrast, the dominating impression gained by the new visitor was of a quiet and restrained city, run-down but with an underlying elegance. The absence of cars was striking; local people simply walked, rode bicycles or used the pedicabs known as 'cyclos'. A few old Russian trucks trundled through the streets, belching smoke; one or two embassy cars manoeuvred their way through the silent traffic. Around Hoan Kiem Lake were a handful of government department stores, bookshops and a few stalls. It was eerily quiet from early evening, deserted by nine o'clock. Westerners stranded in town after dark ventured into the Ancient Quarter to the Piano Bar where two Vietnamese musicians played old European tunes from memory on an upright piano and violin. Food was limited: the inevitable fried egg for breakfast and the ubiquitous eel as soup or fried as a main course with strong tea or coffee. Caviar and Stolichnaya vodka were plentiful and cheap in the markets, thanks to the Soviet presence, a presence that ended abruptly during 1990. Rousing music was played across the roof-tops on the public address system early each morning, and air-raid sirens marked midday. I stayed in the best hotel in central Hanoi, the Thong Nhat Hotel. This is now renovated as the upmarket Sofitel Metropole. Then the rooms reeked of damp, paint peeled on the walls, exposed electrical wiring made using the bathroom life-threatening, and rats ate the soap during the night. Calls home were from a 'Dr Who' phone box installed in the hotel lobby with sometimes an hour's wait to connect with the outside world. It was obligatory to have the police check passports within 24 hours of arrival, and special visas were required to travel outside the city. A trip by jeep to Ha Long Bay, 150 kilometres from Hanoi, took eight hours each way over meandering roads filled with pot-holes, bicycles and bullock carts.

One of my first appointments was with the Australian ambassador to Vietnam, Graham Alliband, at the embassy compound in Ly Thuong Kiet Street. Alliband and Gough Whitlam, the former Australian Prime Minister who visited Hanoi in the mid-1980s, had been key figures in the process that led to the planners at the National Institute for Urban and Rural Planning taking these first steps towards protecting the Old Sector.[6] The embassy is located in the French Quarter laid out by the French colonial authorities in the late nineteenth century. The area's street pattern is typical of French town planning of the time – broad boulevards, neatly kerbed and lined with trees, wide footpaths, decorative iron or masonry fences, and stuccoed villas and administrative buildings.

But within a short block or two of the embassy are other landmark buildings, including several dating from far more distant eras. The Quan Su (Ambassadors) Pagoda stands diagonally opposite, one of the most important, well-patronised and colourful Buddhist complexes in Hanoi. Built in the twelfth century, it is a significant monument from the pre-colonial period when Vietnam enjoyed independence. But is the pagoda culturally Vietnamese – or is it in fact Chinese, a reflection in the landscape of the earlier thousand-year period of incorporation within the Middle Kingdom (111 BC–AD 939) and the longer period of Chinese suzerainty over northern Vietnam?

Left The Australian Embassy, 1995.
Right Quan Su Pagoda, 1991.

A block to the north behind a high stone wall was Hoa Lo, the notorious prison erected by the French to hold those who transgressed colonial law. At the end of Quan Su Street stood yet another contrasting building – the Soviet–Vietnamese Friendship Cultural Palace. This was built in the 1980s according to the principles of the international modern movement as interpreted by its Russian architects. Like others built during the period 1955–90, when the former Union of Soviet Socialist Republics was Vietnam's main source of foreign aid and expertise, its architecture owed little to the local culture; rather, it was based on a prototype developed in Moscow for replication around the Soviet Union and its dependencies.

The Soviet Union's rival both on the world stage and here in Vietnam, the United States, while not a colonial power, has also made its presence felt on numerous occasions and in various ways – during the Vietnam War, during the trade and investment embargo it imposed from the 1970s to 1994, and now during the post-embargo period. Near the Australian Embassy the Americans left a hostile impact at the end of adjacent Tran Hung Dao Street where Hanoi's main railway terminal – the Ga Ha Noi, the word itself deriving from the French '*gare*' – closes off the vista. This is the only major building in central Hanoi obviously to have suffered from aerial attacks during the war years, its main pavilion having been destroyed by a laser-guided 'smart bomb' during an American B-52 raid in December 1972. The two wings were left standing, their French architecture still intact, but are now connected by a concrete block building of little architectural significance.

Reading cities: Ideology and city formation

The area around the Australian Embassy is not atypical. Hanoi's cultural landscape is a complex mix of styles constructed over a thousand-year time span. To make sense of this mix, one can usefully start by appreciating that Vietnamese cultural and, hence, national survival in the face of numerous foreign invasions was only achieved by 'bending with the wind' — that is, by adopting many of the features of the invader's culture while managing, at the same time, to preserve key elements of their own. The survival of language and legends has been particularly crucial, making the intangible heritage as significant to the Vietnamese as the tangible. Another result of this process, however, is that Vietnam's cities today are characteristically multi-layered, each layer the legacy of a period of political and cultural domination by an external power. Hanoi's environment is now strewn with political icons, each regime having produced buildings, streetscapes and whole districts to demonstrate its ideology, and, by so doing, its mastery of the city and its people.

It is this cultural layering and the sense that one feels in Hanoi of the cultural landscape being a kind of palimpsest — a manuscript through which earlier texts keep coming to the surface — that helps to give Hanoi its unique character. Just as Alan Balfour takes an interest in Berlin's 'layers of living residue', the 'ideals, myths and fictions of a culture seen through the reflections of architecture, architects, and artists',[7] so this book uses the architectural vestiges as a way into understanding the cultural development of Hanoi, and by extension Vietnam more broadly. This approach also enables an attempt to be made to explain the significance of the key built elements in today's Hanoi — in other words, the cultural heritage to be found in the Hanoi townscape.

In Hanoi the cultural layers represent different external influences — Western (French colonial, Soviet socialist) and Eastern (Chinese). Much of the influence was indirect — through the setting of tastes in architecture — rather than through actually building public edifices. This means that what we see is not only the architects' and planners' attitudes, but also the attitudes and expectations of their clients, whether government or private, and of the various strata in society in the various periods. Sometimes the impacts are negative — that is, they were destructive rather than creative —

Top Ly Thuong Kiet Street and
Hoa Lo Prison walls, 1991.

Above Soviet–Vietnamese Friendship
Cultural Palace, 1994.

Left Ga Ha Noi
(Hanoi Railway Station), 1995.

as with some of the interventions of the French in the 1890s or the Americans in the late 1960s and early 1970s. To take an example, the Ga Ha Noi might have little architectural significance in itself, but it is a symbolic place: it has high cultural significance as a reminder of a major destructive intrusion in the life of the city and of the constraints on post-war reconstruction due to the imposition of the trade and investment embargo. Very frequently, however, impacts have both positive and negative effects and often the 'binary differentiation', as Christine Boyer in her study of the 'city of collective memory' calls it, cannot be maintained.[8] In Hanoi, it is true that many ostensibly noble acts of urban creativity, especially in colonial times, were made on the foundations of social and economic displacement, both on the specific building site itself and in society generally.

In Hanoi, power, planning and architecture have long gone hand in hand. Architectural drawings and maps are valuable sources of insight into a regime's intentions in the realm of town building. Maps show what the authorities want the user to see. The imperial maps of Hanoi, for instance, showed the royal city but frequently omitted the market town outside its gates. The French Indochinese colonial authorities, and the independent governments of socialist North Vietnam and the post-1975 reunited Vietnam, all used the techniques of city development and map description to provide evidence of their authority and the strength of their political ideology. The maps of Hanoi trace the way government administrators thought about the city and how they wanted the map readers to see the city and their work on it. Each successive regime created new maps of Hanoi, both on the ground and on paper. A townscape is a physical manifestation of the cultural and economic environment in which it developed, and Hanoi's recent physical changes are a clear visual reflection of Vietnam's transformation from socialist and moribund to capitalist and resurgent. Today's planners are creating a new Hanoi, and cartographers are drawing up new maps for a new millennium.

Beyond this, each regime has attempted to define, for the people, which elements of the urban environment were to be regarded as symbolically significant, treasured as part of the city's 'heritage' and protected against physical damage. Much of this heritage is now threatened by the post-*doi moi* urban transformation. The national and international heritage conservation interventions may ultimately be doomed to failure. This book discusses many critical issues applying to heritage protection not only in Hanoi and Vietnamese cities, but in all cities in societies undergoing rapid economic transformation.

In Hanoi the rush to modernise is changing forever the fundament-al character of parts of the city and their environmental assets. The speculative building urge has led, for example, to land reclamation, much of it illegal, around the shores of Hanoi's many lakes and along the dyke roads. Much of the reclaimed land has been for the development of luxury residential units for the Vietnamese nouveau riche and foreign business people. The traditional linkage between lakeside pagodas and the water has been destroyed. New housing has been spreading throughout the Ancient and French quarters and encroaching on the main dyke wall along the Red River. High-rise office, hotel and apartment buildings constructed with foreign funds have already transformed sections of the French Quarter; indigenous investment is doing much the same for the Ancient Quarter.

Some changes are inevitable and desirable in order to bring living and working environments up to modern standards. But a lively and far from finished debate continues about where and what kind of development should be allowed, and what precisely is the urban environmental heritage that should be protected. This debate is not a new one: indeed, there has been a long history of heritage contestation and re-definition in Hanoi reflecting the succession of political regimes controlling the city.

Until the 1990s the urban elite, had it been asked which were the most culturally significant buildings and sites in the city, would probably have identified the Sino-Vietnamese elements – pagodas (chua), dynastic temples (den) and shop-houses, especially in the Ancient Quarter, as well as the Van Mieu (Temple of Literature), Vietnam's oldest university. They would have relegated to second rank the buildings, such as the communal houses (dinh), emanating from rural Vietnamese communities now being engulfed in the expanding city. Their view of the heritage would have excluded altogether the vestiges of French colonial presence, reminders of an era they were then only too keen to forget. For some of the elite, memories of the colonial period were tainted by feelings of guilt about their easy collaboration with the French overlords. For others, especially those who fought long and hard for national independence, memories were coloured by oppression and punitive measures experienced at the hands of the colonial masters.

Under the socialist banner, Vietnam's national government and the People's Committee of Hanoi preferred to ignore the French impact and defined the official heritage as comprising the traditional Sino-Vietnamese (which they simply regarded as Vietnamese) and the buildings and sites that saw the revolutionary movement unfold. By the mid-1990s, however, attitudes were changing towards the French colonial heritage, while it was the Soviet bloc influence that was being down-valued.

Collective remembering: Memory, myth and heritage

These examples – the re-casting of Sino-Vietnamese as Vietnamese and the overlooking of negative colonial effects on Hanoi – demonstrate the problematic nature of separating the 'remembered city' and its heritage from a portrait of the city and its heritage that might meet more universally recognised standards of historical veracity. This task confronts both the reading of a city by the social scientist and the development of policy for the city by Vietnamese politician or planner. In the fields of urban planning and heritage conservation, the analysis of what legacies from the past are significant depends heavily on memory – how people recall and attribute significance to past events and environments. This clearly is not an objective matter, but one fraught with prejudices, unintended misconceptions and deliberate distortions. The nature of memory then, both in the individual and the collectivity (group, community, nation), impacts upon heritage definition. This includes the deliberate distortion of memory for use as a political weapon – 'wilful nostalgia', as Roland Robertson calls it[9] – a form of cultural politics as well as embodying the politics of culture. To control a society's memory largely conditions the hierarchy of power; that is, the dominant group uses images of the past as part of a deliberate strategy to maintain their hegemonic power in the present social order.[10]

Marc Askew has described the manner in which the Thai elite went about creating a particular set of 'national' memories in order to legitimate the regime.[11] This included the establishment of a 'Thai traditional architecture' that is now part of the official heritage. During the French colonial period in Indochina, it was part of the colonial project to discover or invent traditions to bind the subjects into French-defined 'communities' – the Lao, Cambodians, Tonkinese, Annamese and Cochin-Chinese – and then into a totally new piece of geo-space, French Indochina. Panivong Norindr sees French Indochina itself as 'an elaborate fiction, a modern phantasmatic assemblage invented during the heyday of French colonial hegemony in Southeast Asia'.[12] This extended to the creation of the *ao dai* as the national costume for the women of Tonkin, Annam and Cochinchina and to the assertion that the French colonial administration was based on the noblest of ambitions – their *mission civilisatrice* or 'civilising mission'. By contrast, Kammen argues that memory distortion commonly occurs in *post-colonial* situations 'where the creation of national identity is necessary for functional reasons of political and cultural cohesion'.[13]

A frequent conclusion of studies in this area is that societies hold beliefs about their pasts that are based on myths bearing little resemblance to the events that gave rise to them but that, instead, take on a life and 'reality' of their own. Historian Wang Gungwu claims that, in fact, history and myth are interdependent in every culture, but that this is not appreciated in traditional Western historiography.[14] Fanciful interpretations of history become myths; myths become 'facts' and help to shape events, the future's history.

In the field of heritage conservation, myths are important and often totally benign. Indeed, they are themselves part of a society's intangible cultural heritage, as well as giving meaning to places associated with them. To take a prime example, the myth of Venice's perfect union of society and space was propagated by the Venetians themselves and moulded into the landscape of their city.[15] It has become a symbolic landscape of enduring significance for Europeans and, now by its inclusion on the World Heritage List, for the entire world. Hanoi maintains similar myths about its venerability and the uniqueness of its architectural and planning practices, such as the vaunted marriage of water and city. In the case of Hanoi, too, the heritage significance of many buildings lies not in their bricks and mortar but in the myths attached to them, the interventions of the gods and the fanciful tales of kings.

But myths – or information more generally – can also be used as propaganda tools to shape the community's perception. The myths become the 'received truth', their ideological function altering with changes in the regime in power. The use of Burmese historic monuments and sites as icons of Myanmar nationalism by the current junta in Rangoon is a case in point. For Eric Hobsbawm, it is in nationalistic politics that wilful distortion is at its worst: 'The past legitimises. The past gives a more glorious background to a present that doesn't have much to celebrate.' The invented past does it much better! 'Myth and invention,' he writes,

> ... are essential to the politics of identity by which groups of people today, defining themselves by ethnicity, religion or the past or present borders of states, try to find some certainty in an uncertain and shaking world by saying 'We are different from and better than the Others'.[16]

The collective memory is generally propped up by official actions, including support for memory repositories such as archives, libraries, museums and other collections of socially produced artefacts, or the funding of history teaching and research in schools and universities. The past is often memorialised through the erection of monuments, or the observance of remembrance rites. But although constructing cultural objects as memoirs of the past may help to mitigate the fading of memory, they also change the past: turning something into a monument or memorial changes the past in that very process. Memorialisation, Michael Schudson notes, 'moralizes the past, creates out of a chronicle a tradition'.[17] This applies, too, to memorialising an event: memorialisation invests it with extraordinary significance in our conception of the past.

This falsification of the evidence makes the vital role of the historian and historical geographer in heritage conservation a particularly difficult one. On the one hand, they must identify and balance the various, often-conflicting memories in order to write the history of a place, explaining how the place was culturally constructed and how that construction has altered over time.[18] But on the other hand, they also need to maintain a constant watch on the uses to which history is put and, more critically, the ways in which it can be abused. Without this rigorous process, our understanding of the past will be diminished – and our understanding of the past shapes the future. The scholar's role is to help provide an understanding of those traces of the past that have continuing significance so that they can be kept and other places opened up to redevelopment. This is the only recipe for balancing heritage protection and modern development in cities. It provides the theoretical and practical key to the successful practice of heritage conservation in general and for determining Hanoi's urban heritage in particular.

Structure of this book

Each city has its own story. This is Hanoi's biography. It tells the story of the making of Hanoi's cultural landscape, but it does so in an attempt to enable a better understanding of the evolution of Hanoi's cultural landscape and the historic roles and present-day symbolic meanings of sites, buildings and monuments. In other words, this is an applied history clearly referenced against the present day and seeking to provide a more solid basis for the identification and protection of Hanoi's cultural heritage. More precisely, it falls into the new interdisciplinary field of cultural heritage studies – a blend of history and geography, archaeology and anthropology, architecture and town planning – that is emerging in universities around the world.[19] For the purposes of this analysis, Hanoi's history has been divided into six periods during which different external influences prevailed and different cultural layers were put down. Each chapter moves through historical outlines and descriptions of significant monuments and sites to the discussion of key theoretical and practical issues confronting the conservation of cultural heritage in Hanoi.

Chapter 2 deals with the long pre-colonial Vietnamese era from its nomination as capital city by Ly Thai To, the first king of the Ly dynasty, in AD 1010 to the arrival of the French in the late nineteenth century. During this period the dominant cultural influence was Chinese, and a central question is the extent to which a distinctive Vietnamese national culture was able to emerge. Whatever the answer, the fact is that this Sino-Vietnamese amalgam provided the cultural setting which the French found when they arrived and on to which they proceeded to graft European influences. The chapter emphasises the way in which myths merge with history and became and continue to be one of the important bases for heritage evaluation in Hanoi.

Chapter 3 considers the French colonial period up to the Japanese military takeover in 1940. Some scholars divide this period into two sub-periods. Following André Masson's seminal study of early Hanoi, the first sub-period – from 1873 to 1918 – is frequently referred to (not without an element of irony today) as the *période héroïque*. This was a time when the

French, inspired by their 'civilising mission', sought to tame the local environment and its people and to create a European city in the midst of an exotic, tropical and hostile context.[20] The manipulation of Hanoi's image by the French authorities is also discussed, showing how this was simultaneously motivated by the need to satisfy the colonial ministry and parliament back home in metropolitan France, to bolster the confidence of the *colons* in the future of French Indochina itself, and to convince the *indigènes* of the advantages of French rule. The 'real' character of the *mission civilisatrice* is discussed, setting a stage for the emergence of the Vietnamese nationalist resistance. The second sub-period – from 1918 to 1940 – was marked by a softening of French cultural impacts on Hanoi's townscape, but also by growing Vietnamese resistance to colonial domination. The chapter focuses on the sharp discontinuity that the advent of the French represented for Vietnam and Hanoi, the contrast between traditional and modern, and the impacts of globalisation and urbanisation.

Chapter 4 deals with the period of Japanese control over Indochina (1940–45) and the subsequent abortive attempt by the French to re-establish their colonial hold. Although the Japanese permitted the French to continue administering Indochina, it was nevertheless a critical step in dislodging France's hold on their colonies. The anti-French resistance movement under Ho Chi Minh fought on the Allies' side to dislodge the Japanese, who were seen in Vietnam as imperialists rather than, as in the Dutch East Indies, as saviours from Western colonialism. Hanoi was the principal Vietnamese stage upon which the political battle against colonial France was fought and where independence was proclaimed, first in 1945 and more definitively in 1954 following the French loss at Dien Bien Phu.

During the next period, from 1955 to 1990, Hanoi, as the capital of an independent socialist country, fell within Moscow's orbit and became engulfed in America's Cold War attempts to block the expansion of communism. Chapter 5 seeks to give a picture of what life in the city was like during the Vietnam War, how the city managed to function under the constant threat of bombing raids, and what impact the bombing had on the built fabric of the city, including those elements construed as heritage. The theme of memory distortion resurfaces when causes of the disjunction between the mental images of a war-devastated Hanoi held by many Westerners today and the actual impact on the city are discussed.

Chapter 6 partly overlaps in time – 1955–90 – but focuses directly on Hanoi under the tutelage of the Soviet bloc countries, especially the Russians. This was a period when Vietnamese architects and planners borrowed heavily from their Soviet colleagues in reconstructing war-damaged sections of the city, building new suburbs, and creating a new set of buildings and monuments symbolising the country's independent and socialist status. The chapter investigates how this transfer of ideas and methods took place, itself another significant step in Vietnam's globalisation and move away from tradition.

Chapter 7 commences with the Sixth Party Congress in 1986 that represented another dramatic discontinuity in Vietnamese cultural history. Vietnam began again to open up to Western economic, social and cultural (although not yet political) ideas. How has this new *doi moi* ideology impacted on those urban precincts, buildings and monuments that might be regarded as significant components of Hanoi's cultural heritage? The chapter focuses on the contestation that emerged during the 1990s about Hanoi's sense of place and about the conflict between the planning goals of modernisation through redevelopment and the maintenance of the national and local culture through a process of heritage protection. How has the cultural heritage of the city been redefined and who by? What has been the impact of cultural tourism, blossoming in the 1990s, on the way the Vietnamese politicians, planners and public perceive their city and define its sense of place and its heritage assets?

The final chapter elaborates on the context of increasing economic and cultural globalisation that confronts Vietnam. It asks how globalisation is impacting on socio-political attitudes and what that means for collective memories and the Vietnamese sense of identity and community. The chapter moves this on into a discussion of future planning and heritage conservation objectives for Hanoi as it moves with the rest of the world into a new millennium. The convenient French term '*ville millenaire*' is used; in Hanoi's case it is doubly apt, for Hanoi is also approaching its own 1,000th anniversary in the year 2010. Its political status as capital of an independent and united country now seems assured; its prosperity is on the increase. The current Asian financial crisis gives decision-makers time to pause and reflect on the hectic growth of the 1990s and to contemplate at a more leisurely pace how they want the city to develop in the future.

It is argued that the local and national cultural heritage must remain an essential element in visions for Hanoi. Furthermore, since there is no single objective set of memories or no one definitive history of the city, the chapter concludes by urging that the heritage be defined in the most inclusive terms possible. All cultural layers are significant, representing important stages in Hanoi's history. Overriding this, however, is another imperative – that participation in the process of determining what makes up the city's heritage and how the city's future development might proceed should be as inclusive as possible. As Vietnamese society becomes increasingly pluralist, there are signs that a wider range of groups are wanting a say in such decision-making, rather than continuing to depend on top-down direction from the political elite. The increasingly public debate about architectural, town planning and cultural heritage values is one of the important vehicles for the continued democratisation of Vietnamese society.

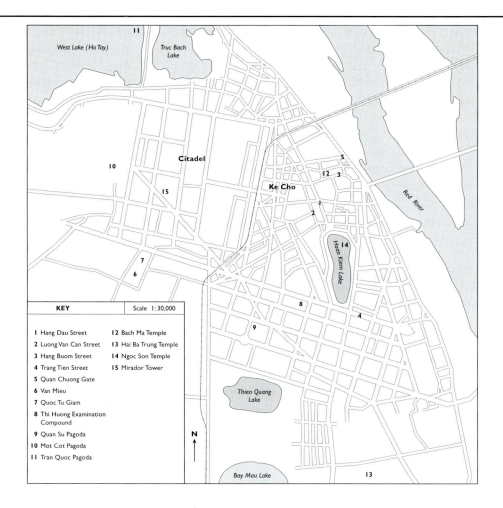

West Lake (Ho Tay)

Truc Bach Lake

Citadel

Ke Cho

Red River

Hoan Kiem Lake

Thien Quang Lake

Bay Mau Lake

KEY	Scale 1:30,000

1 Hang Dau Street
2 Luong Van Can Street
3 Hang Buom Street
4 Trang Tien Street
5 Quan Chuong Gate
6 Van Mieu
7 Quoc Tu Giam
8 Thi Huong Examination Compound
9 Quan Su Pagoda
10 Mot Cot Pagoda
11 Tran Quoc Pagoda

12 Bach Ma Temple
13 Hai Ba Trung Temple
14 Ngoc Son Temple
15 Mirador Tower

N

Chapter 2

Thang Long, the ascending dragon: Pre-colonial Hanoi and the Chinese imprint

Feudal Hanoi: Religion, city and the state

In a central location in Hanoi's French Quarter stands the handsome and well-patronised Quan Su Pagoda, a precinct of interconnected cement-rendered brick pavilions and courtyards. Worshippers gain access to the complex through a three-entrance gate surmounted by a bell tower. The main prayer hall contains numerous altars, including the Nine Dragon Throne, and stands high over a small entry yard with bonsai plants in ceramic pots. Teaching and dormitory buildings surround the hall on three sides. As is common with Vietnam's ancient pagodas, the date of establishment is a matter of some uncertainty, but it was probably erected around the time of Hanoi's foundation a thousand years ago.[1] When it was first constructed, the pagoda stood quite some distance from the royal court, amid rice fields and villages, and it probably also had a cemetery and orchard, typical features of Vietnamese pagodas.

Quan Su translates as the 'Ambassadors' Pagoda', referring to its origins in an era when Buddhism was the national religion and as the place where ambassadors from the adjacent tributary Lao and Champa states came to pay their respects to the Lord Buddha during their visits to the Vietnamese capital. From this illustrious start, the pagoda has gone on to become one of the most important in the country. From 1492 it was the central pagoda for the emerging Buddhist organisational network. Last century, it became the headquarters of the Buddhist Association of Tonkin in 1934 (as part of an Asia-wide resurgence of Buddhism), and in 1981, following the reunification of North and South Vietnam six years earlier, it became the chief seat of the national Buddhist Sangha (Vietnam Buddhist Church). Currently the Sangha controls nearly 14,500 pagodas and 28,500 monks and nuns across Vietnam.[2] The Most Venerable Thich

Quan Su Pagoda.
The pagoda's importance
within Vietnamese Buddhism
ensures its periodic repair
and restoration (most
recently, in 1941 and 1996).

Tam Tich of Quan Su Pagoda was elected Patriarch of the Sangha in 1997.

At the time of Quan Su Pagoda's construction, the Vietnamese kingdom – known as Dai Viet – was confined to the Red River delta area of northern Vietnam, but already its capital, Thang Long, was acquiring significant political status within mainland South-east Asia. As its name suggests, Indochina lies between Asia's two major blocs, India and China, a shatter belt both geographically and culturally, bearing the impacts of Indian and Chinese expansion on the indigenous peoples and their civilisations. Thang Long's physical appearance reflected the resulting split personality. The Chinese had, by the third century AD, annexed Tonkin as its southernmost province and maintained direct control over it until the Vietnamese victory in the first Bach Dang River battle of 938. Thereafter, China maintained a tributary relationship over 'independent' Vietnam for almost another a thousand years. This long duration meant that the Chinese imprint was indelibly established over most aspects of Vietnamese life. By contrast, India's stay was short-lived and it merely sowed the seeds of cultural change, particularly among the peoples who formed the Champa in the middle section of Vietnam, later known as Annam.[3]

Buddhism was, however, one of India's lasting contributions to Vietnamese cultural life. Whether it came directly from India or by way of China is not clear. Some scholars believe the religion entered the region and began replacing the existing animist beliefs in about 300 BC, probably as a result of Indian traders landing along the coast of the Gulf of Tonkin in search of spices and silk. Others, such as D.G.E. Hall, assert that it came from China at the end of the sixth century.[4] Being the Mahayana form of Buddhism rather than the Theravada form that dominates India, the second theory seems to have credibility. But whatever the process of entry into Vietnam, it spread rapidly in the relatively stable and prosperous centuries under the Ly (1010–1225) and Tran dynasties (1225–1400). Indeed, some scholars suggest that the first Ly king adopted Buddhism as the main foundation for the social evolution of independent Vietnam in order to create a deeper separation between his country and China.[5]

Today, Buddhist pagodas (*chua*) are conspicuous elements in the cultural landscape of town and countryside. Early pagodas followed a number of distinctive architectural layouts deriving, like the religion itself, from India, but these have become confused in the multi-style pagodas built in urban areas, like the Quan Su.[6] The Mahayana form of pagoda is characterised by a rich pantheon of transcendent Buddhas or 'enlightened ones', gods of Buddhist cosmology and Buddhist saints. Chu Quang Tru claims the Indian *vihara* (multi-celled monastery) was the source of inspiration for the quadrangular towers that marked the major pagodas of the Ly dynasty. Most of these towers have not survived.

The Hanoi townscape features many significant Buddhist pagodas from this early period. The Dien Huu Pagoda (also known as Mot Cot or One-Column Pagoda) is an exceptional case both in its survival and its unique design in the shape of a lotus flower rising from a pool. It was built in 1049 by King Ly Thai Tong (1028–54) who, according to legend, dreamt of Bodhisattva Avalokitesvara, the Buddhist deity, sitting on a lotus throne.[7] The sixth-century Tran Quoc Pagoda, housing the Ten Kings of Hell statues, served the highest priests of the royal court and was the Buddhist centre of Hanoi until that role was taken over by the Quan Su Pagoda. It was shifted in 1615 from the riverside Yen Hoa hamlet to an islet on Ho Tay to the north of the Royal Citadel. The main pavilion of the pagoda demonstrates the typical Vietnamese method of sitting the timber pillars on stone sockets rather than embedding them in the floor as in Chinese construction.

Rival modes of thought also penetrated from Vietnam's northern neighbour, China, in the form of Taoism and Confucianism. These pre-dated Buddhism, being brought in by the first Chinese rulers, and blended with

Left The Mot Cot Pagoda houses a fertility shrine dedicated to a Buddhist deity. Here the pagoda is seen in a state of disrepair in 1922. (Musée Guimet, Paris. ©PHOTO R.M.N.)

Opposite page Entrance to the main pavilion of Tran Quoc Pagoda on West Lake.

animist and the later Buddhist beliefs to form a single system of morality accepted by many Vietnamese.[8] The result is a degree of cultural confusion that remains today. In the pagodas, for instance, Buddhist deities mingle with Taoist saints, spirits and heroes, as well as statues of Confucius. Taoist temples (*den*) also dot the cultural landscape alongside the Buddhist pagodas. Taoism was originally derived from the philosophical doctrine of Lao-tzu, centring on the metaphysical notion of man's oneness with the universe. In Vietnam it was generally accepted as much as Buddhism and Confucianism until the end of the Tran dynasty, but thereafter began to degenerate into a kind of polytheism with innumerable gods, the supreme one being Ngoc Hoang (Emperor of Jade). Other major gods are Diem Vuong (King of Hell) and Long Vuong (King of Waters), and there are innumerable lesser household gods. This degenerate form of Taoism has left Vietnam with many practices considered superstitious by many in Vietnam and the West alike, including sorcery, witchcraft, horoscopy, chiromancy and geomancy, as well as religious cults.

By contrast, the imprint of Confucianism on today's landscape is more muted. Cults based on the ethical system of Confucius, the sixth-century BC Chinese philosopher, were established in the Vietnamese court in the eleventh and twelfth centuries AD. However, at that time, Confucianism existed in a Buddhist environment and had little influence on imperial policy-making.[9] It was not until the thirteenth century under the Tran dynasty that the influence of Confucianism, along with Taoism and geomancy, can be said to have regained the dominant status they had enjoyed before the rise of Buddhism. During the fourteenth century a Confucian establishment began to emerge out of the cultural confusion, with the first known proclamation being made in 1318 enforcing a Confucian social order – that father and son, husband and wife, master and servant were not to make accusations against each other.[10] By the fifteenth century, the Confucian ethic had clearly triumphed over Buddhism, with the Later Le dynasty kings being totally imbued with Confucian thought. At this point, Confucianism became the official state doctrine.

The relative strength of Confucianism and Buddhism continued to shift over the following centuries. From the fifteenth to the seventeenth century, Buddhism declined further as Confucianism became more formalised.[11] Indeed, the kings deliberately put a brake on Buddhism's growth for fear it would undermine Confucianism (and imperial attempts to re-sinicise the society), and under the Le kings the construction of new monasteries was forbidden.[12] But Buddhism re-emerged during the eighteenth century in the period when the Vietnamese had taken over the Champa lands and moved into the Mekong River delta of southern Vietnam. This was a period marked by a weakened royal court and an intense rivalry between the leading noble clans in the north and south – the Trinh and Nguyen, respectively. This unstable political situation ultimately led to the installation of a Nguyen prince as King Gia Long (1802–20), the establishment of the Nguyen dynasty that lasted until 1945, and the transfer of the royal capital from Hanoi to Hue. Despite the instability, the majority of pagodas that are now referred to as 'ancient' were either built or restored in this period.[13]

Under the Nguyen kings, Buddhism again fared less well, particularly under Gia Long and the long-reigning Tu Duc (1847–83). Since 1955, when independent Vietnam became communist, the religion has been deprived of much of its property, autonomy and centrality in Vietnamese life. Nevertheless, the Buddhist pagodas have maintained an important role in Vietnamese cities and countryside alike, not only as places of worship but also as hospices, retreats and training centres. They also function as the sites of cultural activities such as traditional ceremonies and festivals, helping to strengthen the solidarity of local communities in times of war and economic hardship. Visitors to the more significant pagodas will notice wall plaques indicating official recognition as 'historical and cultural vestiges'. Such protection by a communist state originated with President Ho Chi Minh's 1945 Decree No. 65 which declared that 'it is forbidden to destroy communal houses, pagodas, temples, shrines and other religious places, palaces, ramparts, mausoleums and tombs which have not yet been preserved'.

There is a debate among academics about whether South-east Asian societies had any significant indigenous urban base, or whether cities only emerged under the influence of imported ideas and practices from India, China or, much later, the colonising West. Some scholars regarded the city as an alien implant, 'at least in the Western sense of being an economic and administrative centre and the focus of capital accumulation'.[14] Others contend that, although South-east Asia was overwhelmingly agricultural, some urban centres have long played a major role in the history of the region, culturally, politically and economically.[15] According to Australia's leading Vietnam historian, David Marr, Thang Long was one of these, serving during its millennium under the Chinese a hinterland stretching beyond present-day Guangzhou and Hong Kong. Between the fifteenth and eighteenth centuries it was one of the largest Asian trading ports, comparable in size, it is said, to Venice.

In his study of cultural adaptation in mainland South-east Asia, Charles F. Keyes identifies three different types of ancient cities.[16] The first type comprised 'sacred' or 'temple' cities situated in territories where the agrarian population believed the cities radiated the religious virtue necessary to ensure the people's prosperity. These were characteristic of the Indianised parts of South-east Asia and included Vijaya, capital of the Champa kingdom. The second type were 'entrepôt' or 'trading' cities, like Oc-Eo which had developed by the early Christian era in the kingdom of Funan in what is now southern Vietnam. Such cities may have had some religious role too for the rural population, but they had mostly grown on the basis of regional trade. They were characteristically more cosmopolitan than the sacred cities. Keyes's third type were the 'citadel' or 'garrison' cities, found in the northern part of mainland South-east Asia, such as Tonkin, where the Chinese had established control. Their role was essentially military, political and administrative, although culture came to the service of the regime making the role of royalty and religion more significant than in the case of Western citadel towns.

Keyes sees Thang Long as based on this Chinese model, being the cultural and religious centre, as well as the political centre, of the Vietnamese state. However, the city varied from the theoretical type to the extent that, according to most contemporary observers, the royal city was relatively mediocre and run-down. By contrast, an adjacent market town – Ke Cho – flourished. Nevertheless, although market forces clearly existed as an agency of city formation, they do not seem to have completely determined social life in Hanoi. Relationships were based on kinship, status was derived from both traditional ethnicity and occupations, and townspeople lived in tightly woven and controlled webs of friends and acquaintances that were both local and city-wide in scale.[17] In other words, feudal Hanoi was perhaps more like Terry McGee's notion of the 'composite' city[18] – initially a garrison town, later acquiring something of a religious ('temple') character, but from early days being dominated by the trade and crafts of Ke Cho. During the period of direct Chinese rule, the city's growth was organic, with the planned capital city – the citadel Thang Long – being imposed in the eleventh century.

While cities generally act as growth poles and influence the surrounding countryside, a recurring theme in Vietnamese history has been the frequent re-injection of rural belief systems into the city. Redfield and Singer, in their influential paper on the cultural roles of cities, distinguished between the 'great traditions', determined and institutionalised by the traditional elites, and the 'little traditions' characterised by popular customs, attitudes and practices largely spawned in the rural areas.[19] Confucianism falls into the 'great traditions' category: its significant status was clearly dependent on the urban elite in Thang Long and other cities, and its physical or built manifestations were largely confined to the cities. Buddhism, by contrast, lies across the boundary, being both urban and rural and, with a greater influence on the common people than Confucianism, more like a 'little tradition'. Moreover, as Askew and Logan point out, the 'little tradition' often survived (and still survives) in old localities that have become engulfed in expanding urban cities like Hanoi. In this way, many ancient Buddhist pagodas constructed originally in rural villages and hamlets, as well as rural beliefs and customs, now form part of the cultural heritage of the city.[20]

Tied to the 'little tradition' are myths or legends, being popularly believed but fictitious narratives of historical events, frequently with a supernatural element. Frequently, too, the origins, design or names of cities, buildings and precincts are attributed to mythical events and persons, and it is belief in the myth that gives those urban features their cultural significance. The naming of the new royal city, Thang Long, is one such case. Historical evidence indicates that it was built in 1010, replacing the earlier capitals at Co Loa (275–179 BC, and again from the sixth century AD to 948), 20 kilometres north-east of Hanoi, and Hoa Lu (968–1009) in the limestone mountains of Ninh Binh Province. Myth has it that King Ly Thai To, while alighting from the royal boat to enter his new citadel, saw a dragon rising into the sky and he named the place Thang Long ('ascending dragon'). No doubt he was also keen to erase the name Tonh Binh, given to the area by the Chinese administrators.[21] The rising dragon was also a portent of permanent fertility. Thang Long remained the general name for the urban agglomeration until the nineteenth century.[22]

Chinese overlords

The Van Mieu is one of the oldest and most significant buildings in Hanoi and among the largest Confucian complexes in Vietnam. Its design and use illustrate the Chinese influence that permeated Vietnamese culture. It was erected in AD 1070 in Thinh Hao Village south-west of the citadel and, although metropolitan Hanoi has now grown up around it, it still lies a short way from the centre of town on a flat and narrow, roughly rectangular piece of land.[23] It is also known as the 'Temple of Literature', while the colonial French named it the 'Pagoda of the Crows'. Its dedication to Confucius so early in the Ly dynasty seems to indicate that, while Buddhism had pride of place as the dynastic religion, the Ly were already adopting Confucianism as the basis of their national education policy.[24] High dignitaries came here in spring and autumn to make offerings in honour of Confucius and his eminent disciples. While the initial plan of the Van Mieu had been based on the Temple of Confucius at Qu Fu, his birthplace in China, the complex kept evolving through the Tran and Later Le dynasties, only reaching its most complete form under the Nguyen in the middle of the nineteenth century.

The Van Mieu's Great
Hall of Ceremonies
and Courtyard of
the Sages, Quoc Tu
Giam Street.

The Khue Van Cac Pavilion,
commonly used as the icon
for historic Hanoi.

Like temple compounds in China, the Van Mieu is walled. The main gate, or Great Portico, is said to be 'resolved monumentally' by the use of columns typical of ancient Vietnamese architecture. Five courtyards then follow – another striking Chinese feature. The first courtyard contains two formal lotus ponds – restored in 1992 – and the tree planting gives it a formal appearance. The second is more park-like and ends with the famous Khue Van Cac Pavilion. The third courtyard is the Garden of the Stelae containing a square artificial pool known as the 'Well of Heavenly Brilliance' flanked on the east and west by two rows of stone stelae on pedestals shaped like tortoises, which represent memory. The stelae record the names of successful candidates in the mandarin examinations since 1484. This courtyard is the nucleus of the whole composition, dividing the complex into two parts, the first official section devoid of buildings and the second, more intimate, section where the temple and adjoining offices are located.

The fourth courtyard is entered through the Dai Thanh Mon Gate (Gate of the Great Synthesis). This courtyard – the Courtyard of the Sages – is more traditionally Chinese in style, with two parallel single-storey buildings along either side of the open space and linked at the north by twin pavilions, the Great Hall of Ceremonies and the High Sanctuary. The Vietnamese architects adopted the basics of Chinese pavilion architecture here: a stone terrace, the main part of the building supported by iron wood pillars, a system of brackets, and an overhanging roof gracefully curving upwards at the ends and covered with enamelled tiles and decorated with majolica statues.[25] Two symmetrical dragons facing a lunar disc adorn the roof ridge. The High Sanctuary is an identical building, with the altar to Confucius in the central bay.

The court relied on the Confucian mandarinate to govern the country in imitation of the Chinese; that is, the mandarins would govern according to the universal moral order as described in Confucian classics. The monarch not only had to be a man of virtue, but also had to choose virtuous men from all quarters of his realm to assist him. The measure of virtue was not birth, nor wealth, but learning. This led in China and other Confucian societies to the establishment of a rigorous examination system to select imperial officials, or mandarins. The examinations were open to all men of land-owning families, and in a society where partible inheritance, rather than primogeniture, was the rule, this meant wide access.[26]

The fifth courtyard in the complex came to house the series of educational institutions where students studied Confucian literature and philosophy – hence the alternative name, 'Temple of Literature' – in the hope of passing the examinations for entry into the mandarinate and wealth and fame. Initially, in 1075, a Royal School was opened to educate the royal princes. In the following year the Quoc Tu Giam (National School) was added. Here the royal relatives and mandarins' sons were housed and taught from books and wooden printing blocks. In 1253 the Tran dynasty turned the schools into the Quoc Hoc Vien (National Institute of Learning), attracting the best students from all over the country and leading to the claim that this was Vietnam's first university. It was extended in the fifteenth century with the erection of the Thai Hoc auditorium and a hostel for 300 students.[27] The gruelling triennial mandarin exams were conducted – in Chinese script – at the Thi Huong examination compound near the southern end of Lake Hoan Kiem. This compound had two main enclosures, a large open space with a single small central pavilion, the Thap Dao, for the candidates, and a second enclosure for the examiners' lodgings.

Whereas Buddhist pagodas had flourished under the Ly kings, during the subsequent Tran dynasty larger numbers of temples and tombs were built, marking the increasing influence over the realm of Confucianism mixed with Taoist dynastic or ancestor worship.[28] The temples were dedicated to the worship of heroes, high-ranking officials and military leaders; the tombs were for kings and high officials. During the late eighteenth-century turmoil that led to the establishment of the Nguyen dynasty, there were some attempts to recombine the three thought systems. A number of Buddhist pagodas, such as the Kim Lien Pagoda on the banks of West Lake (Ho Tay), were built according to the Taoist principle of yin and yang in which contrasting parts – male/female, fire/water, earth/sky – make up the whole.

Under the Later Le, another ideological shift occurred that impacted upon the cultural landscape of Hanoi and other urban centres. Concerted efforts were made to rebuild Vietnamese society on Confucian principles of good and efficient government. Villages and hamlets lost their autonomy, and village chiefs were used as representatives of the royal government to collect tax and recruit soldiers. To help co-opt the villages into a centralised bureaucratic system, the Le imported from China a kind of god – the god of the village – who was to be regarded as 'a little king' in the rural areas. In each village the communal houses, or *dinh*, previously used to worship Buddha as well as for meetings of the village notables, councils and justices of the peace and for banquets, now became the village cultural centre with a throne for these little kings.[29] The *dinh* were often built on timber piles and, resembling the houses represented on drums from the Dong-son period found during the excavations of Co Loa buildings, are said to be the most typical Vietnamese architectural structure.[30]

This administrative rearrangement highlights the fact that there was always going to be a problem for Buddhism in a society founded on

As expanding Hanoi
engulfed neighbouring
villages, many *dinh*
(communal houses)
acquired new functions.

Confucianism (or, later, communism). The emperor and his hierarchy of
scholar-officials took the place of both Church and State in traditional
Vietnamese society. There was no room for any other 'established' religion,
either Buddhist or Taoist. In Vietnam, the Buddhists seemed to have lacked
institutional discipline and operated in a fragmented way. However, the
Confucian court needed to keep a watchful eye on the Buddhist sects, as
also on the Taoists, because, as Ralph Smith noted, 'Beneath the surface of
Confucian order, there existed an underworld of secret societies and
political revolt.'[31]

Pre-modern conceptions and configurations of space: Geomancy and feng shui

Much of this sinicisation had been implanted in the period of direct rule
before Thang Long was established. It is often claimed that the Chinese
taught the early Vietnamese how to control floods using dykes.[32] Others
reject the argument on the basis of archaeological evidence.[33] Whatever
the origin, the reclaimed compartments of dry land became the basis of

31

the geographical pattern of villages that soon formed. They had still not been wholly sinicised when the break-up of the T'ang dynasty in China allowed the Vietnamese to assert their independence as the separate country of Dai Viet.[34]

The site on which Hanoi, or Thang Long, was established had been inhabited since Neolithic times and, known as Tong Binh, had been the chief population and administrative centre of the Red River delta region during the period of Chinese domination. A number of Chinese fortresses had been built there.[35] Because the ground on which Thang Long was constructed was below the level of the Red River in the wet season, a network of dykes (known as *La Thanh*) was formed to protect the city. Built in the eighth century and enlarged in the ninth, they remained unaltered until the nineteenth century, and even today remain essential to the city's survival. The main dyke ran along the Red River in the east, along West Lake in the north, and the To Lich in the west. It was a low earthen wall, topped with a narrow carriageway and protected by a bamboo hedge and deep moat bristling with spikes. All Thang Long inhabitants were required to contribute to the maintenance of the dyke in the form of *corvée* labour. During the sixteenth century there were 16 wooden gates (called *cua o*) through the dyke walls, reducing to eight by the eighteenth century. These were closed at dusk for security reasons and manned by soldiers 24 hours a day. Outside each gate a market took shape where farmers from neighbouring villages sold their hens, pigs and vegetables to the townspeople living inside the walls.[36]

Various explanations for the choice of this site for Thang Long have been put forward. Nguyen Luong Bich says the site was neither a random choice nor due to the existence of the earlier Chinese fortress there.[37] In the formulaic language in which historical events were discussed at the height of Vietnam's socialist period, Bich maintains that Thang Long's construction was permitted by the eleventh- century social environment and was demanded by the development needs of Vietnamese society. In other words, the technology of citadel construction existed and political and military considerations were critical: the site needed to be central to the area to be administered and a flat plain had the advantage of allow- ing advancing enemies to be easily seen. French historians Bézacier and Azambre say the site was chosen according to the imperatives of geo- mancy, claiming that these factors were always present in royal building in Chinese and other sinicised societies and, in fact, often outweighed po- litical and military considerations.[38]

Geomancy is a system devised to get the better of Fate, the force determining 'everything under Heaven'. It is still central to Confucianism and Taoism and followed also by many Buddhists. Geomancers, astrologers and spirit mediums have been important in traditional Vietnamese society

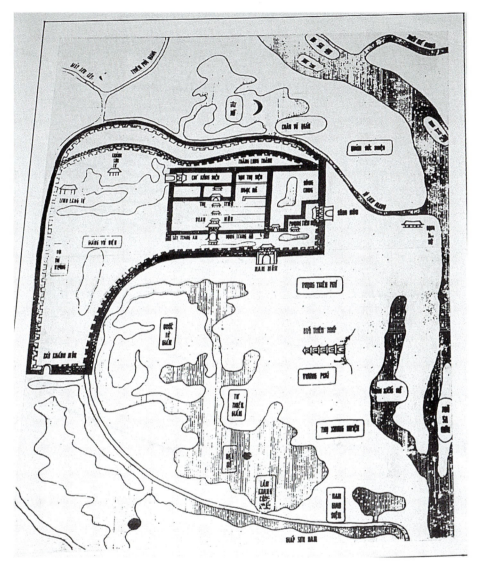

Thang Long 1490 —
stylised map of the
feudal city.

because they claimed to be able to discover what Fate had in store. The
thay-phap (called 'sorcerer' by the French) was universally respected. He
could calculate propitious times for meetings and actions, and he was called
upon to identify the best site for a house or tomb to protect them from evil
spirits.[39] Because society believed this mysterious set of beliefs (*feng shui*;
phong thuy in Vietnamese), the geomancer became a key figure in both

architecture and planning. Generally citadels, palaces and other buildings faced south (although some variation was allowed and the Hanoi Citadel, in fact, faced south-south-west). A 'royal screen' of hills or forest must shield the main entrance, thus blocking the entry of malignant spirits that could only travel in a straight line. Also facing the entrance, two hills or mountains were required – one to the east representing the White Tiger (Bach Ho, the Chinese king of the wild beasts and metaphor for a range of qualities, including courage and dignity) and the other to the west representing the Blue Dragon (chief of all aquatic creatures). A winding river must flow around the site to irrigate the 'magnetic field'. If any of these features was missing in the natural site, it was admissible for people to erect protective screens, raise mounds to provide better surveillance or dig ditches to create magic streams.

The influence of geomancy seems to have peaked around the thirteenth century and, if this is so, it must have substantially altered the conception of the capital as well as the design of pre-existing buildings such as the Van Mieu complex. But there is considerable evidence of a strong, earlier role. The site of the Van Mieu was chosen, according to the official guide to the site, by Ly dynasty geomancers so as to stand in harmony with the Taoist Bich Cau Temple and the Buddhist One Pillar Pagoda.[40] Ly Thai To's royal edict regarding the establishment of Thang Long in 1010, which is quoted in numerous sources and with a variety of wordings, shows clearly the decisive role of geomancy:

> Furthermore, Dai La citadel that is the ancient citadel of Lord Cao Bien is situated in the space between Heaven and Earth, in the location where the dragon is coiled and the tiger crouching. The capital is laid out on North-South East-West axes and is favourably situated with regard to the mountains and river. The site is large and flat, the fields high and well enough exposed. The population is protected against high water and floods. Everything there flourishes and prospers. It is a most beautiful site where men and riches from the four cardinal points converge.[41]

The text continues:

> In the whole country, Dai La is the best place; all paths cross here; this place is worthy of being selected for building an everlasting royal capital. I want to use that site of beneficial geomancy as my settlement place, what do you think about that, my subjects?[42]

The mythical scene that supposedly followed Ly Thai To's decision is described by Hoang Ni Tiep:

> In the autumn of 1010, multitudes of builders began to pour into the capital and to erect walls, fortresses, palaces and all sorts of buildings. At first they gathered together to create a majestic monumental ensemble

such as had never been seen before. It began with the construction of phuong (street blocks) …. The capital grew more beautiful with each day.[43]

In fact, the citadel grew slowly and underwent considerable remodelling following frequent destruction by the Mongols, Cham, Han Chinese and inter-clan warfare.[44] A major process of rebuilding began after Le Loi defeated the Ming forces in 1428 and established the Later Le dynasty.[45] When the Mac dynasty collapsed into the inter-clan hostilities between the Trinh and Nguyen war lords in 1592, the Trinh lord demolished the citadel walls. These were later rebuilt by Gia Long, the first Nguyen king.

Located in the northern part of the walled city, a rectangular structure of bricks surrounded by the then-navigable To Lich River in the north and a moat on the three other sides contained the royal palaces as well as administrative buildings for the mandarinate. This was the Royal Citadel, or *Hoang Thanh*. Within this again was another rectangular set of walls – the Forbidden Citadel (*Cam Thanh*) where the royal family and concubines resided. Initially made of earth, the Forbidden City walls were enlarged and reconstructed with bricks in 1029 and had five gates opening to the south and three gates on each of the other sides.[46] As the original site was flat, mounds had been built to represent the White Tiger and Blue Dragon, but the highest man-made tumulus, the 'Nung Son' ('hill where the dragon sits'), was the site chosen for the king's palace. A large road passed through the southern entrance. This was used for the mandarins to come for audiences with the king and was wide enough for processions of elephants and horses.

The Royal Citadel was enlarged to the south and east in the fifteenth century, doubling its size. According to Nguyen Luong Bich, it was then full of resplendent palaces and imposing buildings.[47] These included the Forbidden City, the Thien An (Heavenly Peace) Palace (built in 1029) where the king met with mandarins to discuss matters of state, the Thien Khanh Palace where the king worked, and the Truong Xuan where the armoury was kept. Outside the Forbidden City but still within the Royal City were numerous pagodas, gardens, trees and lakes for the king and mandarins. In contrast to this description, early European visitors, such as the English trader Samuel Baron in 1685, portrayed the royal palaces and adminis-trative buildings as extensive but mediocre in appearance, being made of wood unlike European palaces.[48] At that point, the triple walls of the citadel were in ruins, but it was possible to see how solid they had once been. The English traveller William Dampier, who visited in 1688, described the walls as being totally hidden by the houses surrounding the citadel.[49]

Sometimes the Royal Citadel is referred to as the 'imperial city'; however, while everything gravitated around the emperor, clearly at this stage it did not look much like a town. Its walls delimited a territory exclusive to the king and high mandarins of the central administration,

Above The Bach Ma Temple in Hang Buom Street, Ancient Quarter.

Below The main citadel gate in the early 1880s as seen by a French artist. (Émile Duboc, *Trente-cinq Mois de Campagne en Chine, au Tonkin: Courbet-Rivière (1882–1885)* (Paris, Librairie d'Education de la Jeunesse, n.d.), p. 47)

La Porte de la citadelle d'Hanoï.

but its physical structure was spread out and made up of isolated monumental buildings, rather than being dense and organic. One modern Vietnamese scholar, Nguyen Duc Nhuan, has likened it to 'an entrenched camp' in the midst of rice fields, gardens and ponds, and giving no impression of a city.[50] As Christian Pédélahore pointed out, the Confucian influence was fundamental, being displayed in the 'creation of rather exclusive spaces whose differentiation was not based on criteria of urban functions, but on the identification of a social rank and an activity'.[51]

However, the eastern road from the main gate of the Royal Citadel led to the Red River. Here an agglomeration of traders and artisans, as well as homes of the mandarins, was emerging along the band of dry land that cut across the chain of ponds and swamps running from Hoan Kiem to West Lake. The buildings were huts of bamboo, reeds and straw. Certainly not a solid town yet, this 'Kinh Thanh' (Capital City) was commonly given the somewhat pejorative Vietnamese name of 'Ke Cho' (after the 'market people') to distinguish it quite clearly from the Royal Citadel. That is, although within the outer walls of the entire settlement of Thang Long, it was *extra muros* in relation to the Royal Citadel, again a reminder that Confucianism gave traders low status compared with scholars and administrators. But this is where the people lived; even the king's children and high mandarins had palaces here. The army was also housed in Ke Cho. This settlement was the kernel of the real urban agglomeration that was to become Hanoi.

Chinese impact on common life

Legend has it that Thang Long's builder, King Ly Thai To, selected the gods of the To Lich River and Long Do mountains as guardian spirits of his new capital, perhaps because they were believed to have caused considerable mischief to the previous Chinese occupiers of the site. During the construction of the citadel, however, the earthen walls collapsed repeatedly as soon as they were built. After making offerings at the Long Do Temple, the king saw a white horse come out of the shrine, circle the site from east to west, then disappear back into the temple. The king immediately ordered the walls of Thang Long to be built on the perimeter traced by the horse's footprints. Since that time the Long Do Temple has also been known as the Bach Ma (White Horse) Temple. The white horse figures frequently in Chinese mythology, once more reflecting the strong Chinese influence on both the courtly and popular urban cultures after the thousand years of domination.

Many temples, like the first commoners living inside the capital city, had belonged to farming villages that pre-dated the construction of the wall.

Around four gates of the Royal Citadel, major markets sprang up, one on each side – Cua Dong in the east (now Hang Buom Street), Cua Nam in the south, Cua Tay in the west (now Ngoc Ha market), and Cua Bac in the north. Here royal edicts were proclaimed, prisoners executed and festivals organised. Markets were both permanent and periodical, and all were controlled by the imperial administration. On the first and fifteenth day of each lunar month, Thang Long's population was swelled by peasants flocking in from the surrounding countryside to attend the major agricultural fair. Traditional farm folk would throng into the temples and pagodas and devoutly pray to their various gods in a haze of incense smoke.[52]

Other temples were associated with early artisan activities. The first such activities were probably connected with the court, either through forced annual labour contributions by the village men or through the permission given to retired women servants to open private workshops where they made brocades (from the eleventh century), fans (fourteenth century) and silk fabrics (seventeenth century). Copper founders, silversmiths and other artisans were forcibly brought to the capital from surrounding provinces to work for the court, and then stayed on in their own specialised communities (*phuong*) eventually to form guilds – family-like organisations based on the Chinese model. Yet other artisans such as dyers, turners and mother-of-pearl inlayers drifted to the capital of their own free will, either creating new guilds based on their village of origin and specialist craft, or joining existing ones.

Nevertheless, the town remained relatively small until the Le dynasty in the fifteenth century because most high-ranking mandarins lived on their estates, except when called to the capital by the king. This seems to have reduced the demand for imported goods and craftsmen in the area. Under the Le, however, the mandarins were forced to live in the town. Most chose to reside south of the Royal Citadel around the Van Mieu. Later, in the seventeenth century, when the Trinh lords assumed power, the high mandarins also lived to the east of the Royal Citadel in 52 east-facing palaces in the area between Hoan Kiem and the river. Whenever royalty or the mandarins wanted to erect new buildings, the commoners were simply evicted from their lands and relocated outside the walls. Conversely, when the city population declined, the court would import workers from outside. Even today, annual rituals see the descendants of these new groups return to their village of origin, despite the passage of up to 900 years.[53]

Almost from its establishment, Thang Long was the most important urban centre in the kingdom, thanks to this *extra muros* activity and population. Trade-based prosperity grew to the extent that, in 1788, the French missionary J. Richard could describe the number of boats in the Red River port as 'so huge that it is difficult to approach the river banks. Our rivers and most bustling ports, even Venice with all its gondolas and

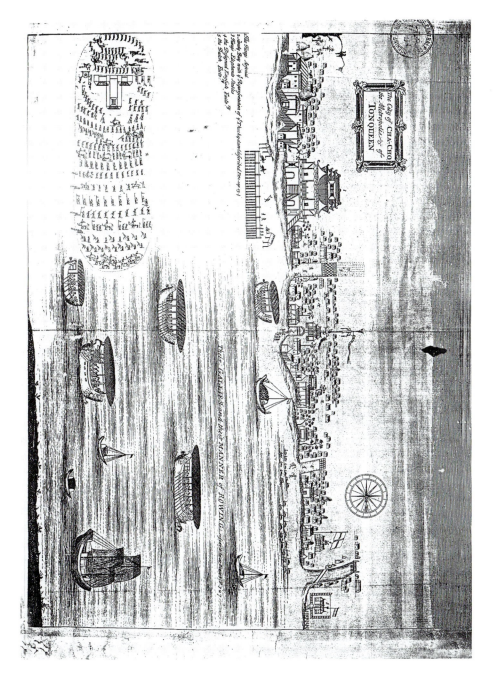

Cachao, or Hanoi, in the late seventeenth century. The flags of the English and Dutch factories can be seen on the extreme right. (Baron 1686; published: Churchill 1746; reprinted in Alistair Lamb, *The Mandarin Road to Old Hue. Narratives of Anglo-Vietnamese Diplomacy from the 17th Century to the Eve of French Conquest* (Chatto & Windus, London, 1970), p. 33)

boats, cannot give an idea of the tremendous movement and activity of the riparian population of Ke Cho.'[54] But even so, the capital city remained the same in structure and functions – with Ke Cho sitting alongside the Royal Citadel. Despite the fact that the market town overshadowed the Royal Citadel in size and prosperity, through to the late nineteenth century maps often failed to identify it and only showed the imperial enclosure, its lakes, temples and surrounding palaces.

Under the Confucian administrative system, the capital and its surrounding territory comprised a unit called *phu*; this was divided into two *huyen* and each *huyen* was subdivided into eighteen *phuong* (quarters), giving the origin of the common reference to the Ancient Quarter as the 'Area of Thirty-Six Commercial Streets'. Each *phuong* was bordered by four streets, and each street had its own headman, police and administration, based on the *dinh* or communal house, where the spirit protector of the community resided and where a school was run.

Travellers such as William Dampier commented favourably on the orderly appearance of the town, with each guild street being separated from the next by timber barricades with small gates that were closed off at night. The names of the streets (*pho*) – Pearl Inlayers Street, Silk Street, Cotton Street, Fan Street, and so on – were written in Chinese characters above the gates, sometimes with good wishes or advice (such as 'May the population in this street enjoy peace').[55] However, in rainstorms, the narrow, largely unpaved streets turned into insanitary bogs, and it was only after the French arrived and Hanoi municipality was created in 1888 that a system of gutters and stormwater drains was introduced. The description given by Richard suggests some improvements may have been made during the eighteenth century: in 1778, he saw the streets of Ke Cho as wide and beautifully paved with bricks, the lanes left unpaved being destined for the passage of royal carriages, horses, elephants and other domestic animals.[56] This sounds more like a description of the Royal Citadel, but may have referred to the Chinese sections of Ke Cho.

In terms of social hierarchy, Ke Cho typified the Vietnamese pattern described by Alexander Woodside: a landed, literate, leisured class of mandarins and related elite with country estates and townhouses; a mass of peasants; a Buddhist clergy; the artisans; and a powerful, alien Chinese merchant class.[57] The better-off artisans worked to foreign orders; others worked for the local market, and the worst off were those who worked for the court as virtual serfs.[58] The more prosperous Chinese traders, who probably initiated trade at Thang Long and who certainly had control of it during the entire feudal period, lived in their own paved streets where they occupied more substantial two-storey masonry houses with tiled roofs and monumental gates. They were in many ways a world apart, with their own temples, schools, festivals and organisations that newly arrived

Chinese migrants had to join. It is estimated that 85 per cent were Cantonese and the remainder Fukkienese.

Dampier calculated in 1688 that there were 20,000 houses in Ke Cho and depicted them as low, with mud walls and a straw, reed or leaf thatch roof on timber columns, although about one-third were built of brick and had tiled roofs. The typical dwellings were single rooms looking on to a street or lane and serving as places of production, storage, sale and residence. Most had a courtyard with an oven-like building into which valuables were put when the common event of fire struck the town. Samuel Baron confirmed that there were few buildings of brick except for the foreign comptoirs,[60] but he seems to have overlooked the Chinese. European traders – mostly Dutch, English and French – were forced to live along the riverbanks outside the town walls, a situation that continued until 1873.

Gradually, by the end of the nineteenth century, the flimsy structures were replaced by more solid ones of brick and plaster, and rooms were added behind, eventually to form the building type known as the 'Chinese compartment' or 'shop-house'. These are also known in Hanoi as 'tube houses' due to their long, narrow form. No doubt having their origin in makeshift stalls on the street line, these houses have widths of around three metres, a limit set by the maximum length of available timber beams. The prominent Vietnamese architectural historian Dang Thai Hoang explains that, depending on the wealth and status of the owner, houses were either one room wide, three rooms wide or, in rare cases, five rooms wide.[61] But their depths were often 60 metres or more, with a succession of residential spaces, storage rooms and workshops, interspersed with courtyards which gave access to light, ventilation and rainwater. The ridge roofs were made to sag, and the houses were separated from each other by projecting parapet walls, giving the streetscape a distinctive look.

Until the twentieth century, these shop-houses were rarely more than two storeys in height. According to the sixteenth-century Hong Duc Code, ordinary citizens were not permitted to build large houses imitating the royal or mandarin residences, to use rare materials, or to decorate them in the patterns that embellished royal buildings, such as the dragon or the phoenix.[62] This restraint on the civilian population was reinforced, until at least the middle of the nineteenth century, by Article 156 of the nineteenth-century royal Annamite Code prohibiting commoners from erecting buildings in brick or of more than a single storey. Doors and windows could not be higher that the shoulders of a royal family member or mandarin travelling in a sedan chair. Attics were therefore uninhabitable, because they were not permitted to have windows, and could only be used for storage.[63]

However, the shop-house form, while it may have had particular local details, was far from unique, being found then and now in cities through South-east Asia where Chinese traders were influential, such as Melaka, Penang, Singapore and Bangkok, as well as, of course, in China itself. Nineteenth-century watercolours of Batavia (Jakarta) also indicate the prevalence of shop-houses in colonial Indonesian cities.[64] This would therefore appear to be yet another impact of Chinese culture on Hanoi's physical appearance and the life of its common people. Certainly, numerous recent studies insist on the critical role of Chinese immigrant communities in the development of South-east Asian cities. But French architectural historian Alain Viaro questions whether the shop-house is, in fact, a Chinese architectural creation.[65] He concedes that there are Chinese elements in the building techniques and especially in the décor of shop-houses in South-east Asian cities. But he argues that the shop-house, as an architectural type, owes its diffusion and the manner of their grouping into terraces to the influence of the European colonial authorities, notably the Dutch in Indonesia and the British in Singapore, Malaya and Burma. There is even some thought that the original inspiration was the similarly narrow houses fronting on to canals in Dutch trading cities. Since Hanoi's shop-houses appear to have pre-dated the arrival of the French, this would mean that the Chinese immigrant community must have brought with it notions of architectural design and knowledge of building technology already established by Europeans in China. Whatever its origin, the French colonial authorities accepted the design sense of the shop-houses and only sought to impose regulations on building materials, amount of ventilation and other performance standards.

The pre-colonial struggle for independence

Alexander Woodside points to the paradoxical nature of cultural contact between the Chinese and the Vietnamese when he notes that there was both 'heavy sinicisation and heavy cultural resistance'.[66] Clearly, a millennium of direct Chinese rule followed by another 850 years of tributary status reinforced Chinese influence in urban areas, especially among the elite. In summary, these impacts ranged from the adoption of Chinese concepts of state and government, to the search for a perfectly ordered society, the establishment of hierarchical social relationships, and the acceptance of the idea that education was more important than economic luxury. So, too, Vietnamese houses, religious and other buildings, and monuments were constructed according to Chinese architectural and town planning models. Although the first rulers of independent Vietnam tried to cast off the heavy blanket of Chinese influence, notably by trying to replace Confucian elements in the administrative and educational apparatus with Buddhist ones, they soon discovered that without such Confucian guidelines they simply could not administer the state effectively. The archaeologist H.H.E. Loofs commented that 'the Buddhist path is well suited for the achievement of individual salvation, but inadequate for running a country'.[67] 'Thus,' he added,

> ... whether the Vietnamese wanted it or not, Confucianism was there to stay, and with it all the other Chinese elements, both spiritual and material, which seemed to be inevitably linked with it, such as the Chinese language and script, Chinese court etiquette, Chinese-style ceremonies, and even the Chinese idea that the Emperor (or King) is at the same time the Chief of all the spirits of the land.[68]

There were periodic reformist movements throughout Vietnamese history, the latest being during the Tay Son Rebellion at the end of the eighteenth century, but Confucianism always quickly restored and remained the key feature of Vietnamese 'official' culture.

How did Vietnamese-ness survive the Chinese cultural influence? Climatic differences, particularly the monsoonal wet seasons, set some limits to the ability to simply replicate the Chinese cultural landscape. It also appears that up to the fifteenth century the Vietnamese elite was influenced culturally as much by the Cham as by the Chinese, especially in dance and music forms and the types of musical instruments. It is said that the Cham influence can be seen too in the way Vietnamese theory and practice of warfare differed from the Chinese. This extended to the contrast between the Vietnamese use of elephants and the Chinese use of horses.[69] The fact that the Chinese impacts were mainly felt by the urban elite but left the popular rural culture largely unaffected is critical. Although the Chinese had made spoken and written Chinese the language of the court, bureaucracy, the urban elite and much of commerce, they had been unable to supplant the Vietnamese spoken language elsewhere. Despite the implantation of tonal pronunciation and many loan words, language became the key factor in the survival of the sense of being Vietnamese. In the countryside especially, the culture therefore remained based on a different language and a set of legends handed down orally. This is a main reason why the intangible heritage is still today given such significant status: it, more than anything, is seen as conveying the true spirit of Vietnam.

One result of the introduction of a romanised script by the first French missionaries in the seventeenth century, allowing them to translate Christian texts more easily, and of the subsequent adoption of this *quoc ngu* as the national script, was that the peasantry were diverted away from acquiring Chinese. The *quoc ngu* was used by the French administration in Tonkin from 1900 so that even the bureaucrats began to abandon

Chinese, and this was accelerated with the abolition of the traditional examination system in 1916. It means that Chinese characters are totally foreign to the vast majority of Vietnamese today.

At times, such as during the Nguyen dynasty, the 'superiority' of the Chinese culture was explicitly recognised. Paradoxically, the active assimilation of Chinese elements by the urban elite followed the Confucian belief that, if Fate looks unfavourable, it is wise not to act, but to wait; that is, to bend with the wind rather than oppose the invasion of foreign cultural influences. Ralph Smith explains the Vietnamese cultural resistance in terms of the philosophy of *thi dung*, again borrowed from the Chinese: while they might imitate the foreigner in matters of utility (*dung*), they maintained their own traditional values in matters of substance or essence *(thi)*.[70] Confucian tradition had always distinguished between the inner and outer affairs of man and allowed a man to be inwardly Taoist or Buddhist so long as he was outwardly a Confucian. So, although the Vietnamese kings were rulers in their own right, making their own sacrifices to Earth and Heaven, they sent regular tribute to Peking without loss of integrity. Receiving in return Chinese diplomas of investiture, seals of gold and access to trade in China, the recognition of Chinese superiority was as much economic as political in intent.[71] This was not what we think of as national independence but was a utilitarian response that held the Chinese at bay. Despite this, on four occasions the Chinese attempted to recapture Vietnam – the Sung in 1077, the Yuan in the 1280s, the Ming between 1407 and 1427, and the Qing in 1788–89.

Cultural resistance continued on in the twentieth century with fairly constant efforts by archaeologists, anthropologists, historians and other researchers to demonstrate that there has always been a qualitative cultural difference between Vietnam and China. In the 1920s and 1930s, archaeological work by the École Française d'Extrême-Orient and the Commission Archéologique de l'Indochine discovered the existence of earlier flourishing 'Indonesian' peoples in the Red River delta region. Named the Dong Son culture after the main site at Thanh Hoa, this early Vietnamese culture was very different from the Chinese in a number of significant ways, particularly in its use of bronze, its practices of tattooing and tooth-blackening, and the chewing of betel nut in ceremonies. Early Chinese visitors had remarked on these differences.[72] There is even some scholarly resistance to the idea that rice paddy cultivation – the economic mainstay of the Red River delta peasantry then as now – was introduced by the Chinese. Moreover, the archaeological confirmation of these observations and the semi-historical legends of pre-Chinese Viet kingdoms took on ideological importance in the twentieth century at a time when nationalist Vietnamese were trying to assert the country's independence. The first signs of a sophisticated Bronze Age culture in the Red River delta fired the imaginations of twentieth-century Vietnamese patriots.[73]

Here cultural resistance flows over into political resistance. Such linkage has occurred at frequent intervals throughout Vietnamese history. One of the most interesting examples relates to another way in which the urban elite maintained a distinction from the Chinese – in the greater freedom allowed to women.[74] Daughters as well as sons could own and inherit land and serve as trustees of their ancestral cult funds. One of the most highly regarded poets, the eighteenth-century Ho Xuan Huong, was a woman. So, too, women are well represented among the most successful rebels against the Chinese overlords – Trung Tac and Trung Nhi, who staged a successful rebellion against the Chinese and ruled briefly in AD 39–43, and Ba Trieu in the second century. In the case of the Hai Ba Trung (Two Trung Sisters), the uprising was a reaction to the Chinese governor's policy of active sinicisation, especially his promotion of the southern Chinese style of irrigated agriculture, use of the plough drawn by ox or water buffalo, and Chinese customs and ceremonials. Chinese colonists had occupied and developed the best lands and had drawn the Vietnamese into service as functionaries and militiamen. The indigenous aristocracy became increasingly hostile, and the execution of a Vietnamese nobleman in AD 40 sparked off a rebellion led by his widow and her sister – the two Trung sisters.[75] The Chinese general Ma Yuan came south to repress the rebellion in AD 43 and it is said that his massive forces met resistance from 65 fortresses or fortified residences.[76] The sisters, on elephant-back, led the Vietnamese armies into a desperate last stand against the Chinese invaders but were crushed, and the Vietnamese people were placed under more intensive Chinese administration and enculturation than before.

However, despite their ultimate failure, the Hai Ba Trung came to be seen as symbols of resistance to the Chinese, in particular, and of the struggle for independence in general for the ensuing almost 2,000 years. The oral legends and the stories by historians such as the thirteenth-century Le Van Huu transformed memories of the Trung sisters, Ba Trieu, Ly Thai To and others into a historical force in their own right. The Trung sisters are memorialised in the temple named after them that is now located in the southern suburbs not far beyond the limits of Hanoi's Old Sector. It had originally been built by King Ly Anh Tong in 1142 on the banks of the Red River in line with the Chinese practice of constructing temples dedicated to heroes and genii. Tran Ham Tan and Nguyen Ba Chi maintain in their detailed study of the temple that the king's dedication makes it the most significant temple in Hanoi.[77]

But there are numerous interpretations of the significance of the Trung sisters, as well as details of the Trung temple's location and construction history. According to common legend, after disappearing in the River Hac, the two sisters metamorphosed themselves into two stone statues that

Left The Hai Ba Trung Temple and forecourt.

Below The Hai Ba Trung Temple: floor plan and cross-section. (Tran Ham Tan and Nguyen Chi Ba, *Den Hai Ba Trung* (Imprimerie Thoi Su, Hanoi, 1948))

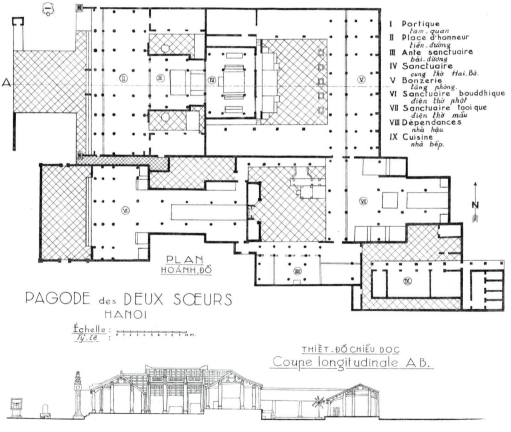

I Portique
  tam-quan
II Place d'honneur
  tiên-đường
III Ante sanctuaire
  bái-đường
IV Sanctuaire
  cung thờ Hai-Bà.
V Bonzerie
  tăng phòng.
VI Sanctuaire bouddhique
  điện thờ phật
VII Sanctuaire taoique
  điện thờ mẫu
VIII Dépendances
  nhà hậu
IX Cuisine
  nhà bếp.

N

PLAN
HOÀNH-ĐỒ

PAGODE des DEUX SŒURS
HANOI

Échelle :
Tỷ-lệ : 0 1 2 3 4 5 6 7 8 9 10 m.

THIÊT-ĐỒ CHIỀU DỌC
Coupe longitudinale A B.

drifted downstream to the Dong Nhan River where they beamed light to scare away enemy boats. In other versions, the two sisters simply disappeared after losing the war against the Chinese and the local people erected a temple to worship them at Hat Mon Village. These sources attribute tremendous supernatural powers to the women, particularly the ability to break drought. It is said that King Ly Anh Tong found that his prayers to them for rain were so successful that he took the statues to Hanoi and built a temple dedicated to them north of the city. Not long after, the sisters appeared before him in a dream asking him to build a temple for them in their native village and the king obeyed. Under the Le dynasty, the two sisters were raised to an exalted status and worshipped at Donh Nhan Temple. From 1819, King Gia Long used this temple as a martial arts school to train his soldiers and it was shifted to its present location with the help of the residents of Phung Cong Village. Every year, on the fifth day of the second lunar month, the locals gather at Dong Nhan Village and walk in procession to the Nhi River to collect water as offerings to celebrate the anniversary of the two sisters. The celebration traditionally lasted three days.[78]

The temple is part of a religious complex housing a Buddhist convent controlled by a Superior (or chief nun). It comprises a square-shaped group of seven long houses surrounding an inner shrine. On the south side is the Vien Minh Pagoda, and on the north is the temple dedicated to the Hai Ba Trung as well as a stele commemorating their good deeds. The partitioning within these houses consists of finely carved timber frames and screens. Paintings and other interior decorative displays describe the services rendered by the two sisters to the country, while a stele gives details of emperor Tu Duc's reign and restoration work on the temple. The inner shrine, which is rarely opened to the public, contains two statues of the sisters. A tall funeral oration room with a red brick floor and gold painted timbers contains an altar dedicated to the founder of the pagoda and has 21 statues of the highly ranking venerables arranged in seven lines. Along both walls are several small altars with stelae and photos of bereaved relatives of worshippers.

The religious complex sits on the western side of a large courtyard. Today there is a small lake outside the courtyard, with a row of betel trees along its banks. However, a 1925 map of Hanoi shows the temple and a larger lake in an unsettled area, part of which was still swamp and paddy, to the east of the European cemetery and Hue Street. It is claimed that the temple had been built to take advantage of its rural setting, with a low, rather rustic architectural style and abundant leafy trees forming a canopy over the roof.[79] While Vietnamese traditional architecture is characterised by its use of water features, particularly reflections to heighten the sense of a building's grandeur, this is certainly no longer the case here. Instead, the Hai Ba Trung Temple lake is the end-product of a swamp infill process designed mainly to create solid ground for new residential construction. It appears that in 1933 the Hanoi municipal authorities decided to develop a road improvement and landscape beautification plan for the temple precinct.[80] It entailed further land infill and the destruction of the bamboo hedges north of the temple. However, the project appears to have proceeded slowly or not at all because, in 1941, the chief nun, Dam-Thu, was still lodging objections to the Tonkin Governor (*Résident-Supérieur*). Her argument was that the temple had control of the surrounding lands, the revenue from which goes to the pagoda's upkeep. This was normal in Vietnam, leading her to insist that, 'In fact, just as one cannot picture an Annamite village without its bamboo hedge, so one cannot imagine a pagoda or temple without its surrounding lands which provide its physical and aesthetic setting'.[81]

Another municipal plan dated 1956 shows a very elaborate design for the precinct, with ornamental lake embankments and other landscaping structures. None of these works can have proceeded, judging by the present state of the area. During the ensuing years, the temple area has been surrounded by government educational buildings and low-quality housing. The courtyard in front of the temple provides an important open space in today's Hanoi and is regularly used by small boys playing soccer and badminton. The large trees blend picturesquely with the columns of the temple entrance gate, but the small lake with its earthen banks is poorly maintained and polluted with sewage leaking from adjacent buildings.

Nineteenth-century neo-Confucianism and imperial collapse

A temple that successfully fulfils the traditional Vietnamese design ambition of marrying town and water is Den Ngoc Son on the small Jade Island at the northern end of Hoan Kiem Lake. The temple also demonstrates many of the Chinese design principles that were again fashionable during the nineteenth century. Dating from the start of the reign of the first Nguyen king, Gia Long, the Ngoc Son Temple was, in fact, a combination of Buddhist, Confucian and Tao elements and was dedicated to a number of deities and heroes.[82] It was extensively renovated in 1864 by the Hanoi scholar-poet Nguyen Van Sieu and connected with the bank by the smooth arch of an openwork Huc bridge. Near the entrance to the wooden bridge, the mandarin also erected a small mount called Dai Nghien (The Inkstone) and a nine-metre-tall tower called Thap But (The Brush) supported by three stone frogs. The Stele Pavilion overlooks the lake, then a welcoming antechamber known as Tien Duong leads to the Sanctuary of Van Xuong, which is dedicated to the Chinese god of literature and literary examinations. Behind this, another sanctuary is reserved for the worship of

Tran Hung Dao, the national hero who defeated the Mongol invaders in the fifteenth century, and Quan De, the Chinese warrior god. The pavilions are dark, with reflected light from the lake entering through the sliding panelled doors and carefully carved wooden barred windows. Today, a small group of trees by the bridge and the free line of the grassy shore overgrown with flamboyant trees emphasise the temple's natural environment.

Hoan Kiem is Hanoi's heart, the place to which people, young and old, flock to celebrate the Tet (New Year) festivities or just to enjoy strolling with friends and family on a balmy evening. Lending atmosphere and significance to this place is the myth of the returned sword. According to the fifteenth-century legend, a fisherman from the village of Thanh Hoa by the name of Le Loi was casting his nets into the lake when he caught, not a fish, but a magic sword.[83] Drawing round him a band of partisans, over a period of ten years he effectively created a popular independence movement against the Chinese and eventually staged a successful revolt in which he used the sword to defeat the occupying Chinese troops.

Den Ngoc Son
(Temple de Jade)
on Hoan Kiem
Lake, c. 1905.

Ngoc Son Temple, 1995.

Having made himself king, he wished to return the holy sword to the lake. As the ceremonial cortege reached the lake, a burst of thunder and flashes of lightning emanated from the sword. The sword rose from its sheath, transformed itself into a jade dragon and dashed into the lake, thus giving it the name 'Lake of the Returned Sword'. Other versions are less elaborate and describe the king in a boat on Hoan Kiem returning the sword to a golden turtle. In addition to the lake's mythological significance, Vietnamese and international landscape architects hail the creation of this public centre around a picturesque lake as 'one of the most successful examples of using nature in the architecture of town complexes'.[84] The protection of the lake, its two islands — Jade Island and Thap Rua (Turtle's Head)[85] — and their temples, the banks and their trees and gardens, and the ring of notable buildings lining the encircling boulevard, has become one of the most important heritage conservation objectives in Hanoi.

In pre-colonial times, the lake was larger, one of the string of swampy lakes and ponds running through what is now the Ancient Quarter. It was bordered in the south-east by the important Bao An Pagoda complex. But during the nineteenth century the lake became increasingly hemmed in by stilt houses and was in a filthy state by the time the French arrived. Indeed, much of Hanoi became run-down during this period. This was largely the

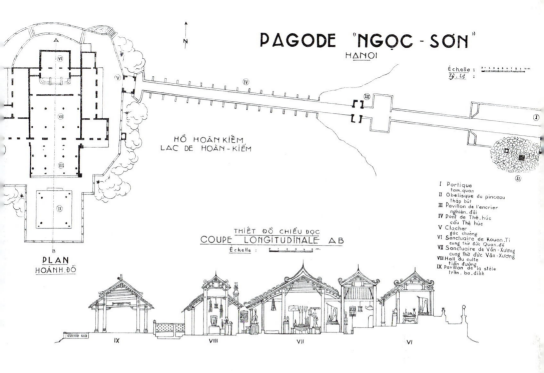

PAGODE "NGOC-SON"
HANOI

Échelle : 0 1 2 3 4 5 10m
Tỷ lệ :

HỒ HOÀN KIẾM
LAC DE HOÀN-KIẾM

PLAN
HOÀNH.ĐỐ

THIẾT ĐỒ CHIẾU DỌC
COUPE LONGITUDINALE AB
Échelle : 1 2 3 4 m.

I Portique
  tam.quan
II Obelisque du pinceau
  tháp bút
III Pavillon de l'encrier
  nghiên.đài
IV Pont de Thê.húc
  cầu Thê.húc
V Clocher
  gác chuông
VI Sanctuaire de Kouan.Ti
  cung thờ đức Quan.đế
VII Sanctuaire de Văn-Xương
  cung thờ đức Văn-Xương
VIII Hall du culte
  tiên đường
IX Pavillon de la stèle
  trấn. ba.đình

Above Ngoc Son Temple:
floor plan and cross-section.
(Tran Ham Tan and Nguyen
Ba Chi, *La pagode de l'île de
Jade* (Imprimerie Thoi Su,
Hanoi, 1948))

Below Huc bridge
leading to Ngoc
Son Temple.

result of the royal capital being transferred to Hue in 1802. The Nguyen, wanting to reorganise the reunited Vietnam, deliberately modelled themselves and Vietnamese society on the Chinese. Confucianism was seen as the perfect model for doing this, and Confucian principles and practices were enforced more vigorously than before. This now went beyond the cities and into the rural villages, where temples were dedicated to Confucius and the high mandarins.[86] The first three Nguyen rulers – Gia Long (1802–20), Minh Mang (1820–40) and Thieu Tri (1840–47) – had themselves saluted at court as '*Hoan De*', the Chinese term for human emperor; they also used the Chinese term for kinship, '*thien-tu*' or 'Sons of Heaven'.[87] Following Chinese practice, they declared that Dragonboat Day would be one of its three great holidays, along with Tet and the emperor's birthday.[88]

Neo-Confucianism was most aggressively pursued by Minh Mang, but reached a peak under Tu Duc (1847–83) as the ideology of the Vietnamese state. The urban impact of this neo-Confucianism on Hanoi and other Vietnamese towns and cities was significant. While the Nguyen built new royal palaces, temples and mausoleums at Hue (using Chinese models), Hanoi was relegated to chief town of Bac Ha, the North. It kept some administrative functions and its triennial examination system still flourished, but the Royal Citadel had fallen into disrepair following the political unrest of the late eighteenth century. It is said that Gia Long would not repair the citadel because it had been built by the usurping Tay Son brothers (1788–1802), and, in 1805, ordered its demolition and construction of a new, smaller citadel using the seventeenth-century Vauban model of fortification.[89] David Marr says that court antipathy towards the Tay Son and lingering uncertainty about the strength of popular support for their government may explain why Gia Long and Minh Mang devoted so much attention to the building of Vauban-style fortresses in modest provincial town centres.[90] Gia Long's down-sizing of the Hanoi Royal Citadel was followed in 1835 by Minh Mang's decision to lower the walls to a height less than those at Hue. This, in turn, was surpassed in 1848 by Tu Duc's decision to dismantle the remaining palaces completely and to transfer to Hue all wooden and stone artefacts of value.[91]

But within the Gia Long's new walls, the Royal Citadel took on a much more extreme geomantic form. Minh Mang erected a new palace – the Temple of Memory – surrounded by a wall housing the funerary stelae of the former Le kings. On the south side of the royal city, on an artificial mound, the Le kings had built a mirador or flagstaff tower, known in Vietnamese as '*cot co*', and dedicated it to the planet Mars and the element of Fire. This was rebuilt during the nineteenth century, and the present tower was not finally completed until 1912. It is a hexagonal brick structure with Chinese motifs, now surmounted by a dovecote-shaped lookout station added by the French.

With the Royal Citadel vegetating, the trading activities of the Ancient Quarter or Ke Cho, although always relatively separate from the royal city, could not remain unaffected. In particular, the court's efforts to exclude foreign traders had the effect of limiting trading opportunities and prosperity in the town. Until the fifteenth century, foreign traders had come from China, Champa, Java and Siam, but the Later Le dynasty had banned them from living in the capital, even restricting the more favoured Chinese to certain quarters. In 1746 a royal edict forbade foreigners from even staying overnight in the city. The Nguyen kings, who persecuted Western missionaries from time to time, again closed Hanoi to foreign merchants. Even so, the level of Ke Cho's trading activities seems to have recovered over the century and, from having been depopulated at the start of the Nguyen era due to the civil war, by the arrival of the French it was described again as crowded.[92]

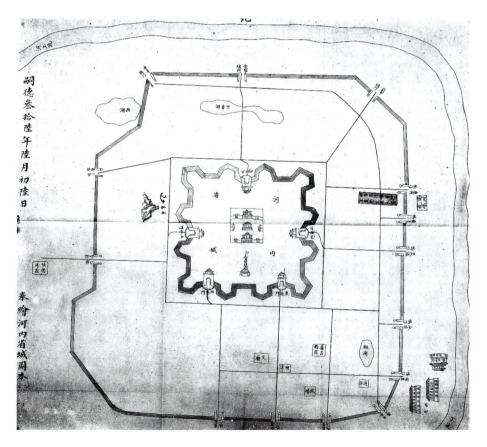

Hanoi's Royal Citadel under the reign of Tu Duc, 1864; drawn in 1913. (Photographic reproduction by the Bibliothèque nationale de France)

The Mirador Tower, one
of the few vestiges of
the Royal Citadel.

Gia Long's Chinese-style legislation also had a major impact on the
way Ke Cho grew. This Annamite Code[93] was written in 1811 and promulgated in 1815 with a preface by the emperor himself. Of the 22
volumes and 398 articles, Articles 156 and 176 had the greatest effect on
the appearance of the town and on the common people's standard of
living. The former declared that the houses of common people could not
be built on a double base, have a double roof, be painted or decorated, or
be made of stone. For the mandarins, the number of entrances and the
kind of decoration depended on their rank. Article 176 reinforced the
hierarchy: the houses, habitations, vehicles and clothing of the mandarins
and the common people were required to differ, again according to rank.
Further, the people of Ke Cho were not permitted to build multi-storeyed
houses – or square houses, since the earth was thought by the Chinese to
be square and only the royal city and palace could emulate the nature of
the earth.[94]

Other works around Hanoi also reflected the neo-Confucianism of
the Nguyen dynasty. One such was the construction of the shrine to
Confucius's parents on the site of the Quoc Tu Giam, or National School.

This had fallen into disrepair during the civil unrest and had been demolished when its royal college function was shifted to Hue in 1807. In the Van Mieu, two entry courtyards were created and, in 1833, adopting another Chinese feature, the entire complex was walled. The overall complex achieved an individuality of design yet a perfection of form in Confucian terms. The low rise of its pavilions manifested humility; its symmetrical layout sought to demonstrate clarity and simplicity. The Chinese concept of harmony lived according to the Confucian 'Middle Path' or 'Golden Mean' was reflected in the balance achieved between the architectural forms and the landscaping of tress, gardens and lotus ponds. The beautiful Khue Van Cac Pavilion was a case in point: built in 1805, its square plinth symbolises the earth, the high two-storey tower with representations of the sun represents the sky, the breezeway through the open pavilion represents wind, and the pool in front of the pavilion symbolises water.

One of the greatest achievements of the Nguyen period was the centralisation of government across the whole of modern Vietnam. This centralisation broke down the old clan and regional loyalties and aided the emergence of a sense of Vietnamese national community. Under Gia Long, the north and south remained relatively free from interference from Hue, but Minh Mang was more ambitious and, despite resistance, insisted on more complete control. He undertook a reform of local government in the early 1830s and, in 1836, ordered a complete revision of the village tax rolls throughout Vietnam. As part of these administrative reforms, he created the province of Ha Noi ('within the bend of the river') and changed the name Thang Long to Ha Noi.[95] Hanoi was reaffirmed as the principal town of the whole of North Vietnam in 1834, and it then became the seat of government of the Kinh-Luoc, or Viceroy, who ensured that Tonkin remained firmly under imperial control.

Benedict Anderson points out that

> ... since the end of the eighteenth century nationalism has undergone a process of modulation and adaptation, according to different eras, political regimes, economies and social structures. The 'imagined community' has, as a result, spread out to every conceivable contemporary society.[96]

This includes Vietnam, where it was perhaps paradoxical that the dynasty that sought to re-sinicise Vietnam should also have witnessed such a flowering of the sense of Vietnamese national identity. That the sense of being Vietnamese should have survived in the countryside is not surprising for reasons already discussed. This separateness was deliberately used for nationalistic purposes in the next century, and a variety of myths and particular versions of history were popularised to assist the nationalist cause. Ralph Smith reports a conversation between Ho Chi Minh and a Russian writer in Moscow in 1923 where Ho, dismissing the Chinese–Vietnamese cultural connections, described himself as belonging to 'an ancient Malay race'.[97] But among the urban elite, memories of the deliberate destruction of the Vietnamese heritage by the Chinese conquerors lingered on and fed the anti-Chinese sentiment.[98] Alexander Woodside claims the adoption of Confucian humanism turned the pre-modern Vietnamese royalty and mandarinate into 'an elite of history-addicted bookworms and bibliophiles', again paradoxically strengthening the sense of difference from the Chinese.[99]

But, in the end, the centralisation of power in the royal court at Hue worked against the Nguyen kings and Vietnamese independence, proving to open up weaknesses that allowed the French to gain ascendancy in the later decades of the century. The ideal Confucian state, in Vietnam as in China, was – to use Jonathan Porter's words about another Chinese-based city, Macao – 'a family-like unit, reflecting the same moral relationships and obligations. And just as kinship ties and tensions create conflicts within the family, so they can disrupt the large society.'[100] The self-contained totality of the world was represented by the Chinese garden – 'a controlled setting, all of the fundamental aesthetics of nature in a balanced harmony' – but the Nguyen court under Tu Duc closed in on itself and became its own totality. The neo-Confucian hierarchical structures, to say nothing of increased taxes, alienated the court from the people. The court appears to have thought that Confucian learning would be sufficient to cope with Vietnam's problems with the French, as it had been in the past with other invaders. Internal disarray ruled out an effective response to the French attack on Da Nang in 1858 and subsequent events leading up the attack on the Hanoi Royal Citadel in 1873 and the capture of Hue ten years later.

Hanoi in 1873: The pre-colonial heritage

The plan drawn in 1873 gives a picture of Hanoi during the reign of Tu Duc at about the time the French arrived on the scene. While still highly stylised, it shows the Royal Citadel with its perfect symmetry and Vauban ramparts lying inside the outer walls of Thang Long. The Kinh Thien Palace and two other palaces – no doubt only a sample of what existed – are found at the centre within the Forbidden City compound. The description by Truong Vinh Ky, who visited in 1876, fills in some of the details:

> First of all we went to the old imperial citadel where, after passing through the Ngu-mon-lau (the principal gateway with five doors), we approached the Kinh-thien Temple. This temple stands on a very high base with a flight of nine steps leading up to it, the whole being built of Thanh-hoa stone.

On either side of the stairway are two dragons, also of stone, with their heads facing downwards. The columns of this temple are large, measuring the whole span of the arms in circumference, and all of them made from ironwood. On investigating behind the temple I saw one or two old palaces in which the Le emperors had once lived, but these are now in ruins and only vestiges remain.[101]

A mandarin probably drew the map and did not bother to show the market town. The large buildings outside the city walls near the Red River to the south-east seem to be European traders' depots.

The number of maps increases significantly from 1873 and portray the city in more realistic terms than the earlier stylised efforts. They show the Kinh Thien Palace taking pride of place within the walls of the Forbidden City. Outside the Forbidden City and immediately to the east were other compounds — the offices of the Viceroy, the chief judge and the military commander. To the west was the larger compound belonging to the tax collector, as well as a temple honouring the military genius, and terraces dedicated to the spirits of the earth, crop harvests, mountains and streams. The elephant stalls were located in the south-eastern corner. The Mirador Tower guarded the Royal City from the front, while behind were two artificial mounds — Tho-son and Khan-son — representing the protective Blue Dragon and White Tiger. Paddy, swamps and pools were numerous within the Vauban fortifications, while the To Lich River flowed through the citadel moat, across the market town, through the external city walls and disappeared into the sandbanks along the Red River.

The Ancient Quarter by this time was bursting with people. The population under Minh Mang was around 50,000, and comprised three-quarters Vietnamese and one-quarter Chinese. Hang Chieu Street leading to the gate on to the Red River seems to have become the main east–west axis, while Hang Dao and Luong Van Can streets have acquired their current role as main north–south roads through the Ancient Quarter. The houses appear still to be mainly of timber, bamboo and thatch, and development is sending out tentacles towards the south-east, enclosing vacant lands. There was still water everywhere. Narrow embankments were topped with muddy lanes, and houses clung on to reclaimed edges. According to André Masson's reconstruction of early colonial Hanoi, 'stinking ponds' occupied the interiors of the Ancient Quarter's built-up blocks.[102]

This was the base on to which the French proceeded to graft their own urban developments from 1873, destroying or changing much as they went. But even as the French were invading, the Ancient Quarter was razed as a last act of defiance by the retreating Black Flags, an army of Chinese mercenaries who had found temporary advantage in supporting the Vietnamese regime. The subsequent decades of colonialism, military

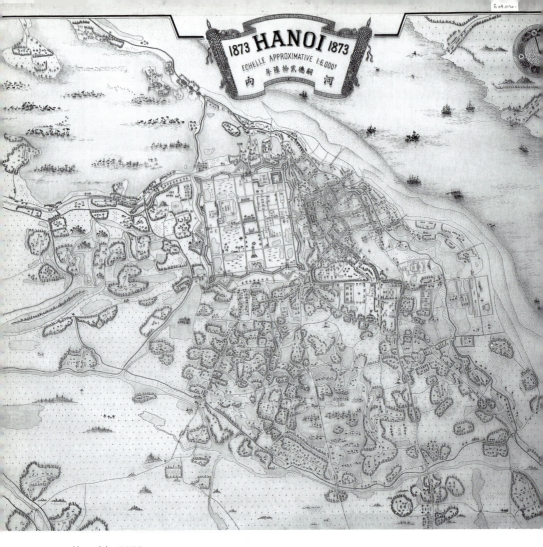

Hanoi in 1873.
(Photographic reproduction by the
Bibliothèque nationale de France)

clashes against the French, war against the United States and its allies,
post-war reconstruction under the influence of the Soviet Union and,
most recently, post-*doi moi* liberalisation have all left their mark, erasing
much of feudal Hanoi. However, the years at the beginning and the end
of the colonial period were the most destructive. The French effort to gain
control over Tonkin saw the dismantling of the Hanoi citadel, the Quoc Tu
Giam and the Thi Huong Examination Hall, while the collapse of the
French regime in the 1950s involved the destruction of the Mot Cot
Pagoda and enormous damage to inner Hanoi streetscapes. Histories by
the French of their time in Vietnam usually make little of this, while
Vietnamese descriptions of Mot Cot highlight its venerability, also leaving
out the fact that it was totally rebuilt in the 1950s and on other occasions.

Authenticity and heritage

What, then, is left of pre-colonial Hanoi that merits inclusion in Hanoi's heritage? At the most fundamental level, the basic division of Hanoi's old sector into the royal city and the commoners' market town is still one of the most prominent features of modern Hanoi. This binary division became a three-way division as the French constructed their own European quarter to the south of Hoan Kiem Lake. Though the Vauban citadel walls were dismantled, their alignment can still be seen in the rectangular pattern of boulevards created by the colonial authorities in the area. Several of today's important roads extend out from where the citadel gates had been: for example, Hang Buom Street originated as the main road linking the East Gate with the port on the Red River. In the market town or Ancient Quarter, the street pattern, though much tidied up by the French as we will see in the next chapter, is still irregular, with narrow roadways and lanes and still dominated by the central markets and a myriad of small retail shops and artisans' workshops. The French Quarter, by contrast, has a regular grid pattern of wide roads lined with pavements and shady trees.

Hundreds of pre-colonial religious buildings — *chua* and *den* — remain scattered throughout the city, often lying tucked away down alleys and surrounded by later accretions. The fifteenth-century Ba Da Pagoda is hidden from public gaze down an alley near the cathedral. The Lien Phai Pagoda, built in 1726 by a Trinh lord in response to a dream, once stood in the broad countryside south of Thang Long. With its ten-storey hexagonal Dieu Quang stupa, which was added in the nineteenth century to hold relics of the patriarch and other Buddhist masters, it is now completely engulfed in the post-1954 low-quality housing of Hanoi's southern suburbs. Despite their surroundings, however, most of these religious buildings are well tended and maintained, and their future contribution to Hanoi's heritage seems assured.

It is a significant fact that in Hanoi there is not much that is old, apart from religious buildings and some tumuli to the west of the old sector. Although the Ly, Tran, Later Le and, to a lesser extent, the Nguyen built extensively in the city, little of Hanoi's pre-colonial architecture remains. Successive invasions and internal conflict led to the destruction of most of their works. Those that have survived date mostly from the mid-seventeenth century or later. Of the Royal Citadel's architecture, only very few vestiges remain today; in fact, only the Mirador Tower and the Cua Bac, or North Gate, are accessible to the general public. Most of the former citadel area is controlled by the Vietnamese army and closed to visitors. There are, however, other relics of the past — a dragon staircase among them — hidden from view. Presumably curatorial attention is being paid to them by the army and when, as has been promised, the army relinquishes the citadel site over the next decade, these relics will again be available as part of the people's heritage.

The dyke system has played an essential role in allowing Hanoi to survive in its watery environment, and is clearly of immense heritage value. So, too, are the remaining city gates, whether physically intact (though much restored) or present only by having been written into the modern street patterns as foci of pedestrian and vehicular traffic. The *dinh*, or communal houses, maintained a village-like or cellular structure in the growing city and for that reason are significant. The French view was that only the *dinh*, along with the fortified imperial city of Hue, stood out as exceptional architectural monuments.[103] Many still exist, but some have been turned to residential use as a result of chronic housing shortages during the last 50 years.

The wind/water theory had a great influence on the spatial arrangements and settings of pre-colonial buildings and should be the basis of evaluation of Hanoi's heritage according to Dam Trong Phuong.[104] Rather than focus excessively on the Ancient Quarter, he argued that buildings and precincts demonstrating this typically Vietnamese design characteristic should be identified and protected. This is certainly important for the Kim Lien and Tran Quoc pagodas with their special relationship to West Lake, the Van Mieu and Hai Ba Trung Temple because of their relationship to the lakes in front of them, and the Ngoc Son Temple with its relationship to Hoan Kiem. However, we will see in Chapter 7 that the construction of new housing in the 1990s for foreign workers and the rising Vietnamese middle class began to cut Kim Lien from its lake. Meanwhile, tourist boats on West Lake threatened the tranquillity of Tran Quoc until the authorities stepped in with restrictions.

Much of the significance of old Hanoi is iconic rather than strictly historical. Myths, ancient and modern, help to make Hanoi as a whole a special city. The heritage importance of the Ancient Quarter lies more in the belief of its historical quality than in the physical reality. It is important to the Hanoi people to hold to this belief; it is part of their intangible heritage and a key to their cultural identity. But Nguyen Vinh Cat outlined in 1993 a recent survey of 33 old streets in the Hoan Kiem district which showed that, of the 2,345 existing houses, only 7 per cent had been built before 1900, 9 per cent were built between 1900 and 1930, and the remaining 84 per cent were newer than 1930.[105]

Religious and ancestral buildings in Vietnam are periodically repaired, repainted, even rebuilt, as a sign of respect. Other changes were to be expected due to political events, the climate, the materials used and the lack of maintenance. Apart from some stone towers, Vietnamese architecture traditionally used timber as the main building material. In

Hanoi, brick, bamboo and thatch were also used, but the bricks were relatively soft and the bamboo and thatch flimsy. The hot, humid climate and the easily inflammable nature of many of the materials meant that buildings did not last long and either experienced frequent renovations or have disappeared. In the Ancient Quarter, only the brick and tile houses of the more substantial Chinese traders survived the Black Flags' last-ditch stand in 1883. Essentially, the trading town had to be built again under the French – and this was apparently done within a year.[106] Only one of the gates in the walls surrounding the Ancient Quarter – known at different times as the Thanh Ha Gate, the Porte Jean Dupuis or Cua O Quan Chuong – has survived.[107]

The gate is an interesting case. Has it, in fact, survived in its traditional form? Or was it at some point reconstructed, like Viollet Le Duc's over-restoration of French Gothic buildings in the nineteenth century, as it should ideally have been rather than respecting the historical evidence? In this case, the published evidence is contradictory and incomplete, as the three following illustrations indicate. If the Fraipont drawing is an accurate rendition of the gate as it had traditionally existed, it would seem that today's gate, heavily restored in the mid-1990s, still maintains the essential original elements. However, the illustration in the 1987 facsimile re-publication of *Les Grands Dossiers de l'Illustration. L'Indochine* shows an entirely different gate, by artist A. Deroy and accompanying an 1880 description of the Tonkin travels of Dupuis. On face value, it looks like an idealised reconstruction had occurred between 1880 and the time of the Fraipont drawing twenty years later. Fortunately, an almost identical illustration held by the National Library in Paris seems to offer a solution. Signed by the artist A. Brun, it gives the location as 'La Porte des Incrusteurs', or Pearl Shell Inlayers Street, renamed Rue Paul Bert by the 1890s and known today as Trang Tien Street.

A broad issue of the lack of historical authenticity of the Ancient Quarter, indeed of most of Hanoi's historic monuments and areas, results from the frequent repair and restoration activities of the Vietnamese religious and secular authorities. This perceived lack of authenticity, or integrity, is mainly a problem for traditional conservationists from the West. For them the significance of the Ancient Quarter is greatly reduced, and arguments for heritage protection in the face of counter-arguments for redevelopment are correspondingly more difficult to make. This bears on differing conceptions of heritage authenticity, where a sharp contrast exists between the Western and East Asian (including Vietnamese) approaches. The traditional Western approach, as encapsulated in the *Venice Charter* adopted by the International Council on Monuments and Sites (ICOMOS), emphasises the authenticity of the *physical fabric*. Where new materials have to be added to a heritage item, they should be clearly distinguishable

Above Jean Dupuis Street and Gate, Hanoi, c. 1900, as drawn by Georges Fraipont for inclusion in Paul Doumer's memoires of his period as governor-general. (Paul Doumer, *L'Indochine française (Souvenirs)* (Viubert et Nony Éditeurs, Paris, 1905), p. 123)

Centre Jean Dupuis Street and Gate, 1880, as published in *Les Grands Dossiers de l'Illustration. L'Indochine* (Le Livre de Paris, Paris, 1987), p. 53.

Bottom Pearl Shell Inlayers Street, as drawn by artist A. Brun. (Bibliothèque Nationale, Paris) This street was renamed in honour of the first French governor of Tonkin, Paul Bert, in the 1890s.

The Quan Chuong Gate after
major renovations in 1994.

from the original. The East Asian approach is encapsulated in the more
recent joint UNESCO and ICOMOS *Document of Nara*.[108] It puts a much
higher emphasis on showing reverence for the monument and its symbolism by maintaining the condition of the building or even reconstructing
it, and on preserving the craft skills required to restore traditional buildings.
In other words, the intangible aspects of a building's or site's history, including mythical and iconic factors, are given greater status in determining
significance.[109]

The Van Mieu, for example, may have been restored and repaired
repeatedly over 900 years, but its original symbolism has been kept and the
interventions have used traditional skills. This has not prevented
considerable adjustment to the original physical conception of the complex.
In the seventeenth century, there were only three courtyards. Under Gia
Long the complex was remodelled to add the first two of today's courtyards.
This created five compartments within the complex, the number five having
special significance in Confucianism (five elements, five virtues, five
commandments, five sorrows, five cardinal relationships, five classics). It
also involved replacing the existing hedges by new walls using bricks taken
from the citadel that Gia Long was also in the process of rebuilding.[110]

This process of change continues to the present day. In 1993–94, eight
pavilions were rebuilt over the Van Mieu stelae that record the names of
those who had passed the mandarinate entrance examinations.
Seventeenth-century documents show their existence at that time, but they

Above The Van Mieu stelae pavilions, reconstructed with American Express funds in 1993–94.

Below Postcard of the Khue Van Cac Pavilion and Well of Heavenly Brilliance, c. 1905. Some of the 82 stelae are seen beyond the pool exposed to the elements.

93. TONKIN — Hanoï
Pagode de la Littérature
Pavillon de l'Eloquence

were gone by the early twentieth century.[111] By Western standards these reconstructions are not authentic; by Vietnamese standards their reconstruction is desirable, not only to keep alive the sense of the historical place but also to protect the stone stelae from further climatic effects.[112] Thus, in 1992, after 20 years of discussions with Vietnamese and international experts, the State Centre for Cultural Building Design and Monument Restoration produced a design for eight pavilions to cover and protect the stelae. No exact drawings of the eighteenth-century pavilions existed, and the restoration proceeded as an attempt to blend in with the existing architecture of the Van Mieu and to use traditional building methods. The reconstruction took place in 1993–94, with half the costs met by the Ministry of Information and Culture and half by the American Express Company. It is often difficult to know which period an evolving site should be taken back to in the restoration process. With the Van Mieu, the Vietnamese authorities have chosen to return the buildings and site layout to how it was in the nineteenth century.

The Van Mieu is perhaps the most significant single heritage item in Hanoi. However, the heritage interest in Hanoi does not lie principally in individual buildings so much as in the ensemble of historical elements and the social life still contained within them. The greatest need faced by modern Hanoi is to tame the development forces currently transforming the inner city. The current rate and type of development will ultimately destroy the character of the area if it does not produce a social and physical implosion first, with the traditional residents moving out in favour of the new middle class and mini-hotels, and with the collapse of the existing infrastructure. A question that bedevils heritage planners across the world is whether such social ambience can or should be preserved. In Hanoi's case, policy-makers are faced with the need to decide the extent to which the old sector can or should be turned into a museum town, frozen in time.

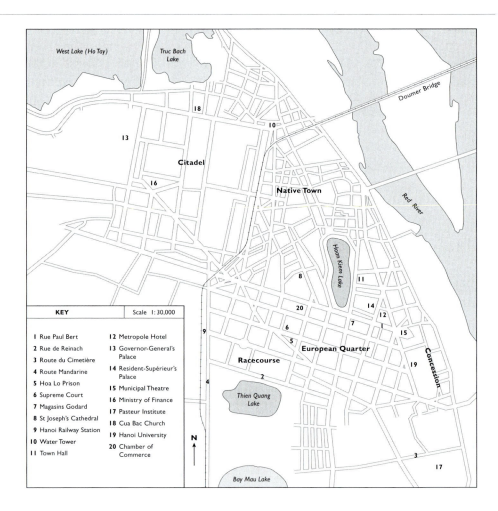

West Lake (Ho Tay)

Truc Bach Lake

Doumer Bridge

18

13

10

Citadel

16

Native Town

Red River

Hoan Kiem Lake

8

11

20

14

12

9

6

7

1

15

5

European Quarter

Racecourse

19

KEY		Scale 1:30,000

2

Thien Quang Lake

4

N
↑

1 Rue Paul Bert
2 Rue de Reinach
3 Route du Cimetière
4 Route Mandarine
5 Hoa Lo Prison
6 Supreme Court
7 Magasins Godard
8 St Joseph's Cathedral
9 Hanoi Railway Station
10 Water Tower
11 Town Hall

12 Metropole Hotel
13 Governor-General's Palace
14 Resident-Supérieur's Palace
15 Municipal Theatre
16 Ministry of Finance
17 Pasteur Institute
18 Cua Bac Church
19 Hanoi University
20 Chamber of Commerce

3

17

Bay Mau Lake

Chapter 3
Hanoi: Building a capital for French Indochina

La période héroique: Taming people and environment

If the Nguyen from time to time persecuted Christian missionaries and harassed Western traders, this was not on the scale of the mistreatment the Vietnamese population experienced under French colonialism. The prison in central Hanoi, known as Hoa Lo (literally 'Hell's Hole'), still stands today as testimony to this record of forced 'pacification' and commercial exploitation conducted in the name of spreading *la mission civilisatrice* to the natives. Attributed to the chief government architect Auguste-Henri Vildieu[1] and built in 1886–89, the prison was given the bland name of 'Maison centrale'. (Later, with further irony, it became known as the 'Hanoi Hilton' by the captured US airmen held there during the Vietnam War.) Originally designed for 450 prisoners, by 1954 it held more than 2,000. The French were doing no more than was expected of colonial powers in the 1880s and 1890s, but this is no justification in the eyes of some older Vietnamese who still remember the colonial times with bitterness.

The first Europeans to arrive in Vietnam from 1626 were Portuguese, Dutch and English traders. Wanting to buy silk and spices in return for European goods, they found the markets poor and the location too distant from major shipping routes, and they disappeared again by the end of the century. It was left to the French to colonise this part of South-east Asia in any more permanent sense in the context of the nineteenth-century competition between European countries to add to their imperial territories and international prestige. However, in the case of the French in Vietnam, missionaries – starting with Alexandre de Rhodes at Hanoi in 1627 – preceded the traders. Despite Vietnamese imperial bans on proselytising, the priests had considerable impact, including the introduction of the *quoc ngu* romanised system of writing the Vietnamese tonal language. It was harassment of the missionaries which, only much later, was the pretext for the first French military intervention in Cochinchina in 1858–59.

Hoa Lo Prison, now reopened as a museum highlighting the colonial oppression that led to the emergence of the twentieth-century nationalist movement.

In the case of Tonkin, by contrast, the provocation was related to trade rather than the church. The story of the 'Dupuis Affair' has been told by Masson and others.[2] Dupuis wanted to use the Red River as a commercial route to the potentially lucrative markets and supplies of southern China. The imperial court in Hue objected and the Governor of the French colony of 'Cochin-Chine', deciding to intervene, despatched Lieutenant Commander Francis Garnier to Hanoi. Landing at the trading quay in November 1873, Garnier declared the Red River open to general commerce. He was determined to put in place immediately a *de facto* protectorate and, with a contingent of only 212 men and without authorisation from Paris, captured the citadel.[3] Piling outrage upon outrage, he commandeered the royal palace (Kinh Tien) for his own accommodation, describing it as reasonably comfortable once he had subdivided its large interior.[4] His audacious actions led to immediate hostilities: the Vietnamese Kinh Luoc (Viceroy) called in the Black Flag mercenaries, but the French troops succeeded in taking the citadel. Within weeks, Garner paid for his reckless actions with his life in a skirmish with the Black Flags on the outskirts of town.

The French government in Paris, apparently traumatised by its loss in the 1870 Franco-Prussian War, hurried to sign a treaty with Hue, abandoning those Vietnamese who had aided them to the swift vengeance of the mandarins.[5] Under the 1874 Philastre Agreement the French troops were withdrawn to a concession on the banks of the Red River. Here the French began creating a settlement along European organisational and architectural lines under the control of the military and with a consul in charge of commercial interests. Another concession was granted at Haiphong on the coast, a town that eventually assumed the role of Tonkin's main trading port. Until 1883, it was only in these two concessions that Europeans were permitted to reside.[6]

France's military power was quickly demonstrated by the development of its Hanoi concession. An area of 18.5 hectares, it was bounded in the north by a narrow road (later renamed Rue de la France by the colonial authorities) which ran from the river to the gate of the imperial mint (renamed Porte de France). On the west, it was bounded by the dyke rampart along today's Ly Thai To and Le Thanh Tong streets, and on the east by the river. In the south, the boundary was an irregular line taking in the Nguyen Cong Tru area that became a European cemetery. The whole western part — where, later, Hanoi University and the Municipal Theatre (Opera House) were built — was swampland. In the eastern part beneath flamboyant trees, inexperienced indigenous labourers were used to build a private residence for the regimental commander, officers' quarters and barracks for the men, the chancellor's quarters, the engineering officer's house, a mapping unit and a hospital. A customs service was established to control the movement of imports and exports. The private house of the first consul was also built here, soon to be enlarged to accommodate the first *Résident-Supérieur du Tonkin* (Tonkin Governor) and the *Gouverneur-Général* (Governor-General) of the French Indochinese Union. The residences were simple, spacious two-storey houses with wide verandahs.

European merchants and missionaries took refuge in the concession during the periods when Hanoi was under the control of the Black Flags. In these years the French population consisted of a handful of administrators and customs officials and the French military. In the mid-1880s there were only four other Europeans: von der Heyde, a well-dressed German representing a German company in Hong Kong; 'two poor French devils eking out a living — Perrin who ran a small café next to the concession, and Peretti, a Corsican, of unclear occupation'; and Mme de Beire, a 'strange adventurer and probably fallen character, flotsam from the Dupuis expedition'.[7] Described as around 55 years old with a 'worn and ravaged face', Mme de Beire claimed to be Belgian and was evidently well educated. She lived in a hut about a kilometre from the concession, near the mission, and drank with the military men who made her hut the target of their evening walks. During the conflict with the Black Flags, timber stockades were set up around the Concession and these remained in place for several years, giving it an embattled look. Inside, the paths were muddy and the buildings far from inspiring. Nevertheless, weekly parties at the consul's house helped to keep up morale and the appearance that all was well.[8]

There was panic in the Concession in April 1882 when rumours were heard that the Black Flags were moving down from Lao Cai on the Chinese border to Son Tay where they were within two forced marches of Hanoi.[9] Four hundred troops under Commandant Henri Rivière were despatched, and the citadel was seized and held for a year until Rivière was killed in another Black Flag ambush on the road to Son Tay, not far from where Garnier had died ten years earlier. The French authorities were incensed and continued to build up reinforcements. In August 1883, there were 3,750 French troops in Tonkin; by December there were 9,000 in six towns – Hanoi, Haiphong, Hai Duong, Nam Dinh, Ninh Binh and Quang Yen – although the Black Flags were still the real masters of the delta.[10] When the Tonkinese authorities demanded an explanation for the doubling of troops in the garrison, the reason France gave was that its troops and missionaries had been too frequently insulted by the Black Flags acting, it was alleged, for the mandarins.[11]

Eventually the long and difficult campaign against the Black Flag troops was won, the imperial representatives either fled or committed suicide, and Quan An – the mandarin in charge of justice – took over the running of the city under the French.[12] The establishment of a French protectorate over Tonkin was recognised by Hue in August 1883 and by China in June 1885. Hanoi became the French capital of Tonkin and, in 1887, capital of the French Indochinese Union that eventually comprised Tonkin, Annam, Cochinchina, Cambodia and Laos, a status it enjoyed until after World War 2. Despite these political milestones, however, French rule met with a mix of passive resistance and open rebellion, and a pacification campaign lasting 20 years was needed to consolidate colonial control.

In his 1929 attempt to reconstruct Hanoi's early years, André Masson labelled the first phase of French settlement from 1873 to 1888 the 'période héroique' – a period characterised by bold steps to tame the place they had now acquired, to subdue the indigenous population and to overcome the most urgent of Hanoi's many environmental problems. From the late 1890s, the French turned to improvements of a more sophisticated nature, much more a reflection of the ideas current in metropolitan France or adopted in other French colonies than a reflection of Hanoi's specific characteristics. Both periods left distinctive marks on the townscape – sets of icons that say much about the prevailing attitudes of the colonial authorities and the architects, town planners, engineers and builders who worked for them.

One of the first impacts – a drastic remodelling of the Royal Citadel – showed who held the reins. Not only were the walls and moats removed to make way for a new grid of road reservations, but in 1886–87 the royal Kinh Thien Palace was demolished and the artillery headquarters were constructed on its site.[13] The Thi Huong examination compound (*camp des lettrés*) was turned into a military post. Confronted by this vandalism, the poet Tu Dien Dong lamented:

> This nation had existed for many thousand years
> Before the Ly dynasty chose this place for its capital.
> Alas! Of the five gates, only Cua Bac is left
> And atop the Tower flutters only the French flag![14]

A well-protected road was established to link the Concession and the citadel, thus setting in place Hanoi's key east–west axis, today's Trang Tien and Trang Thi streets. This was then 1.5 kilometres of tortuous road, quite built-up near the citadel gate but with only a scatter of houses among paddy towards the examination compound.[15] At Hoan Kiem Lake, housing development was more continuous but paddy fields filled the interior of street blocks. The eastern section of this road was called Pearl Shell Inlayers Street by the Vietnamese. It was widened in 1886 at the cost of the Vietnamese houses along it and the historic gate at its eastern end, and soon became Hanoi's main commercial thoroughfare.

The army's main role during this period was the pacification of the natives. Hoa Lo saw many rebels incarcerated in its dark cells. Its architecture, according to Vietnamese architectural historian Dang Thai Hoang, was especially formidable: with its walls of stone 'making it look so strong, [and] by puncturing the surrounding ... walls with iron-barred

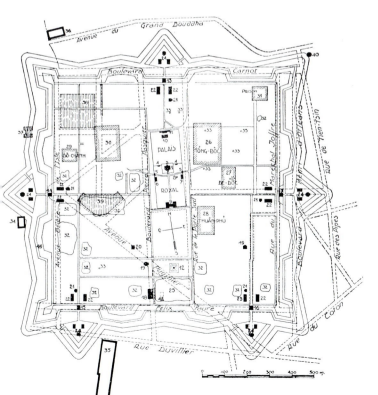

The French redesign of the citadel area. (Les Amis du Patrimoine Architectural du Vietnam, *Hanoi: Ville et Mémoire* (APAV, Paris, 1993), p. 9)

portholes, the French must have sought to create, especially for those outside, a most terrifying impression of life within'.[16] In the years 1900–1906, almost next-door to the prison, the Palais de Justice (Supreme Court) was erected with similar visual intent. Again the design was by Hanoi's chief architect, Auguste-Henri Vildieu.

Civilian government commenced in 1886 with the installation of Paul Bert as first Resident and, from 1888, Hanoi began to expand and take on the appearance of a modern town. Security within the town was improved. In the Ancient Quarter the internal gates between guild sections were removed and the old wall, at that time still running along the eastern side of the city, was dismantled. The streets were widened and straightened, allowing better access by troops, the fire brigade and horse-drawn carriages. The channel stones down the centre of roads were removed and footpaths and gutters installed. The residents were forced to comply with orders to conform to the new street alignments with no form of compensation. Although physically modified, the market town managed to keep its street life and the pattern of street specialisation persisted.

A major concern to the south around Hoan Kiem was cleaning up the environment for health and aesthetic reasons. When the French arrived, they found that Ke Cho and the area around Hoan Kiem Lake had no

Postcard view of the citadel area
and Mirador Tower, 1907.

166. TONKIN - Hanoï — Tour de l'ancienne citadelle

natural drainage system other than the partly canalised To Lich River.[17] But the To Lich was unable to flow into the Red River in dry seasons, and stagnant pools of waste water were left lying everywhere. For most of the year, the waste waters simply ran into the interconnecting swamps and spread across the southern outskirts of Hanoi in a series of marshes and ponds. Georges Dumoutier painted the scene around the lake in 1883:

> ... native huts crowded its shores; to go down to the water it was necessary to weave through narrow alleys, leaving the city's passable roads ... to run into a thousand detours [formed by a jumble of] ... straw huts where a destitute population swarmed, to hop among stinking puddles and piles of garbage; and often at the end of an hour after patient detours as in a labyrinth, the bold explorer found himself yet again at his starting point without having reached the shore. And even if he caught a glimpse of a little bit of the lake ..., he was not tempted to approach ... [because one commonly] encounters an unhealthy lagoon at a street corner or behind gloomy huts in old Hanoi.[18]

Ten years later, Lucien de Reinach, describing Hanoi's living conditions to his family back home in France, wrote of the terrible heat that kept him in his hotel room until late evening.[19] Even there, life was made miserable by tropical insects:

The Beaux-Arts façade of the Supreme Court, c. 1907. Two wide staircases led to an imposing waiting room (*Salle des pas perdus*) on the first floor.

125. TONKIN - Hanoï — Palais de Justice

Never have I seen such a variety of animals walk across the walls. If only they would stay there, but no; they recognise my flesh as good for biting, and give themselves over to all sorts of exercises on my body. The mosquitoes among others are so relentless that they bite me through my clothes. Then when there are no mosquitoes, there are cockroaches ... or more green, pink and yellow flies.

L'ÉVOLUTION DE HANOI EN UN DEMI-SIÈCLE

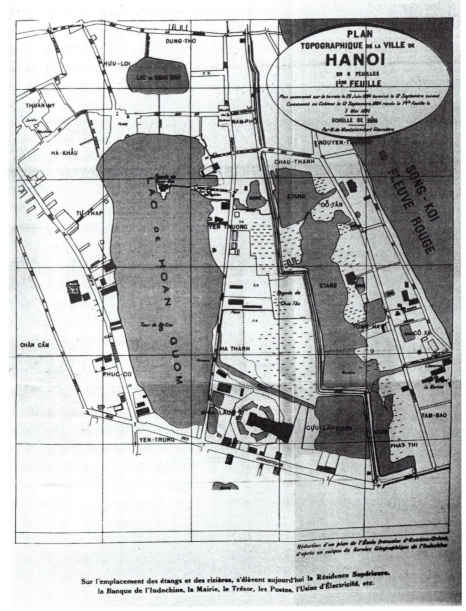

Sur l'emplacement des étangs et des rizières, s'élèvent aujourd'hui la Résidence Supérieure, la Banque de l'Indochine, la Mairie, le Trésor, les Postes, l'Usine d'Électricité, etc.

Opposite page The Hoan Kiem area in May
1885, showing the location of ponds, swamps,
rice fields and pagodas. (Plan topographique de
la Ville de Hanoi en 6 feuilles, Sheet 1, by M.
de Montalambart, Surveyor, reproduced in
André Masson, *Hanoi pendant la période
héroique (1873–1888)* (Librairie Orientaliste
Paul Gueuthner, Paris, 1929))

Above Coolies transport river
sands for the colonial swamp
reclamation program, 1904.
(Photographic reproduction
by the Bibliothèque
nationale de France)

The civil authorities were afraid that the physical health of the
colonists and indigenous population would be affected and so set about
freeing Hoan Kiem's banks of the ring of shambling stilt huts and
diverting household wastes into deep cesspits and, later, a sewerage
system. According to de Reinach, the 'Petit Lac', as the French called Hoan
Kiem, was surrounded by grass, trees and greenery and had become a
pleasant place to wander when the sun went down.[20]

Hoan Kiem's connection with the To Lich River and Lake Truc Bach by
way of a series of swamps and ponds was cut off by the French program
of filling in the hundreds of swamps and ponds in and around Hanoi,
generally with sand from the Red River. By 1902 the only buildings
resisting removal from the banks of the lake were a former pagoda, now

owned by the Protectorate and used as the public lending library, and the properties of Hanoi trader, Godard.[21] Eventually, once the government afforded him compensation, Godard concentrated his efforts in the site at the corner of Rue Paul Bert where he proceeded to establish Hanoi's largest department store. His Magasins Godard (later Grands Magasins Réunis) followed the department store architecture made fashionable by the Parisian Galeries Lafayette and La Samaritaine with a domed ceiling, grand staircase and balconied upper floors. Around Hoan Kiem and elsewhere in Hanoi, the construction of water channels and pumping stations helped to reduce the problems of malaria and dysentery. Work had started on a system of fresh water supply, and major streets were lit with gas, then in 1895 with electricity. An electric tramway system was established in 1900, serving various suburbs and peripheral villages, the markets and workshops. The first public urinals were built in 1902.

As well as being concerned with physical health, the French *mission civilisatrice* included the saving of native souls. Such spiritual activities were focused in the mission area established west of Hoan Kiem, beyond the Ba Da Pagoda. The French missionaries' early efforts seemed to bear fruit in 1886 when Monseigneur Puginier inaugurated the square-towered St Joseph's Cathedral.[22] But when Governor-General Paul Doumer — often described as the Father of French Indochina — arrived in Hanoi in 1897, he was shocked to find that the Vietnamese population, while more or less under control, still 'readily seized any opportunity or a moment of weakness on our part to try to throw off the yoke'.[23] This was despite the peace, stability and improved well-being that he imagined the French had brought. Even the mandarins were not to be trusted; indeed, according to the French, the mandarins were now able to blame the colonial regime for the high taxes and other demands that in fact they were imposing on the general populace.

Doumer set about defining a plan of action, putting as his highest priority finding a cure for Indochina's financial position and creating a unified fiscal regime across the whole of Indochina. His other aims were to complete the pacification of Tonkin, and to organise the government and reform the administration of the Indochinese Union. In addition, he wanted to build the infrastructure that would allow the realisation of Indochina's economic potential, and to encourage industrial and agricultural production using French management skills and indigenous labour.[24] Consequently, from 1900, when Doumer began to commission more grandiose public buildings and infrastructure projects, Hanoi entered the second phase of its colonial urban history. Railway lines and improved roads to Lang Son and Lao Cai in the north and Vinh in the south were opened up, the fluvial port was dredged, and a customs house was opened. The main Hanoi railway station began operating in 1903.[25]

The Pont Doumer, drawn by Georges Fraipont. (Paul Doumer, *L'Indo-Chine française (Souvenirs)* (Viubert et Nony Editeurs, Paris, 2nd edn, 1905), p. 312)

The Pont Doumer (now the Long Bien Bridge) was built at this time – a major engineering feat, being nearly 1.7 kilometres long and spanning a river that shifted from year to year across a bed of sand, gravel and stones. Many people credit the design of the bridge to Gustave Eiffel. According to Doumer's memoirs, the company of Daydé et Pillé, from Creil in Oise Department, won the tender and started work in 1898.[26] Dang Thai Hoang claims the bridge was 'built to an Eiffel Company blueprint'.[27] Laurent Weill refers to the Doumer Plan (1898–1902) generating numerous projects for the Compagnie des Etablissments Eiffel.[28] But Gustave Eiffel had resigned from the company in 1893 following the Panama Canal scandal in which he had been embroiled and the rejection of his company's bid to undertake the Paris Metro.[29] Is this another Hanoi myth, one designed to bolster the pedigree of the French impact on the city? Certainly the myth is exploited by Gustave's Restaurant in Trang Tien Street near the Opera House, using the Eiffel Tower as its motif.

Such development expenditure was highly speculative. Indochina did not bring in revenue for the French coffers, at least in the early years; in fact, it was proving extremely expensive, and many metropolitan politicians opposed the continual outlay. The ability to increase existing taxes was limited, especially as the traditional imperial monopolies on rice alcohol and salt were publicly hated and not sufficiently lucrative from the government's point of view to be worth taking over. Encouraging the development of traditional handicrafts as a source of trade and tax revenue was written off as early as 1884.[30] Establishing a modern industrial base was even less feasible, due to opposition from French industrialists back home who wanted to maintain an exclusive market for their goods. French merchants also wanted to preserve the established pattern of shipping manufactured goods to the colonies and taking back raw materials for French industries. In fact, French dominance of the Indochina trade was only achieved after World War 1 when effective protectionist barriers were established. But in the 1880s and 1890s, hope shone brighter than reality. The French presence in Tonkin and the four other components of Indochina survived only after last-minute appeals by the French government to the legislature to pass colonial money bills – not in the name of economic logic, but for the sake of national prestige.[31]

The acclaimed *mission civilisatrice* that impelled the French effort in Indochina had two components. First, it aimed at the cultural assimilation of the various Indochinese peoples through the provision of education and inculcation of respect for French culture. Secondly, it was hoped that, by developing administrative organisation and economic activities, Indochina would eventually be assimilated functionally into the French Republic.[32] But behind both were the colonialist goals of national glory and economic advantage. As William Duiker pointed out in his study of Vietnamese nationalism and revolution, this led inevitably to the emergence of serious contradictions in the running of Indochina. In particular, there was a large gap between the 'publicised goal of the white man's burden and the more pragmatic objective of exploiting the economic resources of the colonial territories for the benefit of the home country'.[33] The result was mealy-mouthed statements that must have fooled few Vietnamese. Paul Bert's 1885 call to the Vietnamese is a case in point:

> Our peoples are not made to fight each other but to work together and each provides what the other is lacking. If the French have come to settle in your territory, you should understand that it is not at all with the thought of taking your lands or your harvests from you; on the contrary, the intention is to increase the general wealth by raising the value of your lands, by facilitating your agricultural production, … by the creation of easy lines of communication, by the development of the resources now lying hidden in your mines, and by the protection which we will accord your overseas commercial transactions. The French have the means for doing this, which the Annamites do not yet possess — the capital, the machinery, the engineers and a long experience in business; the French will be your elder brothers.[34]

The hypocritical quality of the *mission civilisatrice* has been demonstrated by numerous scholars.[35] The Vietnamese historian Pham Cao Duong says 'it was merely a myth' and noted that the vaunted educational and medical improvements were largely confined to the affluent urban elite and did not extend to the mass of peasants or even the poor living in urban areas.[36] The way Doumer tried to accomplish his primary goal demonstrates that the French effort was far from being an altruistic rescue mission. His public works program was funded by a system of state-controlled distribution of three commodities understood today to be potentially destructive to the health of the individual and of society in general – tobacco, alcohol and opium.

A new state monopoly on opium, in particular, seemed to Doumer to have the most lucrative taxing possibilities and had the potential to expand. He set about developing state control over all aspects of the supply system – importation or cultivation, manufacture, wholesale and retail trade – except the sale of the final product, which he left to the Chinese who had traditionally cornered the opium business in Indochinese towns.[37] He complained that, despite its population being larger than that of Cochinchina and Cambodia, Tonkin consumed less government opium, partly because much was smuggled across the Chinese border from Yunnan.[38]

In establishing this trade, of course, the French administration was not alone. The English had, also for commercial reasons, introduced opium by force into China in the nineteenth century, as well as into its other Asian colonies, and it appears that Doumer looked to British Singapore as the model to follow. Nor, in fact, was the exploitation of opium completely new in Indochina. The Cambodian king profited from a monopoly on supply of opium and rice alcohol. Also, although Minh Mang and, early in his reign, Tu Duc prohibited opium on pain of death, the latter turned to the licensing of Chinese opium farmers in the north of Vietnam in order to find funds to pay war indemnities forced on him by the victorious French in Cochinchina.[39] By 1888 the Cochinchinese colonial authorities had assumed the opium monopoly and required all purchases to be conducted through French companies established in Calcutta. It was this as much as anything that forced traders in the 1890s to seek alternative sources in southern China.

The opium trade had unintended political consequences. Both the encouragement of opium consumption and the severe repression of smuggling outraged Vietnamese nationalists, who saw it as one of the most hideous and detestable forms of colonial oppression. The trade acted as a catalyst to the nationalist movement and indirectly to the incarceration of political prisoners in Hoa Lo. It even rated a mention in Ho Chi Minh's 1945 Declaration of Independence. A further consequence resulted from the French authorities' attempt to buy off the ethnic minorities, especially the White Thai in Tonkin and the Hmong in Laos, by turning a blind eye to their opium smuggling. This was to become a source of political instability through much of the twentieth century, and public health and social problems associated with opium production, smuggling and consumption among these groups still persist today.

Images of Indochina: Cultural values and vandalism

Not only was the attitude of the French Indochinese authorities, like all colonial regimes, imbued with paternalism and their *mission civilisatrice* impelled by mixed motivations, but many French colonists treated Vietnamese culture with extreme condescension. Even many French scholars regarded it either as mediocre, provincial Chinese or as merely a transition between Indian and Chinese; in either case, it had no distinct identity of its own.[40] The relics of the indianised Champa and Angkor kingdoms were much preferred. Again, as M. Christine Boyer shows, a general disregard for Asian art was widely held throughout Western Europe in the mid- and late nineteenth century. The 'great' nineteenth-century English art critic, John Ruskin, for example, thought all Asian art to be inferior, largely because tropical areas with their enervating heat were not conducive to what he considered as truly noble art. 'The Chinese and Indians, and other semi-civilised nations, can colour better than we do,' Ruskin maintained, but 'all intellectual progress in art has been for ages rendered impossible.'[41]

One of the results of this disdain has already been mentioned – the almost complete demolition of the citadel walls in 1894–97. The motive for this act of vandalism cannot have been the desire to eliminate a military threat to France's hold on Hanoi, for Vauban walls had long been rendered ineffective by advances in military technology, particularly the development of cannons firing explosive shells.[42] The citadel seems to have been destroyed because it represented the wrong symbolism – the old Vietnamese imperial regime. Its demolition was accompanied by the destruction of other equally significant Vietnamese townscape features and their replacement by new buildings and monuments that signalled and soon celebrated France's arrival.

In 1883 the French pulled down the Thi Huong examination compound and reused the site initially for troop barracks. Later, as part of the colonial policy of indirect rule – Tonkin was a protectorate, rather than a colony – the French authorities built a palace on the site for the Kinh Luoc. Before he had moved in, the Viceroy put the palace and grounds at the disposal of the organisers of the first Hanoi Exposition, held in March–April 1887.[43] In 1897 the building appears to have been occupied by the first Chamber of Commerce, but in 1919 it became the offices of the Indochinese Archives and Libraries Department. Hanoi's National Library now stands on the site of the former Thao Dap Pavilion.

The fate of the Quoc Hoc Vien school was no better, although its destruction came later: it was razed by French troops in 1947. However, the education of the royal princes had already been transferred to Hue in the nineteenth century, and the Quoc Tu Giam transformed into the Khai

Thanh shrine to Confucius's parents. Today only a few remains of the shrine are left, standing in an empty space behind the Van Mieu. Nor did the small lake called the Van Ho, opposite the Van Mieu's Great Portico, fare any better. Another important example of the Vietnamese skill in achieving harmony between fluid water and solid form in their architecture, this lake formerly had a small island and pavilion where literature students used to meet. According to poems engraved on a stele, apricot, orange and lemon trees, pomegranates, frangipanis and peonies grew there in the seventeenth century. Later, however, the lake silted up and became overgrown with shrubs and bushes.[44] It was restored by the Vietnamese rulers in 1883, the year before the French established their colonial rule over Tonkin, and again in 1940.[45] It is now once more reduced in size, cut off from the Van Mieu by a busy roadway and almost totally hidden by recent buildings and a plant nursery.

The Catholic Cathedral was built on the site of the Bao Thien Pagoda demolished by the French. The Bach Ma Temple lost almost half of its site because of colonial road alignment and footpath construction works in the Ancient Quarter during the 1890s. Other temples and pagodas suffered similarly.[46] In the 1880s the administrative buildings on the Concession were relocated to a new government precinct at the south-eastern corner of Hoan Kiem Lake on the east–west axis. Old cultural symbols were demolished in the process, including the imposing Bao An Pagoda and its complex of Buddhist buildings.[47] Erected in 1842, its main building had been surrounded by circular ponds overgrown with lotus and it had numerous bell-towers, porticoes and turrets. André Masson referred to it as the most remarkable of Hanoi's pagodas.[48] But it gave way to a new post office, treasury buildings and the Resident's palace and adjacent offices designed by Hanoi's chief architect, Vildieu.

A nineteenth-century Vietnamese watercolour of the Bao An Pagoda. (Musée Guimet, Paris. ©PHOTO R.M.N.)

The only remains of the Chua Bao An
today is the Thap Hoa Phong (Tower of
the Favourable Wind), a small, elegant,
brick gatepost on the lake edge.

Hanoi was proclaimed a municipality in 1888. To construct a town hall (1897–1906) further north along Boulevard Francis Garnier, the Chua Tao, or Temple of Supreme Reason, was torn down. This pagoda had been built to memorialise the wars against the Cham. Its elaborately decorated sculpted friezes, stelae and two notable statues of bird-women playing lutes were dismantled and subsequently lost.[49] The town hall design was again by Vildieu who, though his Hanoi work rarely deviated from his neoclassical European training, was — so we are told by Louis Bézacier — extremely interested in Vietnamese traditional architecture.[50] Indeed, he is said to have made a measured drawing of the Bao An Pagoda before it was demolished. Unfortunately, his drawings have also been lost. Next to the town hall, a long rectangular park — Paul Bert Square — was created in 1890, complete with a circular bandstand for weekly concerts and a statue of the heroic Paul Bert resting on a Vietnamese figure. The Chavassieux Fountain was erected in 1901 in a pocket-handkerchief square on to which the Hotel Métropole coffee shop looked. The Treasury and several private mansions completed the profane rebuilding of this once-sacred precinct.

Paul Bert contemplates Hoan
Kiem Lake. Behind the statue
is the Hanoi Post Office,
erected c. 1905.

Paul Bert Street, today's
Trang Tien Street, leading
to the Municipal Theatre
or 'Opera House', c. 1912.

The Vietnamese imperial mint occupied a large site covering roughly two of today's city blocks. It had access to the Street of Pearl Inlayers (Rue Paul Bert) by a bridge over the surrounding moat. The colonial authorities resumed the site initially for troops.[51] The strategic importance of the Street of Pearl Inlayers, especially in the conflict with the Black Flags, has been mentioned previously. In 1883, the street was described as a 'stinking sewer ... no wider than two or three metres' with a few European houses among the straw huts, two or three Chinese shops, a line of covered stalls and the occasional 'filthy counter of one of those "liquor merchants", shameless Oriental bazaar-keepers'.[52] Within two years, however, it had been macadamised and widened to 16–18 metres. Almost all of Hanoi's European retail shops opened here, as well as a hotel and several cafés. In January 1887 the Resident issued a decree ordering all straw houses on Paul Bert, Jules Ferry, and several other adjacent streets, to be replaced within 12 months by brick and tile buildings.[53] In 1887, brick kerbing was installed. The newspaper *L'Avenir du Tonkin* the following year therefore gave a completely different picture from 1883: 'We are witnessing the transformation of this quarter; everywhere elegant brick houses and beautiful stores are being erected on ground formerly occupied by sordid, Annamese agglomerations, homes of fire and epidemic.' In 1893, Lucien de Reinach wrote that nearly all the Europeans lived in this one street.[54]

In 1891 the administration ordered the felling of trees around various Hanoi pagodas in order to facilitate road works, as well as to provide the city's match factory with timber. The Kinh Luoc was furious and argued that the trees must be preserved to perpetuate memory of the past. In this he was supported by the colonial Director of Indigenous Affairs. They were both concerned too by the growing uniformity in vegetation as a result of the French felling and replanting practices, and they feared particularly for the trees around Hoan Kiem. We start to see here a division of opinion about the merits of Vietnamese civilisation that complicated the local colonial decision-making from the Governor-General down. On the one hand, there were those who dismissed the indigenous culture as crude and worthless. On the other hand, some, like the authors of an 1898 report on colonisation in Indochina, understood better the long and rich cultural traditions of the Vietnamese. 'Tonkin and Annam are not new countries; the Vietnamese are not savages', the 1898 report declared.

> These are two facts that must be understood if one does not wish to commit serious blunders capable of seriously affecting relations ... The population ... enjoys an advanced civilisation; if to be civilised means — as we believe it does — to have a homogeneous political organisation, a solid and respected family structure, and historic traditions. It certainly doesn't have an understanding of our marvellous scientific discoveries and of their not less surprising industrial applications; but it is capable of assimilating them, if it suited them to envy us them, which does not seem to have happened ...[55]

In the tree-felling case, the Resident responded favourably and took conservation concerns even further:

> In consequence [of your submissions] I have the honour of informing you that I forbid in the most formal way the felling of large trees existing on lands belonging to the Protectorate or the Town (or those that they might acquire). Furthermore, demolition of monuments, destruction of gardens, etc. having a religious or historic character, may not be undertaken before an inquiry has been carried out on the suitability of the measure and without receipt of my specific authorisation in writing. Essentially I insist on questions of this type not being decided hastily or without time for me to obtain the advice of the Annamite authorities, which is indispensable to the matter.[56]

Clearly, there were differences in attitude between the Resident and the municipal council and the officials responsible for engineering works. Some of the Governors-General, including Paul Doumer, also clashed with the council. Doumer's approach often appears contradictory, however, as shown by the decisions he took with regard to his own palace. Such contradictions can perhaps be explained by his overwhelming passion to construct a colonial capital that would reflect the glory of France. A complex character driven by expansionist dreams, Doumer nevertheless at times showed an intense appreciation of local history and traditions.

On Doumer's orders, a new Governor-General's palace was constructed between 1901 and 1906 on a corner of the botanical gardens. According to Dang Thai Hoang, it was 'built to emphasise the "sacred authority" of the ruling regime' with an imposing façade and architectural decorations.

[To] make the political message crystal clear, the colonialists chose to position this symbol of authority on a beautifully high and dry piece of real estate in the city's northern sector, practically adjacent to Ho Tay (West Lake) and the Botanical Garden ... [at that time] called the Flower Farm.[57]

The land – 20 hectares of private property – was obtained by confiscation, the lawful owners simply being ordered to move out. But construction of the new palace also necessitated the demolition of the substantial Mieu Hoi Dong Pagoda, which Vietnamese elders claimed was over 1,000 years old. The pagoda was an important site of religious festivities, being the object of twice-yearly pilgrimages by the indigenous administration of Hanoi province. Appeals from the Vietnamese were left with Doumer who, apparently not to be swayed, resolved that the pagoda should be demolished but that the owners should be compensated and provided with an alternative site for a new pagoda.[58]

The architecture of the new building was again typically Beaux-Arts[59] in design, its classical building form and baroque ornamental details straight out of provincial France. It had no connection with the Vietnamese culture and was in many ways quite ill-suited to Vietnamese climatic conditions. The building is sometimes erroneously attributed to architect Vildieu.[60] The 1900 drawings kept in the National Archives in Hanoi and the foundation stone on the building itself indicate that, while Vildieu was head of the Public Buildings Service, the architect in fact was Charles Lichtenfelder.

In contrast to his anti-conservation approach to the Mieu Hoi Dong Pagoda, the destruction of the citadel walls was being completed when Doumer arrived in the colony in 1897 and drew his sharp criticism:

I arrived too late to save the interesting parts. The gates in particular merited being preserved. They had great character to which were added ... the historic memories associated with them. They would have beautified the future quarters of the town, and would have no more impeded traffic or broken the street alignments than the Arc de Triomphe de l'Étoile does in Paris.[61]

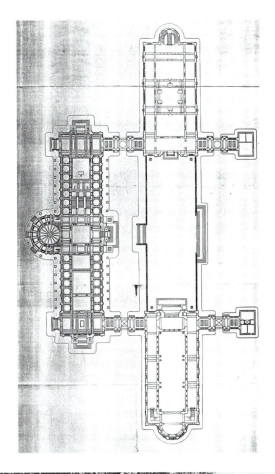

A grandiose complex of domed main pavilion, residence and offices, Vildieu's 1895 design for the Governor-General's palace did not proceed. (National Archives Centre No. 1, Hanoi)

The Governor-General's palace as constructed, c. 1907.

Reception Hall in the
Governor-General's palace.

He also thought it was a mistake to have demolished the citadel, thinking that it might have housed the French military, and dismissing the argument that it prevented the expansion of the town. But he conceded that there was ample justification for removing the walls because they blocked the circulation of fresh air and made the enclosed area an unhealthy living and working environment for Europeans.

These early impressions of Hanoi's redevelopment seem to have led Doumer to a determination to get better advice in future on matters that we call today 'cultural heritage'. Consequently, in 1899, he established the École Française d'Extrême-Orient (EFEO), initially in Saigon but soon transferred to Hanoi. This research school comprising historians, archaeologists and ethnographers turned out to be a major force in Hanoi's cultural life. It built on the work of Gustave-Émile Dumoutier, the protectorate's chief education officer who, acting on instruction from Paul Bert, began recording and collecting examples of Tonkin's ancient treasures. The EFEO continued to document, classify and, most importantly, protect the city's pre-colonial cultural heritage.[62] This enabled the Vietnamese residents of Hanoi to maintain their cultural links with the past — or, at least, with those elements that EFEO and the French authorities deemed worthy of maintaining as Vietnamese heritage. By the end of the 1920s it had built up a library of 25,000 volumes in English, 17,000 in Chinese, 4,000 in Vietnamese and 9,500 in Japanese, as well as 1,600 maps and manuscripts in various Asian languages.[63] It had also established a number of museums in the principal towns, including the Louis Finot in Hanoi, and it had begun to draw up a list of important monuments that were to be protected by official preservation decrees.

This listing exercise was the result of a political campaign it waged in 1905 to save the one remaining city gate – the Thanh Ha or Jean Dupuis Gate, as it was then known.[64] The Hanoi municipal council had voted for its demolition in order to put through a wide avenue that would enable the neighbourhood to be cleaned up. The Mayor wrote to the Resident that 'Now the Jean Dupuis Gate is a pile of bricks and it seems to me as difficult to classify this shapeless heap as a historic monument as it would be incomprehensible ... to conserve a gate in the fortifications of Paris'. The four 'Annamite' councillors had opposed the demolition motion. The EFEO successfully enlisted the support of both the Resident and the Governor-General, claiming that this was 'one of the last and most prestigious vestiges of old Hanoi'. The EFEO also, however, noted that another main reason was that this was the gate through which Francis Garnier had made his triumphant entry into the city. A newly created Commission of Antiquities, with EFEO involvement, drew up the inventory of monument required by the Governor-General as a prerequisite to his placing a conservation order on them. The gate was on the list.

The first local decree was announced shortly after, in November 1906. More importantly, the first general classification for Indochina was proclaimed on 23 December 1924 which applied to Indochina the December 1913 French law relating to the classification and protection of historic monuments.[65] By 1926 the official list contained 89 items in Tonkin, of which 19 items were located in the municipality of Hanoi while several others, such as the Van Mieu, were in non-municipal parts of the Hanoi urban area.[66] These items were all religious buildings of some antiquity, with the exception of the few elements remaining from the former Royal Citadel and two communal houses. The list shows that the EFEO displayed a very distinctive bias: not only did it, in general Indochina-wide terms, regard the Indianised Cham and Angkor heritage as more significant than the Sino-Vietnamese, but old age was clearly a determining criterion. Urban landscape features from the recent past were overlooked, with the single exception of the wooden bridge leading to the Ngoc Son Temple and the Thanh Ha Gate. Similarly, while the classical artistic merit of individual items was important, on the whole the vernacular constructions of the common people were not.

THE EFEO CLASSIFICATION OF HANOI'S CULTURAL HERITAGE, 1926

Den Tran Vu (Grand Bouddha) (1010; reconstructed 1768; repaired nineteenth century; classified 1906)	Den Bach Ma (ninth century; shifted eleventh century; re-constructed, restored and repaired eighteenth–nineteenth centuries)	Islets and banks of the Hoan Kiem, including the Den Ngoc Son, Chua Qui Son	Remaining gate (Thap Hoa Phong) to the Chua Bao An (Quan Thuong or Pagode des Supplices) (nineteenth century)
Den Hai Ba Trung (twelfth century; reconstucted and repaired 1812, 1893)	Chua Mot Cot (eleventh century; restored nineteenth century)	Den Ba Da (fifteenth century; destroyed c. 1790; reconstructed 1847; repaired nineteenth century)	Chua Am (Pho Quang) (Le dynasty; reconstructed 1824)
Chua Hoa Giai (Hong Phuc) (Li dynasty; reconstructed 1683; restored 1899)	Chua Tran Quoc (1625; reconstructed 1628, 1639, 1842)	Chua Ly Quoc Su (Ly dynasty; restored Le dynasty and 1855)	Thanh Ha Gate (Porte Jean Dupuis) (nineteenth century)
Chua Ha Kao (eighteenth century; restored by Gia Long)	Stelae of the Nam Giao (1680)	Inscription at Dinh Hoa Loc (1706–21)	Two phoenixes at Dinh Dong Ha
Two phoenixes on tortoises and two chimeras in the Botanical Gardens	Chua Van Phuc (1037; reconstructed 1687 and 1846)	Van Mieu (Pagode des Corbeaux) (1070; repaired early fifteenth, mid-seventeenth and early nineteenth centuries; classified 1906)	Citadel mirador, Chinh Bac (North Gate; 1803), Doan Mon Gate and various other vestiges

The EFEO was also active in the restoration of numerous pagodas. One of these was the Van Mieu. Here a street alignment program in 1899 had not only led to the removal of straw huts encroaching on the site but also, according to Ngo Huy Quynh, to the destruction of the precinct's geomantic arrangement.[67] But in 1920, the EFEO made partial amends by carrying out an extensive restoration program, following this up with further repair work in 1946.[68] The EFEO campaigned to save the few remaining traces of the citadel. These included the Mirador Tower; the North Gate bombarded by Francis Garnier in 1873; the Doan Mon (Portico of Honour, the central door to the former royal palace); the six dragon banisters leading to the Artillery Division; and a bronze bell and engraved canon at the entrance of the Artillery Division workshops. The Hai Ba Trung Temple was restored in 1921 and the Mot Cot Pagoda in 1922. Much of their work was subsequently undone during the military conflicts that engulfed Hanoi two decades later.

Paris de l'Annam: The French project of distraction

France seemed uncertain whether it wanted Indochina as a colony of settlement or just a short-term base for exploitation. The latter only required the kinds of administrative, commercial and security installations that the colonial authorities had been building in Tonkin since 1884. By the time Doumer's governor-generalship ended in 1902, the vision had moved on. Various schemes for the town had been put forward and more substantial public amenities were being built. The changes were dramatic; indeed, many commentators saw urban development as the most striking of all the geographical transformations wrought in Indochina by the French. According to Georges Maspéro, the French were the 'great builders' – 'They have built solidly and for the future'.[69] They were producing something identifiably Gallic, about which great pride was felt then (as indeed now) by fellow Frenchmen. This was already noticed in the 1890s when Prince Henri, Duc d'Orléans, visited:

> When we Frenchmen colonise ... there are certain good qualities that we
> carry with us wherever we go ... In the first place, we have a knack of
> cleaning up a native town, and of constructing next to it something both
> clean and elegant ... from nothing at all we obtain a pretty result; the taste
> of the Faubourg Montmartre shopgirl reappears in the work of the [French]
> pioneer in California or the non-commissioned officer in Cochinchina. This
> subtle, imperceptible element that is part of our temperament, of our very
> essence, means that with little money we have cleared, put back as new
> and partially reconstructed two of the most beautiful towns in the Far East,
> Saigon and Hanoi.[70]

The thinking behind the building of colonial Hanoi evolved through several relatively distinct phases. The first decade was necessarily characterised by a functional approach when planning and construction were carried out by military engineers. From 1896–97, towards the end of the pacification campaign, Commander Hubert Lyautey began advocating the development of a low-density garden city with scattered two-storey buildings on piles encircled by verandahs and nestling among the vegetation.[71] Lyautey was one of the key French administrators advocating a new policy of 'association' to replace the assimilationist approach commonly being used in the colonies at the time.[72] This was a sharp break from the town building then going on in metropolitan France, and appears to have owed something to visits made to British Singapore. However, from the time of Doumer, when Hanoi entered a second colonial phase lasting to the 1920s, Vildieu was the head of the new *Service des Bâtiments Civils de l'Indochine* (Indochinese Public Buildings Service). As noted previously, his work between 1897 and 1906 was mainly on public buildings designed in a classical style. He was, by contrast, more adventurous in town planning terms, shifting from the early single concentration of administration in the Rue Paul Bert–Hoan Kiem Precinct to scatter some of his new buildings, such as the Governor-General's palace and the Supreme Court, further out in the growing city.

In the nineteenth century, the French authorities focused much of their land reclamation, urban planning and infrastructure development in the area south of Hoan Kiem as far as today's Nguyen Du Street (Rue de Reinach) and Ham Long Street (Boulevard Doudart de Lagré). Here in the 1890s they laid out a generous grid pattern of streets 20–30 metres wide, and large housing blocks designed to give the French settlers the healthy suburban lifestyle then coming into vogue in affluent Western cities. Hue Street (Rue de Hue) had also become a busy commercial street as far as Nguyen Cong Tru Street (Route du Cimetière) where a European cemetery had opened. West of Hue Street, in the Bay Mau area, a first subdivision was created in the early years of the twentieth century as a series of narrow north–south running streets. A racecourse had been established south-east of the intersection of Le Duan Road (Route Mandarine) and Tran Hung Dao Street (Boulevard Gambetta).

The European Quarter began to fill with two-storey detached villas based on regional housing from France – whitewashed with green shutters behind iron picket fences. The senior bureaucrats, bank representatives, opium farm agents and rich colonial settlers (*colons*) enjoyed not only these spacious villas but also horse-drawn and later motorised carriages and teams of servants – the *boys* (manservants), the *beps* (cooks) and the *amahs* (nannies). French women were few in the early days and still only numbered 200 by 1900. French men had their *congaïs* instead, or frequented the *garçonnières* along the Route du Grand Bouddha (Quan Thanh Street). Little has been written about the *métis* (children of mixed blood) who resulted from this period, but they were apparently not as large in number or as historically significant as the Anglo-Indians or the mixed population in the Dutch East Indies. Later, the increase in numbers of European women led to the establishment of more usual family units and stereotypical colonial social patterns such as the *heure de l'absinthe* (cocktail hour) and summers for women and children at the Tam Dao and Sa Pa hill stations.[73] Even so, there was a fairly constant struggle against the climate, sunstroke, mosquitoes and fevers.[74]

If the sweet life of the colonies was something of a myth for the Europeans, living conditions were far more rigorous for the Vietnamese. Christian Pédélahore describes the typical villa in the French Quarter as comprising a main building set in the centre of the allotment facing the gate and generally surrounded by a wall as required in early regulations for European quarters.[75] Behind the house there was another building where the indigenous servants lived and worked. He points to the parallels between social status and living environment: 'In the foreground, the wide, light, functional and hygienic living space of the French colonist. In the background, the narrow space, the dark and dirty places for the native.'

Nevertheless, French Hanoi began to see itself as the 'Paris de l'Annam'. While not all the designed buildings were yet completed, in 1902 the colony celebrated in style its growing status with a major 'exposition'. Another of Paul Doumer's grandiose ideas, the exposition was designed to show off Tonkin's agricultural and industrial products and the cultural artefacts of Indochina and the Far East.[76] The racecourse was commandeered for the construction of a major complex of buildings.[77] The project put Hanoi's municipal budget into the red for more than a decade, but it was seen as a necessary 'politique de prestige' aimed at making Hanoi a 'little Paris'.

The art nouveau fashion was imported from metropolitan France and added flourish to neoclassical buildings such as the new Resident's palace opposite the Hôtel Métropole. But of the new public buildings built in this second phase, the most extravagant was the Municipal Theatre (Nha Hat Lon, commonly known as the 'Opera House'). Designed by an unknown architect in 1896 and built between 1901 and 1911 on the landward side of the French Concession, it was characteristically French both in its architecture and its siting. It seems to have been inspired by Charles Garnier's opera house in Paris. Certainly it reflected the swelling cultural ambitions of the colonial authorities at the turn of the century. A folly of grandeur according to critics, 'a troubling symbol ... where all our faults

Above The Second Empire-style 'Opera House' in 1990. The last opera was staged in the 1950s before the French left.

Left The palace of the Résident-Supérieur, a neoclassical building with Napoleon III and art nouveau elements, completed in 1918 and under restoration in 1993.

come together: love of pleasure, of artifice, of the artificial, unreflective enthusiasm, and a careless lack of foresight'.[78] It was sited in baroque town planning fashion on Foch Square at the convergence of important roads and closing off a key vista along fashionable Rue Paul Bert. During construction, the theatre suffered budget cuts and lost some of the proposed features, including expensive stonework and the two annexes that had been intended to frame the main building.[79] Nevertheless the theatre ended up a massive structure, with a pillared façade, twin-domed slate roof, decorative balustrades and acroteria, and a high baroque interior with a grand staircase, lofty reception rooms and marble floors. Having seats for an audience of 870, it was intended to accommodate most of the 2,500 or so Europeans residing in Hanoi at the time.[80]

The growing elegance of the city was noted by American Harry Franck and his family who travelled through Indochina in the mid-1920s:

Hanoi, northern capital of French Indo-China, is somewhat larger and less obviously tropical than its southern rival, Saigon. It is quite a city, with expensive modern buildings, electric street-cars — found nowhere else in the colony — railways in four directions, many automobiles, both of the taxi-cab and private limousine variety, several excellent hotels; in short, it is a little Paris of the tropics, with some advantages that even Paris does not have.[81]

Rue Paul Bert had some 'very up-to-date government and private buildings, well-stocked stores, and cafés overrunning the sidewalks'. Hoan Kiem Lake was 'delightfully blue and restful, bordered by a stone-faced embankment space with huge old trees'. It had a flower market in one of its well-shaded corners, especially busy on Sundays, with black-toothed Vietnamese women in long cinnamon-brown coats, and every bit as charming as the flower market at the Madeleine in Paris.[82] At the same time, in the Ancient Quarter,

[The] rush and swirl of street life ... was even more nearly incessant than that of hotter Saigon. Hawkers, improvised restaurants, hundreds of rickshaws, most of them thumping their wooden wheels on the ill-fitting axle, queer carriages, wheelbarrows again for the first time since leaving China, man-drawn freight-carts, automobiles bellowing their demanding way through flocks and shoals of pedestrians, all bore testimony to the importance of the northern capital.[83]

Superficially, everything was French, down to the tiny gasoline bottles required for French cigarette lighters that Franck saw displayed in native as well as French shops.

Flower sellers beside
Hoan Kiem Lake in 1936.

French colonial achievements were celebrated in the famous Exposition Coloniale of 1931 held in Paris. The Indochinese stands lavishly recreated scenes of Angkor Wat and Vietnam, and the catalogue provided by the government in Hanoi was not shy in announcing that 'There is no doubt that the production and general wealth [of Indochina] has been built up enormously through the actions of France'.[84] One of the distinguished visitors, Vice-Admiral de Marolles, responded as the French colonial authorities would have wanted:

> One of the facts that would have struck the visitor to the exhibition has doubtless been the marvellous development that Tonkin has made in less than fifty years. While admiring the results obtained in such a short time, one finds it difficult to imagine what this little known country was like in 1882, given over [as it was] to administration by Annamite mandarins, so lamentable that there was not even a road link between Haiphong and Hanoi.[85]

Despite the concerns of the politicians in France about the financing of the French Indochinese Union, there was a growing fascination with Indochina among the French. One of the manifestations of this was the development of tourism to Indochina. This got off to a slow start in the early decades of the twentieth century when it was decidedly for the more adventurous. Game hunting was one of the favourite activities. The Indochinese authorities were keen for tourists to come to see the progress being made and complained in 1910 that not many French tourists were going beyond India despite the easy sea voyage. The sights were wonderful, they insisted, especially Angkor, which rivals Egypt, and Ha Long Bay. One visitor that year agreed, commenting that

> They don't know how nice it is to come into contact with the yellow race, with the exoticism, with the tropical flora and temperature, all the while keeping the company of our compatriots, having the pleasure of hearing French spoken ...

But he warned that 'it's an error to regard it as a paradise' and pointed to the summer heat, fever, sanitation problems, shortage of European fresh foods and the general lethargy of life.[86]

Nevertheless, reports such as the following from Henry G. Bryant, President of the Geographical Society of Philadelphia, in a 1909 issue of the monthly magazine *Travel and Exploration* helped whet the traveller's appetite to visit Tonkin and Hanoi:

> After visiting many cities in the Far East, I must affirm Hanoi made a distinctly favourable impression. It is indeed a creditable creation of the French colonising spirit, with its broad avenues, stately government buildings, sunny parks and good hotel ... Should fate decree that I should be exiled to the French colonies in Asia, Hanoi would be my choice as an abiding place.

He, too, commented on the immense attraction of Hanoi to the French —
an attraction that evidently survives today judging by the continuing flow
of French tourists to the city.

> The intense patriotism, which never permits the colonist to forget the
> fatherland or to adapt himself irrevocably to new conditions, has often been
> urged as one of the factors which make against success in the French colonies.
> [However] If there is any city among France's colonies where the exile should
> be reconciled to his lot, that city is Hanoi, with its boulevards and magasins, its
> race-course and subsidised opera, its soldiers and the gay life of the cafés.[87]

Tourist numbers increased after World War 1 and, in 1921, the Colonial
Tourism Committee of the Touring-Club de France published a booklet titled
French Indochina: Sites, Monuments, Types of People, Virgin Forests. It
emphasised the local colour, the numerous races and ethnic groups ('In type,
manner and religion, these groups present different specimens of mankind,
each with a character of its own') as well as mountains, plains, sea and
forest. 'Hanoi with its pagodas' is billed alongside Hue and its Royal Palace
and Angkor. By 1924, Hanoi's annual report to the President of the French
Republic noted the importance that tourism was starting to have in
Indochina but expressed concern about the 'active commerce in local
curiosities'.[88] More tourists were coming to see the artistic and
archaeological heritage that was still being discovered and popularised in
Europe. One such was André Malraux who was imprisoned in Saigon for
smuggling Khmer artefacts out of Indochina. It is an irony that he later
became the French Minister for Culture from 1959 to 1969. In this role he
is particularly noted for introducing the first historic precinct legislation in
France — the so-called *Loi Malraux* that has become widely accepted as the
model for area conservation in the francophone world.

From assimilation to association

Back home, the debate over colonialism in the French parliament had
escalated. The debate focused on both the economic and moral nature of
colonialism and revolved around two opposing approaches to colonisation:
assimilation and association. Raymond Betts, who made one of the most
thorough studies of this debate, believed that it was not entirely over when
France lost Indochina after World War 2.[89] Cultural differences between
the colonists and the colonised, and what were the best policies to handle
those differences, were at the heart of the debate. The early colonial
administrations tended to emphasise assimilationist policies that pushed the
adoption of forms of government and cultural norms that were those
followed in metropolitan France. The pursuit of such policies had undercut
indigenous political, economic and social structures. The position of the

Kinh Luoc was terminated in 1897, the mandarin examinations were abolished, and French schooling and the French language were imposed. Assimilation was also seen in architecture and planning. Christian Pédélahore directs this criticism at Vildieu in particular:

> Abandoning the utilitarian rationalism of the constructions of the 1880s, he [Vildieu] drew upon the massiveness and decorative vocabulary of neoclassical architecture in order to subjugate the native masses and demonstrate without doubt the superiority of the new power, at the same time symbolically assuring its longevity.[90]

It was simply expected that the Vietnamese would come to value these examples of a superior culture.

But gradually there was a shift in the attitudes of politicians back home and of Tonkin's rulers – or at least of reformist Governors-General in the 1920s and 1930s like Maurice Sarraut, Maurice Long and Alexandre Varenne. Indeed, already by April 1909, the Chamber of Deputies had called for new policies in all colonies based on giving more visible attention to the needs, wishes and cultures of the colonised peoples.[91] The softer approach that came to dominate colonial thinking was that of 'association', a term never sharply defined according to Betts, but imputed in the idea of a colonial protectorate rather than straight-out colony.[92] It suggested that colonial policy should be guided by geographic and ethnic factors, as well as recognising the state of social development existing in that time and place. Indigenous groups should be allowed to evolve along their own lines. This was not a wholesale rejection of the *mission civilisatrice*, but merely a modification of it – really a way to win over the hearts and minds of, at least initially, the small Vietnamese elite.

Confronted by this new approach, the Governors-General remained determined to continue their modernisation programs, but to do so in ways that would win greater support from the indigenous population as well as the colonists, these last usually fighting against any liberalisation with vehemence. Some scholars, such as the American historian Gwendolyn Wright, author of several works linking power and architecture in Indochina and other French colonies,[93] see a linear shift from assimilation to association. In Vietnam, architecture and town planning were clearly part of the effort to modernise by using associationist means. This modernisation included the development of the first comprehensive 'master plans' for Hanoi and other major cities, with attention being given to land-use zoning and to traffic circulation. In 1921, Governor-General Long asked Sarraut, by then the French Minister for Colonies, to establish a central architecture and planning service in Hanoi. He was hoping to introduce policies like those developed by the colonial planners Henri Prost and Marshal Lyautey in Morocco in order to expand the administrative precinct in Hanoi and to draw up a plan for Da Lat where Doumer had long ago decided to create a new 'summer capital'. The request was approved in 1921 and a Town Planning and Architecture Service was established within the Public Works Ministry in 1923.[94] But Long also seemed to see Hanoi as something of an experimental laboratory for the demonstration of the latest planning ideas and regulations introduced in France itself. This included the law of March 1919, which had been principally designed to facilitate France's reconstruction after World War 1, as well as the supplementary law of July 1924 setting out the regulations for implementing subdivisional, improvement and extension plans and for forming urban property owners' syndicates.[95]

The administration claimed to be showing a greater sensitivity to the local peoples in its attempts to preserve the traditional cultures by bolstering communal leadership structures, preserving historic monuments (through the work of the EFEO) and using indigenous motifs in architectural decorations. Gwendolyn Wright sees these changes in approach as part of a self-serving scheme in which the colonial officials

> ... hoped to preserve an established sense of hierarchy and propriety, buttressing it with what they perceived to be traditional rituals, spatial patterns, and architectural ornament, believing that this would reinforce their own superimposed power.[96]

This judgment is supported to some extent by a study of the ideas and practices of the principal architect and planner employed in the 1920s to head a new Town Planning and Architecture Service, Ernest Hébrard.

Cultural relativism: Hébrard in Hanoi

Ernest Hébrard had an established reputation as an outstanding Beaux-Arts-trained urbanist when he arrived in Hanoi in 1923. He was a member of the small Société Française des Urbanistes and had worked on plans for the rebuilding of Thessalonika and the design of a number of futuristic 'World City' projects.[97] Long had invited him in 1921 to come to Indochina to advise the municipal authorities, and his major works there consisted of the master plans for Hanoi (completed in 1924), Saigon, Phnom Penh and Da Lat. In Hanoi, Hébrard's influence was felt both in architectural and town planning terms. He was responsible for the design of a number of significant buildings that introduced a cultural-relativist element by incorporating Indochinese decorative features based on his extensive Asian field research and photography, reading, and discussions with historians and archaeologists at the EFEO. Through the use of verandahs, window canopies and ventilation devices, his designs were better suited to the local climate than had been the usual French designs with their small windows, mansard roofs and attics.

The Ministry of Finance building
in Dien Bien Phu Road.
Constructed by Verneuil-Gravereand,
it was opened in May 1928.

Five buildings stand out as Hébrard landmarks in Hanoi today. The first is the Ministry of Finance building, erected between 1925 and 1927 and now home to the Ministry of Foreign Affairs. The second is the Louis Finot Museum constructed between 1925 and 1932, now the National History Museum. Less well-known are the Pasteur Institute, erected in 1925–30, the Cua Bac Church built in 1925, and the original main building of Hanoi University built in 1926. The Hanoi Pasteur Institute was one of four Pasteur institutes in colonial Indochina, the others being in Saigon, Nha Trang and Da Lat. It was built well beyond the southern limits of the French Quarter, on the site of the former lepers' village, and was encircled by gardens, a carriageway and a fence.[98] Eventually, Hébrard designed a wide, tree-lined approach which, today, presents an attractive vista through a green, open space. Dang Thai Hoang casts doubt over who was responsible for the Institute's design, listing as the architect not Hébrard but Gaston Roger, the Deputy Architect.[99] The original documents held in the National Archives Centre No. 1 in Hanoi show, however, that while it was Roger who signed off the final plans, the preliminary drawings were by Hébrard.[100] In the case of ecclesiastical buildings, Hébrard was highly critical of the habitual French use of Gothic architecture and considered it particularly inappropriate in Indochina's climate and culture. Consequently, his Cua Bac Church abandons tradition and is eclectic in style, with strong art deco influences. In the Hanoi University design, Hébrard again broke from his classical European training to use a more traditional Vietnamese style.

Above The Louis Finot Museum (now the National History Museum) under construction. (National Archives Centre No. 1, Hanoi)

Left Ernest Hébrard combined art deco and design elements from different parts of Asia in the Louis Finot Museum.

Opinion is divided over the significance of Hébrard's architectural contribution. French commentators treat him favourably. Christian Pédélahore, for example, sees the development of the *style indochinois* as the main legacy of Hébrard's architecture.[101] By contrast, Gwendolyn Wright (whose judgment of Hébrard becomes increasingly harsh as she moves from her 1982 work to those of 1987 and 1991) attacks his use of traditional design elements as being no more than a resort to superficial decoration.[102] She argues that he was fundamentally concerned with the evolution of French architecture, which he thought could be revitalised by the use of 'history and a certain cultural sensibility'. As a consequence, 'his buildings usually resemble a pastiche of exotic details superimposed on a Beaux-Arts plan, rather than the more radical change in direction that he advocated'. Such a view allows Wright to interpret the Louis Finot Museum with its Japanese, Indian and Indochinese design elements as 'a hodgepodge of architectural motifs ... [and] a statement of cultural dominance'.[103] This is perhaps an odd judgment to have been made in the 1990s era of postmodern architectural design when eclecticism and pastiche are more acceptable than in any previous period.

This debate flows over into Hébrard's impact on Hanoi's urban planning and civic design (or *urbanisme*, to employ the useful French term). Here his chief significance, according to Pédélahore, was to be the first planner in Indochina to push beyond mere physical design into urban policy-making and management. He was also said to be more concerned with spaces and groups of buildings than with the architectural details of

The Hanoi Pasteur Institute (now known as the Hanoi Microbiology Institute) in Y-Ec-Xanh Street. (Centre des Archives d'Outre-Mer, Aix-en-Provence)

buildings or the engineering details of road and bridge construction.[104] Hébrard is portrayed as seeing his work as one of synthesis, drawing together the relevant elements of economics, statistics, physical and human geography, hygiene and epidemiology in order to achieve a higher level of urban planning and management than had been previously seen in the colonies. This contrast with the more limited practitioners operating in the colonies and at home leads Pédélahore to hail Hébrard as an exceptional figure in the history of French architecture.

Hébrard's urban planning achievements in Hanoi included the organisation of the Town Planning Service created by Governor-General Long. He prepared the first master plan for Hanoi in 1924 with large extensions of the built-up urban area covering the suburban zones to the west and south, and almost doubling Hanoi's size. With this master plan he introduced the concept of land-use zoning to Indochina and established a rational hierarchy of roads across the city. He created the monumental political and administrative precinct in the Ba Dinh area on lands acquired (some compulsorily) by Long in 1922. Hébrard's design for this area was based on a new Governor-General's palace, three times larger than the existing one, and the clustering of administrative offices for the Ministries of Finance, Education and Public Works, and the Secretary-General. The old Governor-General's palace was to become home to a new Indochinese Council, and a green belt of parks and sporting facilities was proposed, stretching up to and round the northern end of Ho Tay.

The Governor-General's precinct, c. 1925. The large circular 'square' was named after Hébrard in the 1930s and 1940s. (National Archives Centre No. 1, Hanoi)

Four general criticisms have been levelled at Hébrard's urban planning approach. The first relates to his handling of racial segregation issues. While his plans sought to keep incompatible land uses apart, they also involved the separation of European from 'Annamite' residential areas. In his 1928 article, 'L'urbanisme en Indochine', Hébrard argued forcefully that 'specialisation of residential districts is necessary, especially in relation to the native districts which for a variety of reasons must not be mixed with the European districts'.[105] Elsewhere, he reasoned that:

> We should not forget that the Europeans [in Indochinese towns] need the Natives in order to survive ... Domestic servants live in their master's houses, but every day go to the market for their shopping, or to a native village to see their families and friends. Around every European settlement one or more native agglomerations always form; these correspond, in fact, to the groups of shopkeepers and workers in our modern cities, who are, in truth, separated from the bourgeois neighbourhoods without a definite line being drawn on a map.[106]

He saw interracial contact as inevitable in the colonial city but, according to his critics, he wanted to organise it.[107] In other words, so it is claimed, he clearly continued to support racial and class segregation in his planning.

It is clear that Hébrard followed the concept of the 'dual city' espoused by Marshal Lyautey in French North Africa, where the traditional town (*ville indigène*) was maintained alongside the Western imposed town (*ville moderne*), with a buffer zone between them. Such a planning approach demonstrated an associationist rather than assimilationist philosophy, one that was widely seen in British as well as French colonial town planning.[108] Hébrard recognised that the planner's actions need to be built upon what exists already:

> It would be a great mistake to think that developing a town plan in a colony could be done without a preliminary investigation of the places and a study of the existing conditions of the city to be created or the native town to be organised and extended. Without a site inspection, one would end up with one of those off-the-rack plans reminiscent of the geometric drawings of the architects of the Renaissance.[109]

However, in practice, his approach in Hanoi seems to have been largely design-oriented, devising aesthetic roads schemes with little regard to pre-existing settlement patterns. In this way, he still fitted into the nineteenth-century Haussmannian approach of cutting through the existing fabric, charged up with visions for the future and apparently thinking present social disruptions a price that was worth paying. He was also continuing the approach used by Hanoi planners before him who had proceeded to 'tidy up' the Ancient Quarter, the Van Mieu precinct and other areas without regard for the negative consequences.

The second and third criticisms are that he largely ignored the suburbs where the bulk of Hanoi's population lived, and that he lacked interest in suburban industrial development. In particular, he is said to have had no interest at all in designing cheap housing for the majority of Vietnamese residents. The final criticism is that, even though he set up and taught at the architecture section in the Hanoi College of Fine Arts (founded 1924), he focused on narrowly inculcating his *style indochinoise* and apparently never saw the Vietnamese architects and planners developing a national style for themselves.

While it is possible to see elements of these failings in his works, by comparison with the work of other prominent planners in France and the French colonies in the 1920s, Hébrard's faults seem moderate. It is perhaps too easy to make the kind of retrospective judgments that Wright does, ignoring the fact that his work was for government and done in an intellectual and political context that was both time- and space-specific. The paramount task set by his employer was to create a capital befitting the stature of the French Indochinese Union. So, when Long suggested to him that Hanoi needed new buildings and open spaces 'worthy of a great colony', they both inevitably had the Paris model in mind. They envisaged an elegant Hanoi constructed to a plan of wide tree-lined axial boulevards with green spaces and vistas enclosed by imposing monuments associated with French history in Hanoi, such as the Jean Dupuis Gate and the Water Tower dating from the Concession period or the proposed Governor-General's palace.

Hébrard's work reflected the intellectual climate of the times and, in particular, contemporary views about the control and management of colonies. Colonialism was considered by most administrators and colonists as an enterprise that had to find methods to manage the indigenous society with a minimum of intrusion. The French were constantly comparing their methods with those tried by the British and Dutch in the hope of finding a 'proper system' that would fit the needs of French colonial rule in Indochina and elsewhere. Hébrard's answer was to extend land-use zonation into social and racial controls as a way of achieving a smooth-running city.

Hébrard's apparent lack of interest in industrial planning can also be explained as a result of his acceptance of the contemporary view of likening the running of a colony to the management of an enterprise. There is no doubt that Hébrard was irritated by the lack of rational land-use zonation that resulted in the presence of factories in the heart of Hanoi and by the inefficiencies resulting from factory annexes being scattered over numerous sites rather than consolidated on a single site. He

General view of the Ancient Quarter from the
cathedral, c. 1930. The regularity of building
height, sloping tiled roofs and whitewashed
parapet walls is striking.

did try to reduce air pollution by shifting the manufacturing industry and
utilities scattered around Hanoi to Gia Lam on the left, or eastern, bank
of the Red River. He was probably also frustrated by the too-deep street
blocks that gave rise to the development of 'veritable ghettos' behind the
main rows of houses. Today, in Western liberal democracies at least,
solutions to these problems would be sought by engaging the stakeholders
in the planning process; in the 1920s, this would have been revolutionary
in the developed world, let alone in colonial Asia. Instead, Hébrard relied
entirely upon land-use zonation techniques to rationalise the industrial
pattern. But colonial policies were not geared towards encouraging
the expansion of industry in Indochina. The President of the French
parliament in the first half of the 1880s, Jules Ferry, had made this very
clear when he declared that 'Colonial policy is a child of industrial
policy'.[110] Governor-General Doumer had taken a similar line, as had
subsequent Indochinese Governors-General. Hébrard's actions in Hanoi
merely conformed with the official view.

In the end, the political context in which he worked proved
overwhelming. In 1932, he raised in his retrospective account of his time
in Indochina what appears to have been a key stumbling block – the
enforcement of land-use zonation in his planning schemes.[111] Easy to do,

French colonial orderliness in
the Ancient Quarter, c. 1930.
(Centre des Archives d'Outre-Mer,
Aix-en-Provence)

he noted, when the planning area belongs to the state, municipality, single owner or multiple owners who agree on goals, but impossible where every private owner is principally motivated by the desire to make maximum profit from his property. Many *colons* were unimpressed by Hébrard's cultural-relativist works and preferred the Beaux-Arts architecture of his predecessors. He also appears to have made lasting enemies of the Public Works engineers shortly after his arrival. With a dictatorial patron like Doumer, he might have succeeded; but under the more democratic Governors-General of the 1920s, his political support proved inadequate.[112] Budgetary constraints added to his woes.

Consequently, Hébrard did not stay long in the Indochinese colonies, leaving in 1929 with his Hanoi master plan only partially implemented and several major ministerial buildings no more than designs in progress. It was only some years later − in 1942 − that the municipal council expressed belated gratitude towards Hébrard, declaring that 'Little by little, following the extension plan drawn up by Mr Hébrard, Hanoi has taken on the physiognomy by which it is known today'.[113] If he had done nothing else, he had forced the municipal and ministerial authorities into a more detailed and politicised level of debate about the nature of the city and its management.

The Bay Mau Quarter, south of the French Quarter, was developed in the late 1920s and 1930s as a result of the Hébrard plan. In a municipal council session in February 1930, the southern extension was described as:

> ... destined to become if not the most beautiful, at least the most pleasant in the Town. It includes in fact the management of two lakes, one being the very large Bay Mau Lake, the other being the smaller Thien Khuong [Thien Quang] that are separated by a broad botanical tract and bordered by streets and lawns constituting a place for promenading which is unique in the centre of Hanoi.[114]

The area became a chief location of the middle-class Vietnamese working for the colonial administration and private enterprises.[115] They occupied two-storey L-shaped houses with small courtyards built in the transitional architectural styles of the 1930s – a mix of classical and art deco. This housing stock represents a highly significant part of Hanoi's twentieth-century architectural heritage. But it owed little to Hébrard's architectural design ideas. In fact, the implementation of most of Hébrard's grand ideas was halted by the Great Depression in 1929 that hit Indochina severely in the years 1931–35.[116] By then his cultural-relativist architectural work was completely out of line with the universalist principles of the international modern movement that was reshaping Western architectural practice. Hébrard's architecture is perhaps better suited to today's postmodern world where repackaging of traditional with more international elements is again the vogue.

The clinic built on Ly Thuong Kiet Street for Dr Vu Ngoc Huynh in 1936 is a prime example of Hanoi art deco.

Only slowly in the late 1930s did Hanoi pull itself out of the depths of economic crisis. Industries recovered but, despite Hébrard's best intentions, remained scattered throughout the city. Electricity plants abutted residences. The French-owned Distilleries de l'Indochine occupied a large site in the middle of the French Quarter, a site that houses the French Embassy compound today. Small-scale sugar, soap, silk spinning and weaving, embroidery and lace, carpets, leather, button and match factories created minor levels of noise and air pollution.[117] Social problems such as unemployment, poverty and prostitution remained serious across the decade. These are generally not well documented in official archives but are reflected in the autobiographical works of contemporary Vietnamese writers, such as Tam Lang's picture of the 1930s' life of a cyclo-driver or Vu Trong Phung's portrayal of domestic workers.[118] It was these social conditions that account for the independence and socialist movements that grew rapidly in this period and that came to a head in the 1940s.

Hanoi bipolarity: The imposed colonial city in Asia

Almost 20 years ago, Richard O'Connor studied South-east Asian cities in an attempt to see if there was a typical pattern of indigenous urbanism. He was responding to the view commonly held by Western scholars of Asia that cities were not natural to the region but were a colonial import. In his study, O'Connor insisted that there are few essential discontinuities in South-east Asian urban history. In particular, he argued that history and symbolic meanings play as important a part in the development of South-east Asian cities today as ever before and there has been 'no break, no time when the past was erased and the present became simply "rational" instead of symbolic'.[119]

These assertions are debatable in the case of Vietnam and the cultural landscape of its capital city, Hanoi. While not denying the continuing adherence to Tao and Confucian ideals or to the luck-bringing principles of *feng shui*, or the parallels that can be drawn between Confucian and communist administrative approaches,[120] there have indeed been several sharp discontinuities in Vietnamese history. These are points of time when the pre-existing political and social order was suddenly transformed and when abrupt changes in the symbolic meaning given to townscape features saw the downgrading of 'traditional' environmental values, especially in terms of official policy. Such systems of symbolic meaning define and delimit the city's cultural heritage of buildings, monuments and sites. The 'heritage' is constantly being changed. At the present time, as outlined in Chapter 8, Hanoi's heritage is under pressure from the potent forces of economic and cultural globalisation flowing from the introduction of the *doi moi* (renovation) policies by the Sixth Party Congress in 1986. But, rivalling this in its significance in terms of its impact on Vietnamese economics, culture, society and city formation, was the sharp break associated with the arrival of French colonialism a century earlier.

The result of French town planning and construction activities in Hanoi (and other Indochinese cities) was to create discontinuity on the ground – to build alongside the established indigenous town a new European town. There is growing international interest in the colonial or 'imposed' city type found today in much of ex-colonial Asia, from Yogyakarta and Semarang to Delhi and Amman, where modern and traditional activities sit side by side. But while the two parts were physically separated, they were held together by a complicated set of economic and political relationships. Some academics have begun to focus on the 'shared' nature of the bipolar cities created through colonialism.[121] Others operating in a postcolonial paradigm, such as the 'subaltern' school in India, have set about analysing the political intent behind the colonial cities. This includes exploring the thinking behind the drawing up of the typical rectangular patterns of European quarters, which they see as linked to the English (or even European) cultural 'obsession with naming, with demarcation, and with segregation'.[122] Much of the interest focuses on the role played by the urban centre as the primary location for the dismantling of pre-colonial social, political and economic systems.

In Indochina, new economic ideas and connections tied the cities into international networks, a new phase in the region's increasing economic and cultural globalisation. In the case of Hanoi, the colonial period brought a sudden influx of merchants, manufacturers, professionals and civil servants who congregated in the city to prop up the new extractive economy geared back to France.[123] The particular French type of urbanism in Hanoi, as in other major Indochinese cities, was conceived as a project and Hanoi was seen as an experimental laboratory for achieving the perfect colonial society. This not only involved the assimilation–association debate, but it was also seen, especially in the 1920s and 1930s, in the attempt to find the best spatial arrangements within urban centres to achieve that end. Thus, in many ways, the modern elements being introduced through colonialism represented a total rupture of the traditional society. Hanoi came to reflect on the ground both the best and worst aspects of colonialism. This was a colonialism and a colonial city imposed by force, and, by becoming (or being perceived as) the symbol of oppression, the bi-polar city became the rallying point for the nationalist movement that in the end helped to bring the colonial regime tumbling down.

But this was mostly how the Vietnamese intellectuals saw the city. It is unwise to oversimplify the cultural role played by the city during the colonial period; in fact, the Vietnamese city generally did not present a single dominant cultural image in this period. The French deliberately fostered a social hierarchy in order to divide and rule more easily: white European; the *créoles* from French India; the *métis* or mixed Franco-Vietnamese; the Chinese, Indians, naturalised Vietnamese; and then the rest – Vietnamese, Khmer, Lao, the ethnic minorities from the mountains. Each group saw city life in a different light according to its particular place in the colonial order of things. For the French *colons*, the city was where they tried to recreate the European way of life. For the Vietnamese elite, the city was a window on to a new world where the French value system dominated. Pierre-Richard Feray described the elite's perception this way:

> More than just an economic centre, the town was first and foremost a cultural meeting place. From the first instant that the Vietnamese gained wealth and lived in the town, he began to become gallicised. He tried to speak accentless French. He ate, lived, breathed French. If he was Catholic, his first concern was to take on a European first name: Jean, Roland, Georges, Marie; his second was to look for a French spouse; the third was to become, by naturalisation, French.[124]

This social class was the product of the web of colonial policies: land allocations, political favouritism, restricted educational opportunities, even the urban zoning plans Hébrard drew up and implemented. For the poor, by contrast, the city offered escape from the poverty-stricken countryside, where they could make good – or at least where they could pretend to be making good until, as many finally did, they returned to the village birthplace.

In short, the cultural role played by Hanoi, and the other major cities of Vietnam, during the colonial period was an ambiguous one. They were the points of most intense Western impact from which modern ideas were diffused to smaller urban settlements and to the countryside. But they were also the places where indigenous cultures met and mixed with other non-colonial, immigrant cultures, as well as the points through which largely Western-educated political radicals began to create mass resistance leading to revolution. O'Connor concludes that out of cultural dialectics such as this emerged the different varieties of South-east Asian nationalism and national identity. The cities were beginning to resume their 'orthogenetic' role; that is, their role in defining and disseminating the essence of indigenous national cultures. And this was to be reflected in the further emergence of a new set of national symbols in the urban cultural landscape. But before Hanoi could fully resume this new cultural role for the Vietnamese nation, it became embroiled in wars that were to last a generation.

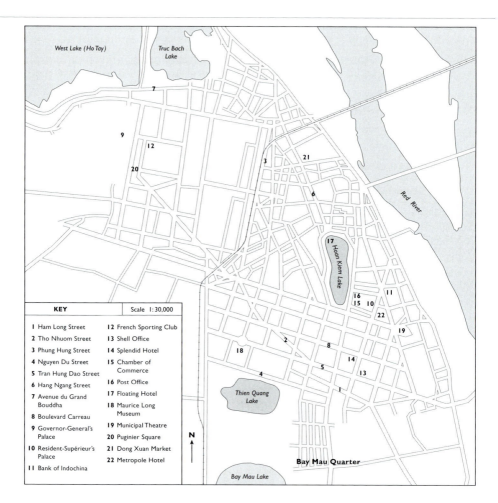

West Lake (Ho Tay)

Truc Bach Lake

Red River

Hoan Kiem Lake

Thien Quang Lake

Bay Mau Lake

Bay Mau Quarter

KEY	Scale 1:30,000

1 Ham Long Street
2 Tho Nhuom Street
3 Phung Hung Street
4 Nguyen Du Street
5 Tran Hung Dao Street
6 Hang Ngang Street
7 Avenue du Grand Bouddha
8 Boulevard Carreau
9 Governor-General's Palace
10 Resident-Supérieur's Palace
11 Bank of Indochina

12 French Sporting Club
13 Shell Office
14 Splendid Hotel
15 Chamber of Commerce
16 Post Office
17 Floating Hotel
18 Maurice Long Museum
19 Municipal Theatre
20 Puginier Square
21 Dong Xuan Market
22 Metropole Hotel

N

Chapter 4
The Japanese interlude: Vietnamese resistance, French collaboration and collapse

Viet Minh and the Communists

The period of direct Japanese intervention into Vietnamese affairs was brief – less than five years – but it was a momentous interlude. During their period of military victories and economic expansion, the Japanese taught a new lesson of 'Asia for the Asians' and fostered anti-colonial movements in much of South-east Asia. While the relationship between Japan and anti-colonialism was never so simple in Vietnam, this short period of Japanese intervention did untie France's hold over its Indochinese possessions. It led up to what David Marr has called the most important year in modern Vietnamese history – 1945 – when a millennium of rule by imperial dynasties came to an end.[1] Not only was the monarchist ideology swept aside, but ideas of modernisation and materialism, linked to the imported Western political ideologies of capitalism and communism, replaced or at least distorted traditional Confucian beliefs.

House at 5D Ham Long Street – headquarters of the Vietnam Revolutionary Youth Association where the Vietnamese Communist Party was formed in March 1929.

The nationalist activities that eventually culminated in the establishment of the communist Democratic Republic of Vietnam in 1955 had grassroots origins and were carried out through a network of political cells operating in suburbs and villages. The 'little people' now take centre stage and the buildings, monuments and sites associated with their struggle for national independence and a socialist order are commonly humble in scale and design. The question of heritage significance moves away from issues of imperial and colonial prestige and architectural and urbanistic merit to criteria of social significance. Later the leaders of these groups became leaders of the new independent Vietnam, but the buildings and sites reminding us of their humble origins take their place alongside the grander monuments of other periods.

One such place is No. 5D, Ham Long Street in the French Quarter of Hanoi – a far cry from the buildings designed by Ernest Hébrard. It was in this small house, one of a set of four, that a provisional Vietnamese Communist Party was formed and a manifesto drawn up in May 1929, about the time that Hébrard was quitting Indochina. Decisions were also taken to begin publishing a newspaper and to translate documents from the Russian October Revolution for distribution to other supporters.[2] The house appears to have acted as a front for these political activities for several years, with Comrade Quoc Anh and his wife, Comrade Lien, being appointed to live there as 'normal residents'. It is now officially recognised as part of the Hanoi heritage.

The efforts by the French administration to soften its assimilationist policies and adopt an associationist stance proved totally ineffectual in stemming anti-French sentiments among the Vietnamese. Such feelings went back to the nineteenth century and were by now well entrenched in the popular psyche. Members of the scholar-gentry class had led much of the early resistance in the years 1885–1925.[3] Confucianism was the focal point of these first anti-colonial movements, which might seem paradoxical given its underlying search for peace and harmony. However, many members of the Confucianist mandarin class had traditionally exerted a rapacious hold over the peasantry and they resented the foreigners' intrusion. The last of the scholar-inspired insurrections against French rule in central Vietnam in 1916 failed and its leader Tran Cao Van, a well-known Confucian scholar, was decapitated for his role in urging peasants to resist higher colonial taxes.[4]

By the time Doumer left in 1902, Vietnamese life had already changed immeasurably. The pacification campaign had officially ended, although it was never completely successful. The monarchy had failed to resist the French and was humiliated in the eyes of much of the Vietnamese population. The later Nguyen kings, Thanh Thai (1889–1907) and Duy Than (1907–16), had tried courageously to reassert themselves but had been outwitted and dethroned. The old mandarin ruling class was declining along with the monarchy, both because the French authorities had undercut its functions and because collaboration with the French discredited it. A unified and strong colonial administration now covered the whole of Indochina and a new class system was emerging. This featured a small Vietnamese middle class, a Western-educated intelligentsia, the landless peasants, and an industrial proletariat. Together these groups formed the basis for the successful nationalist and communist movement later in the century.[5]

The intellectuals ironically included students who had come home from French universities. That they had had to study in France was a direct result of the assimilationist colonial policies which limited the availability of university places within Vietnam and encouraged students to enrol in metropolitan France. They brought with them new ideas, rejecting the modernisation and Westernisation seen in the *mission civilisatrice*. For Vietnamese intellectuals, modernisation was bound up with the struggle for independence and for identifying a non-monarchical system of government. This was a steep learning curve for many, since the Western concepts of nation, economic development, constitutional government and revolution were new to Vietnamese language and thinking.[6]

But not all the influences flowed directly from the West; some came from neighbouring China, which was going through its own period of political unrest. The Chinese nationalist leader Sun Yat Sen had stayed briefly in Indochina in 1907–8. His early tactical ideas based on terrorism in the towns and subversion in the army greatly influenced the Vietnamese intellectual, Phan Boi Chau, who is seen by many as the founder of Vietnamese nationalism.[7] Phan Boi Chau established the Vietnam Independence Association (*Viet Nam Phuc Quoc Hoi*) in 1912 and, operating out of China, was able to build up a loyal support group in Tonkin, Annam and in the Vietnamese communities living in southern China and Siam. But his attempted army mutiny at Thai Nguyen in 1917 was quickly suppressed.

By the time of his death in 1925, Sun Yat Sen had swung towards the Leninist view that a revolutionary party needed to be organised through a secret network of cells, and it was this strategic approach that was taken by the Vietnamese Marxist, Nguyen Ai Quoc. The son of a minor official, this man, who was to be known as Ho Chi Minh from 1942, had had a chequered career to this point. After a classical and French education in Hue, he had taken unskilled work both aboard ship and in Europe and became a political activist in France among the Vietnamese student and political exile community, as well as in Moscow. He spent some time imprisoned in the Santé gaol in Paris along with other Vietnamese revolutionaries and became a founding member of the French Communist Party in 1920. He had also attempted to petition President Wilson at the Versailles peace conference in support of Vietnamese independence.

When he arrived back on the Asian scene in 1924, Nguyen Ai Quoc was about 30 years old and brimming with political ideas, enthusiasm and energy. From a base in Canton, his task was to engineer the spread of communism in Vietnam. By 1925 he had organised the Vietnam Revolutionary Youth Association (*Viet Nam Cach Mang Thanh Nien Hoi*), initially by recruiting younger followers of Phan Boi Chau. By 1929 he had enlisted an estimated 1,000 members in Indochina, of whom 200 had gone to Canton for revolutionary training. He took over the Revolutionary Party (*Cach Mang Dang*) that had been established in 1925 in northern Annam and southern Tonkin. In February 1930 he brought these components together and formalised the Vietnamese Communist Party (VNCP) from the provisional party created in No. 5D, Ham Long Street, 11 months earlier. In October 1930, the VNCP was renamed the Indochina Communist Party (ICP or, in Vietnamese, the *Dong Duong Cong San Dang*).

House at 90 Tho Nhuom Street – headquarters of the Provisional Vietnamese Communist Party, 1930.

House at 105 Phung Hung Street – home of the Indochina Communist Party, 1936–39.

Other houses around Hanoi's Old Sector were used by the clandestine organisation. Between May and August 1930 the Central Committee of the VNCP had operated out of a house at No. 90, Tho Nhuom Street. This was then the house of a high-ranking French official who failed to suspect that in his basement the first General-Secretary of the Party, Comrade Tran Phu, was busy at work or that political meetings were being held. Among those who met and stayed there was the schoolteacher Comrade Tran Van Lan, later to become known as Vo Nguyen Giap, the military leader of the North Vietnamese communist forces.[8] Between 1936 and 1939 the ICP headquarters operated from a two-storey house in Phung Hung Street, then Rue Henri d'Orléans, a wide but relatively quiet street on the edge of the Ancient Quarter. It was also the office of the ICP's propaganda and campaign newspaper, *Tin Tuc* (*Information*).

The 1930s were a period of anti-colonial unrest and retaliation by the French authorities using troops and aircraft. In 1930 an uprising at Yen Bay, north-west of Hanoi, was put down ruthlessly. It had been organised along Sun Yat Sen's ideas by the Vietnamese Nationalist Party (VNP; *Quoc Dan Dang*), led by Nguyen Thai Hoc. Even the May 1938 Hanoi Exposition was marked by a massive demonstration of 50,000 people and 25 organisations. During the decade, as a result of the VNP's failure, the ICP began to emerge as the main force within the revolutionary movement in Tonkin. Already by April 1931 it counted 1,828 full members and 35,770 in associated organisations. The colonial authorities realised the ICP's destructive potential and outlawed the party in 1939. It was not until the end of World War 2 that the ICP finally dominated the Vietnamese nationalist revolution, but even as late as 1954 it still did not dominate the whole of Cochinchina. The ICP's lesser impact on the south was the result of many factors, including the rise of the two new sects of Caodaism and Hoa Hao Buddhism and the antipathy felt within Vietnamese communist circles between the Trotskyite south and the Stalinist centre and north.[9]

An important step along the way to communist dominance was the establishment of the Viet Minh (*Viet Nam Doc Lap Dong Minh*, or Vietnam Independence League). This was formed following an ICP conference at Chin Si in China's Kwangsi Province in May 1941, less than a year after Vietnam had been drawn into World War 2 by the Japanese occupation. The secretary was Nguyen Ai Quoc and the membership was predominantly communist, although its program was more nationalist than socialist. One of the first actions of the Viet Minh was to form guerrilla units, under the direction of Vo Nguyen Giap, to operate in Vietnamese territory against both the French and the Japanese. The non-communist elements in the Viet Minh were riven by factionalism, again leaving it to Nguyen Ai Quoc to force the pace, which he did from a prison cell in China where he was held for all of 1942 and January 1943. Exiting under the new name of Ho

Chi Minh, he now became leader of a new, ostensibly non-communist, alliance called the Vietnam Revolutionary Alliance (*Viet Nam Cach Mang Dong Minh Hoi*). The alliance was supported by the Chinese Kuomintang government, which needed Vietnamese intelligence on Japanese activities in Tonkin.

Ho used his position in the Alliance to strengthen his hold on the Viet Minh. Popular support was strengthened by the brutal French and Japanese persecution of communist members, including the killing of Hoang Van Thu, a member of the ICP Central Committee, at the Bach Mai execution field on the southern outskirts of Hanoi in May 1944.

Japan and France in Indochina

The capitulation of France to Hitler's German army in June 1940 brought Indochina into the war on the side of the axis powers. French Indochina, like France, had been unprepared for the outbreak of World War 2. When it came in September 1939, local reserves in Indochina were called up and France provided 15 combat aircraft and a lone light cruiser, the *Lamotte-Picquet*, to protect the open coast of Vietnam and Cambodia. Vietnamese men were, however, drafted into French armies to fight in Europe. Communication links between France and Indochina were reduced to a telegram service; Indochina was now effectively operating independently from Paris. The Japanese occupation began in June 1940, and the Japanese worked in collaboration with the Vichy French colonial administration for almost five years until March 1945.

Japan had sought to forge an agreement with French Indochina since November 1939 when the Japanese Foreign Ministry sent a detailed proposal to the French Ambassador in Tokyo, Arsène Henry. Three aims motivated the Japanese move. The principal aim was to block off the aid, mainly from the United States, that was passing along Tonkin's Yunnan railway to Chiang Kai Shek's nationalist troops in China. But Japan also wanted to remove or lower the tariff wall against its economic expansion into French Indochina, and to impose upon Indochina a Japanese inspection mission charged with ensuring these matters were implemented.[10] Ambassador Henry's advice to Hanoi dated 19 June 1940 was that 'The only way we could avoid an attack against Indochina would be to let the Japanese do what they want'.[11] French troops in Indochina were less numerous than the Japanese army in Canton, and the French would have to fight on two fronts – the China border and the Gulf of Tonkin. Although Great Britain and the United States were opposed to Japanese expansion, they were not particularly interested in assisting Vichy France and declined to become involved. Indochina was left cut off from outside help. Governor-General Catroux decided to cede to Japan's demands – sacrificing national pride for national interests, as Japanese historian Sachiko Murakami puts it.[12] The Vichy government was displeased by Catroux's attitude and replaced him by Admiral Jean Decoux.

But Catroux's decision enabled the Japanese to occupy the French Indochinese territories without using military force. The Japanese inspection team arrived in Hanoi on 22 June 1940 and, in accordance with the Matsuoka-Henry Agreement signed on 30 August, the Japanese dispatched its army, navy and air forces to Indochina on 5 September. Reactions to the Japanese occupation were complex. It suggested to other Asians that they, too, could overthrow their Western masters. But it did little to demonstrate Japanese support for national independence for, under the French–Japanese pact, it was only a military occupation and the French colonial authorities were left to continue running Indochina on a day-to-day basis. From Tokyo's viewpoint, making use of the colonial administration was seen as the cheapest, most skilful way to administer the territory.[13] The Japanese army headquarters regarded it as the most effective way of maintaining calm and allowing it to get on with military operations in the country, as well as elsewhere in East and South-east Asia.[14] Tokyo installed Japanese officials to shadow the French – a shadow Governor-General, shadow Residents in Tonkin and Cochinchina, senior bureaucrats at the Ministry of Foreign Affairs, and two Japanese representatives on the colonial Council for Indochina.[15]

From the French point of view, it seemed agreed that France would retain its colonial rights in Indochina. Indeed, the Japanese government's decision in July 1941 to replace the military mission there with an apparently diplomatic one appeared to vindicate the French decision to save Indochina by diplomatic rather than military means.[16] Troop numbers were never very high: on the eve of the Pacific War (December 1941) they numbered only 75,000, and even before the Japanese coup of 9 March 1945 were still only 40,000.[17] French trading interests, damaged by the loss of markets in Europe because of the war, were well served by the Japanese connection and the dire need Japan was experiencing to find new supplies of food and raw materials. Indochina's share of the total value of Japan's imports rose from less than 1 per cent in the 1930s to 12.8 per cent in 1942, before falling back to 1.1 per cent in 1944 and zero in 1945.[18] Rice was a critical import for the Japanese, but after 1943 the demands of the Japanese war economy increasingly encouraged the French colonial landowners to cultivate jute, caster beans, hemp, flax and cotton, and to step up the exploitation of Indochinese forests and mines.[19]

As well as revealing Japanese attitudes to the native peoples of Indochina, the documents prepared by the Japanese Foreign Ministry's Indochina experts provide further evidence that Japan was not interested in turning Indochina into a full colony in the way that it had done with

Korea and Taiwan. In one proposal written in 1940, for example, Yasukichi Nagata wrote:

> The people [of French Indochina] are now in a sorry state, having lost their erstwhile vigour, forgotten their culture, forfeited their wealth, and reverted to a primitive and uncivilised state. The majority of the land is given over to wild animals and poisonous snakes. France claims to be guiding and enlightening backward peoples and introducing them to European culture, but this is nothing but empty propaganda directed at the outside world ... From the positive viewpoint of the growth of [Japan's] national strength, development and exploitation of their resources hold great promise ... Our ultimate objective should be to take advantage of this opportunity to grant the Annamese independence (whether Cambodia and Laos are to be subordinated to Annam can be considered later) and include them in our planned East Asian community [that is, the Greater East Asia Co-Prosperity Sphere].[20]

But for the time being, the Japanese priorities were firmly fixed on achieving an easy military arrangement and obtaining food and raw materials; supporting Indochinese nationalist movements had to wait.

As mentioned, on 30 August 1940, the Vichy government and Japan signed the Matsuoka-Henry Agreement, a pact recognising Japan's 'pre-eminent position' in the Far East but leaving the Administration of the Vichy-installed Governor-General, Jean Decoux, to run day-to-day affairs in Indochina. On the night of 7 December 1941, detachments of troops moved quietly into Hanoi, occupying the crossroads and encircling public buildings, including the Governor-General's residence, now known as the Palais Puginier. Others were stationed in towns and at various strategic points along the roads, railway and river routes between Hanoi, Haiphong, Vinh and towns further south. Generally, however, very little was seen of them in either the cities or the countryside, and where they were stationed near French troops they tended to keep aloof.[21] According to the eminent Vietnamese historian Professor Phan Huy Le, life under the Japanese was outwardly almost normal.[22] The French remained responsible for tax collection, the armed forces, justice, police, customs, post and telecommunications, transport, education, and the right to appoint all civil and military officials.[23]

Many of the policies and actions of Admiral Decoux have been described as 'frankly fascist' by Bernard Fall.[24] In fact, the Decoux record is decidely mixed and included a number of progressive steps. Fall acknowledges that the most remarkable of these was the transformation of the Indochinese Grand Council into a Federal Council in 1941 and the appointment to it, in May 1943, of a majority of Indochinese members. Fall sees this as a clear victory over the anti-liberal *colons* who, because of the war, could no longer call on the support of their friends back in France to block change. The Indochinese parliamentary institution was moving towards a more democratic composition, and, although Decoux had full dictatorial powers, it seemed to Fall in hindsight to promise a stronger base for full democratisation after the war was over. For the time being, moreover, because new French nationals were no longer coming to the colonies to fill jobs, a number of Vietnamese rose to increasingly senior posts in the administration and with full salary parity.

The fact that Japan allowed France to administer Vietnam meant that the Japanese had very little direct impact on Hanoi's built environment.[25] Urban development and town planning were left to the French colonial authorities. In his 1949 account of his period in office, Decoux made a list of his major achievements in the cities of Indochina — a list, he said, that would 'strike the imagination of both the elite groups and the masses, demonstrating to them by hard facts that the French effort has not been dimmed but, on the contrary, shines across all its territories with a new light'.[26] At the top of his list was the creation of a *cité universitaire* in Hanoi, an integrated university campus in the North American or Australian sense. A new library for the École Française d'Extrême-Orient was followed by improvements to the *Résidences-Supérieures* in Hanoi and Saigon (so that the official representatives of France could be housed in 'conditions of dignity and sufficient comfort'). He completed his list with references to public works carried out on the royal palaces and residences at Hue, Hanoi, Phnom Penh and Luang Prabang. The Governor-General's efforts were particularly praised by the *colons* in Hanoi, with the city's mayor in 1942, Henri Guiriec, describing Decoux's vision for Indochina in the following glowing terms:

> Confident in Indochina's destiny, concerned to foster the rapid expansion that, before the war, its privileged position and natural resources gave the Union, the Admiral would like Indochina's activity to be resolutely directed towards preparing for a future even more fertile than that of the past, open to a perspective of greatness and prosperity.[27]

International modernism and Cérutti's war-time Hanoi

In reality, the next major phase of development in Hanoi had been under way since the late 1930s as Indochina recovered from the effects of the Great Depression. The Chief of the Town Planning and Architecture Service was by this time Henri Cérutti-Maori, his deputy was Louis-Georges Pineau and, in Western architecture, the international modern movement and the International Style were in vogue. This movement, which had been established in Europe and North America by architects such as Le Corbusier, Walter Gropius and Mies van der Rohe, sought to break from both traditional and classical architecture. It wanted the form of a building to clearly express its function, and it rejected the superficial decorative treatment of façades characteristic of nineteenth-century architectural design. In Hanoi, the International Style tended to be closely linked initially with art deco exterior and interior detailing. Governor-General Decoux, in his desire to show that Indochina was progressing, was keen that its architecture and planning should keep abreast of the trends in France. Consequently, Cérutti and Pineau found in Decoux a leader well attuned to their international modernist approach and it was during this period of French–Japanese collaboration that they did their most productive architectural and planning work in Hanoi.

International modernism in Hanoi predated Cérutti's period in Hanoi, having already begun to find expression in the late 1920s. Of the early Hanoi buildings, the best known is the Bank of Indochina by architect Georges André Trouvé and built between 1925 and 1930. The banking chambers still possess today their elegant art deco features. But others include the streamlined French Sport Club (Cercle sportif français) in the Ba Dinh area, designed by architect Jacques Lagisquet and constructed in 1930. In the French Quarter, the Shell Office, built in 1925–30 on the corner of Tran Hung Dao and Ngo Quyen streets, is now the Ministry of Science, Technology and Environment. The Splendid Hotel (now the Hoa Binh Hotel) retains its original function on the corner of Ngo Quyen and Ly Thuong Kiet streets; unfortunately, it has lost most of its stylistic originality as the result of extensive remodelling in the mid-1990s. Further south, the René Robin Hospital, named after another Governor-General, was constructed between 1930 and the early 1940s to a design by the little-known architect Christian. It is now the Bach Mai Hospital, which became well known internationally during the Vietnam War.

The sleek lines and geometric shapes of Georges Trouvé's Bank of Indochina heralded the arrival of international modernism in Hanoi.

Cérutti appears to have been an advocate for the construction of a set of new buildings around Hoan Kiem Lake to replace the existing 'antiquated and inadequate buildings'. He included in his scheme a new town hall — one that would be worthy of the capital and give this central focus of the city a 'monumental character without diminishing its special flavour'.[28] In 1942 a complex bringing together the central Post Office and the Hanoi Chamber of Commerce was under construction, to plans drawn up by Cérutti.[29] The first part completed — the Hôtel de la Chambre de Commerce de Hanoi — was probably the most stylish of his colonial buildings. It was clearly functional and made use of clean lines and geometric shapes both in its plan and the treatment of its façade. Little reference was made to local cultural traditions in this design — but then this was a key point of the international modernist movement. The result was a sharp break with the Hébrard line and, in building form at least, a move closer to the Soviet-inspired monuments of the next period in Hanoi's cultural history. The design of the Chamber of Commerce building was to have been carried through into the adjacent Post Office, but the project was interrupted by political events. When the Post Office was finally built in the 1960s, it was in yet another style reflecting the values of the newly installed communist regime.

Left The second, international modern Chamber of Commerce on Hoan Kiem Lake. Henri Cérutti-Maori's conception was not followed through with adjacent buildings.
Below The first, neoclassical Chamber of Commerce building, erected at the Examination Compound in Trang Thi Street. It is now the National Library.

The 1942 Hanoi master plan, with its important extension to the Bay Mau district beyond Lake Thanh Nhan to the line of today's peripheral ring road, was his major planning achievement. Work on the so-called Cérutti Plan seems in fact to have spanned the years 1941–44.[30] It was characterised by a renewed emphasis on the Haussmann-inspired urban design ideas employed by Hébrard. In the southern extension this included radiating boulevards focusing on a new square at the intersection of Hue Street and Dai Co Viet Road. According to Pineau, the intention was to create a monumental view cutting right through the Bay Mau Quarter from Rue Hallais (Nguyen Du Street) across Lake Thien Quang to an ornamental park and the newly created Lake Bay Mau.[31] The plan also included design controls for façades, porticos and other aspects of new buildings, as well as site coverage regulations. On the latter, it recommended a maximum 30 per cent site coverage, a compromise between the municipal council's vision of 50 per cent or more and Cérutti's own preference for a low-density 25 per cent such as he had seen enforced in French Morocco. The council was concerned that such low site coverage would work against resolution of the growing housing crisis and would be too costly to implement.

The Cité universitaire, in which Decoux took such pride, was also part of Cérutti's southern extension plan. In an extensive tract of land south of Bay Mau Lake and Dai Co Viet Road, he drew up four land-use zones and outlined the kinds of buildings to be constructed in each. The most innovative was the zone for public administration, the university and *grandes écoles* (specialised tertiary education) – the modern conception of a multidisciplinary campus with recreational and sporting facilities, and a sharp contrast to the old Hanoi University and to the scattered buildings making up universities in Paris. A commercial zone allowed for new shop-houses along lower Hue Street, while a residential zone was set aside for new traditional village- style buildings – a strange departure from the international modernist philosophy. The fourth zone was for open space and public gardens. As with Hébrard's master plan, the Cérutti Plan was never fully implemented. Its failure was due largely to its heavy reliance on the mechanism of land-use zoning. In the Cité universitaire area today, only the road alignment, with its square of streets offset against the orientation of the main boundary roads, still reflects his intentions. While the area has become the home for a number of Hanoi's universities (Polytechnic University, Construction University, National Economics University), they were not built to Cérutti's designs, nor on the specific sites he proposed.

Cérutti's land-use zoning recommendations met resistance from Vietnamese property owners who now appear increasingly assertive in civic matters. One of the first records of Vietnamese engagement with the planning process is the lengthy submission to the municipal council by Nguyen Xuan Thai, Director of the Nam Ky Bookshop, dated

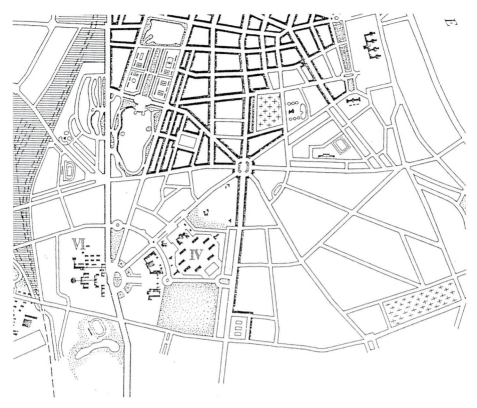

Cérutti's Cité universitaire.
(*Indochine. Hébdomadaire illustré*,
nos 164–65, 28 October 1942)

25 January 1943.[32] The submission took a conservative line, arguing for minimal change in the planning system already existing. In particular, Thai objected to any further entrenchment of the concept of land-use zonation in Hanoi's planning. His argument was that business and industrial entrepreneurs were currently enjoying the benefits of being scattered throughout the city, and that attempting to draw them together into zones would hamper their development. New business preferred to open up in areas away from existing enterprises that would offer competition.

He contrasted the recently developed precincts of modern European-style villas and large gardens with the Ancient Quarter where the houses were cramped, insanitary, and poorly arranged along dangerous and narrow streets. The proposal made in the Cérutti Plan that new areas of 'Asian residences' be built to relieve pressures on the inner area was met with a degree of alarm. It was Thai's opinion that such buildings would destroy the harmony of neighbouring quarters and would be strongly opposed by the existing property owners. Thai speaks in the plural form, but it is not clear whether in fact he speaks for himself alone or for a wider group. In either case, the opinions appear to be those of the Vietnamese elite, well adapted to the French colonial presence and learning how to make use of opportunities for public participation in the planning process to make their views known. This reflects the moves made by Decoux's administration to encourage the development of a Vietnamese middle class, including bringing local Vietnamese into more senior positions within the bureaucracy. No evidence has been found of similar involvement by Vietnamese working-class residents in the planning of their sections of town.

Right House at 84 Nguyen Du Street designed by Nguyen Xuan Tung — an attempt to find a modern Vietnamese style of architecture.

Below The Floating Restaurant on Hoan Kiem Lake by architect Vo Duc Dien. The second storey was originally a pergola-covered terrace.

Among this burgeoning middle class were a number of young Vietnamese architects whose ideas contrasted with the international modernist approach and were more in line with those of Nguyen Xuan Thai. In fact, these belonged to the first generation of Vietnamese architects trained at the College of Fine Arts in Hanoi who had come under the influence of Ernest Hébrard. They sought to establish a Vietnamese national style of architecture using the similar design technique of blending indigenous and Western elements.[33] The villas at 84 Nguyen Du Street by Nguyen Xuan Tung and 17 Thuyen Quang Street by Nguyen Cao Luyen exemplify the work of this group, with their use of upturned eaves, canopies and porticos. The Refreshment Club (Floating Restaurant) on Hoan Kiem Lake by Vo Duc Dien is a non-residential example of this neo-traditional style. A two-storey structure jutting out over the waters of the lake, the restaurant was used by the Americans and other expatriates during the dying years of the French colonial period and has been rehabilitated smartly in the 1990s for a new Hanoi middle class and Western tourists.

The efforts of this group were subsequently both praised and condemned. The architectural mainstream under the communist regime, as typified by Ngo Huy Quynh, seems to have taken the line that they were merely imposing superficial pseudo-Vietnamese, really Chinese, characteristics on to European structures. The square first floor of the Refreshment Club and the type of door frame of the house in Nguyen Du Street were said, for example, to reflect the character of Chinese palaces.[34] Quynh also criticised these new architects for 'satisfying the taste of the new breed of capitalists' that had emerged under French rule.

Doc lap! Independence!

The Decoux years were a time of multiple collaborations – French colonial authorities, property owners and entrepreneurs with the Japanese occupiers; and the Vietnamese middle class with the French. Or that, at least, was how the growing number of Vietnamese nationalists interpreted the situation. This set of relationships came to an abrupt end in March 1945 when the Japanese occupiers staged a *coup de force*, overthrowing the French civil administration, disarming the French troops and police, and taking full control themselves. The relatively peaceful times Indochina had been experiencing were over.

Events on the world stage were changing quickly. Vichy France had fallen, Paris was liberated in August 1944 and, on 30 August, General Charles de Gaulle established a provisional Free French government. Having already declared that 'The territories of the Empire, no matter where they are or what they are, belong to no-one but France',[35] De Gaulle proceeded to repudiate all agreements between Vichy and Tokyo. Decoux responded by quickly ordering all photos of Marshall Pétain removed from government office walls throughout Indochina. Nazi Berlin was now threatened by the Allied advance, and Japan was essentially on its own in the Pacific War. The Allied forces in the Pacific, led by the United States, focused attention on severing the Indochina link in Japan's South-east Asian network. Fearing an invasion by General Macarthur's forces based in the Philippines, and suspecting that the colonial regime was preparing to switch its allegiance to the Free French,[36] the Japanese in Hanoi launched their surprise Operation Mei. At precisely 7 p.m. on 9 March – ironically, as David Marr points out, the very night of the most fatal American air attack on Tokyo[37] – the French army headquarters and the Hanoi airbase at Gia Lam were seized.[38] While the French authorities in Hanoi resisted until the following afternoon, generally the French surrendered with little resistance. The 90,000 French and Indochinese troops were quickly disarmed by Japan's 40,000 soldiers, and nearly all civilian officials and the military were taken prisoner, including Governor-General Decoux.

After the coup, French citizens were required to live in designated quarters in the main cities, and those who had been active in the Resistance were rounded up. However, a large number of French stayed in their jobs, as the Japanese had encouraged them to do. In fact, it seems that, thanks to continued Vietnamese and French collaboration, business was back to normal in Hanoi and other major Vietnamese cities within two or three days.[39] The Vietnamese elite simply transferred their loyalties to the Japanese – bending again with the wind. Japan once more asserted that it had no permanent territorial ambitions in Indochina[40] and, on 17 April, it established an 'independent' Vietnamese government under the leadership of Tran Trong Kim, with Bao Dai as the puppet 'Emperor of Annam'. Cambodia and Laos also revoked their connections with France and recognised Japanese domination.

In order to demonstrate that the days of French colonialism were over, and in line with the Confucian principles of 'rectification of names', the new Japanese-sponsored regime in Vietnam ordered all French place names to be replaced by Vietnamese names.[41] It was at this time that Vietnamese became the official language of government and the bureaucracy, as reflected in the abrupt disappearance of the French language from the archives from the period. However, the Kim government proved short-lived and collapsed when Japan surrendered in September 1945. While the Japanese had not intended to support a nationalist movement in Vietnam, and certainly not a socialist one, their intervention had the effect of undermining the 80-year-old French colonial rule and giving the nationalists, under Ho Chi Minh, a fighting chance of taking control of the country.

No building in Hanoi tells this story better than the Maurice Long Museum that once existed on Tran Hung Street, the southernmost avenue in the first French Quarter subdivision. Its site had consisted of swampy rice fields until the 1890s when the colonial authorities drew up its plans for the European Quarter. Then the site was drained, filled and used briefly as a racecourse before being taken over to house Doumer's 1902 Hanoi Exposition. André Bussy, a Hanoi Public Works architect, designed a magnificent neoclassical centrepiece, surrounded by temporary pavilions and display stands. The building's colonnaded façade was more than 100 metres long. A painted dome dominated the entrance hall, and a grand staircase led to the galleries upstairs. After the exposition, the building was converted to a museum and later named after the progressive 1920s' Governor-General, Maurice Long. It was here, on 1 May 1938, that a meeting of many thousands of Hanoi workers demanded 'freedom, democracy, the right to organise trade unions, the improvement of the quality of life', a key event in the build-up to the First Indochina War against the French. During the Japanese occupation, the complex of buildings was taken over as barracks for the Japanese troops. As a consequence, it became a prime target for Allied air attacks on the city and was hit by American bombers in 1945. Although damage to Hanoi does not appear to have been extensive in this early American air attack on the city, the museum building, in parallel with the fate of the French colonial regime, was devastated. The museum's site further represents in microcosm the history of Hanoi when, during the period of Soviet influence over Vietnam in the 1970s, it was chosen as the location of the Soviet–Vietnamese Friendship Cultural Palace.

The central building designed by André Bussy for the 1902 Hanoi Exhibition. It later became the Maurice Long Museum.

With the routing of the French colonial regime and an end to the Japanese empire obviously in sight, a political vacuum had been created. This provided a brief chance for the Viet Minh to assert itself before the Chinese Kuomintang, representing the victorious Allied forces, arrived to occupy northern Vietnam or British forces could be shipped from Calcutta to take over the south. The Viet Minh seized this opportunity and, in August 1945, formed a National Liberation Committee and decided to seize Hanoi. This led to the famed 'August Revolution'. To the chagrin of many

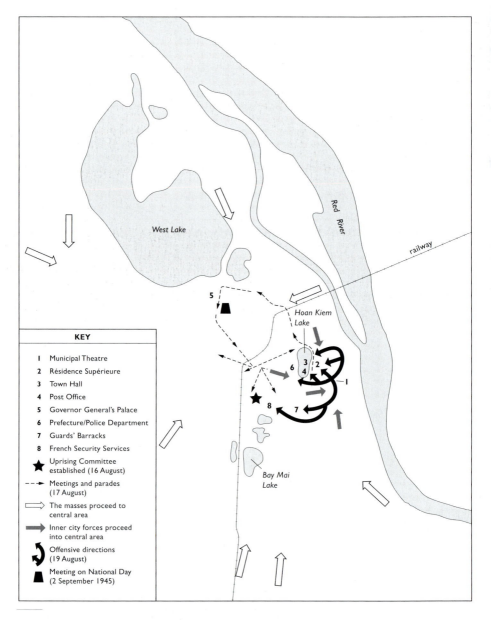

KEY

1	Municipal Theatre
2	Résidence Supérieure
3	Town Hall
4	Post Office
5	Governor General's Palace
6	Prefecture/Police Department
7	Guards' Barracks
8	French Security Services
★	Uprising Committee established (16 August)
---▶	Meetings and parades (17 August)
⇨	The masses proceed to central area
➡	Inner city forces proceed into central area
↻	Offensive directions (19 August)
◼	Meeting on National Day (2 September 1945)

Above Revolutionary flags disrupt the Kim government's mass meeting outside the Opera House. (Centre Militaire d'Information et de Documentation sur l'Outre-Mer, Versailles)

Right The house at 101 Tran Hung Dao Street — home of the communist regional committee at the time of its decision to take Hanoi.

Opposite page The August Revolutionary Enthusiasm. (*Atlas: The Thirtieth Anniversary of the Liberation of the Capital, 1954–1984* (Tong Hop Publishing House, Hanoi, 1984), p. 5)

old-guard Vietnamese historians, David Marr has portrayed the event as more of a general insurrection than a full-blown revolution.[42] In this, Marr built on the observations of eyewitnesses such as Archimedes Patti of the American Office of Strategic Services, who summed up the 'revolution' as being 'no coup d'état, [and having] no bloodshed, no reprisals, no French resistance, no secret plot or arrangement with the Japanese, not even substantive Vietnamese aid from outside Hanoi'.[43] The legend of a full-blooded revolution lives on in Vietnam today, serving well the ideological needs of the communist regime.

On 17 August 1945, the Kim administration called a mass meeting of the Central Committee of Civil Servants to hear anti-communist speakers support national independence under the Japan umbrella. The communist regional committee, then meeting at Tan Trao on Hanoi's outskirts, gave the Hanoi revolutionaries the go-ahead for an uprising. They proceeded to break up the mass meeting in front of the Opera House by unfurling their red flags with the gold star and shouting 'Support the Viet Minh'.[44] The crowd then processed through the Ancient Quarter, along Quan Thanh Street, past the Governor-General's residence and back to the centre. This was the first public and unopposed appearance of the Viet Minh as a political force.

Storming the palace of the Tonkin Résident-Supérieur. (Centre Militaire d'Information et de Documentation sur l'Outre-Mer, Versailles)

In a small upstairs room at 48 Hang Ngang Street, Ho Chi Minh and the ICP Central Committee wrote the Vietnamese Declaration of Independence.

Early on 19 August, members of the Armed Propaganda Brigade moved through the suburbs urging people to attend another rally in front of the Opera House. By mid-day, two assault groups were detached from the rally, one taking the Résidence Supérieure and the other the Garde Indochinoise (Indochinese Security Garrison). In neither case was the use of force required. Eventually the whole of Hanoi was captured on 19–20 August without a shot being fired. With successful actions being taken in other parts of the country, the Viet Minh virtually became the provisional government of the country. Of the 14 National Liberation Committee members, 11 were communist. At 11 a.m. on 19 August, from the balcony of the municipal theatre, Nguyen Huy Khoi proclaimed to an enthusiastic crowd that it was now urgent to establish a Vietnamese revolutionary people's government – the 'Vietnamese Revolution' had begun. Ho Chi Minh entered Hanoi and, according to Marr, was 'whisked to a clandestine residence on Hang Ngang Street in the Ancient Quarter to guard against pre-emptive strikes by opponents'.[45] By the end of the month the abdication of Bao Dai had been secured, and on 2 September 1945 Ho read the Declaration of Independence of the Democratic Republic of Vietnam in Hanoi's Puginier (later Ba Dinh) Square at the apex of the administrative quarter's colonial street pattern.[46]

David Marr provides a brilliant sketch of the setting of this momentous event.[47] The day was clear and hot, with a light breeze from the west. The people, knowing in advance the importance of the occasion, treated the day like Tet, cleaning their houses and exploding firecrackers. Peasants poured in from surrounding villages. A high platform decorated with red and white bunting had been hastily erected. Following the singing of the national anthem and flag raising, the newly proclaimed Minister of the Interior, Vo Nguyen Giap, introduced Ho who read the Declaration. Marr describes the Declaration as containing 'a dramatic world view, a capsule of history, some bold assertions, vivid phrases, and emotional imagery' that captured the imagination of those present and those who heard or read about it later.[48] Its wording drew on the 1776 United States Declaration of Independence and the 1791 French Declaration of the Rights of Man and the Citizen. Archimedes Patti and three other OSS officers attended as observers and stood among the local dignitaries in front of the stand. Jean Sainteny, Resistance hero and the senior Free French officer in Hanoi, watched from the Governor-General's Palace, perhaps realising that France would eventually have to cede to the Vietnamese cry for '*doc lap*' – Independence!

The First Indochina War

In January 1946, elections were held for a Vietnamese assembly in Hanoi.[49] But Vietnam was in the grip of a disastrous famine, and relief activities kept Ho and his new, second government busy until February. There is some dispute about the basic cause of this famine that killed nearly one million Vietnamese. One view is that it was largely the result of the Japanese diverting rice and other provisions to feed its beleaguered troops.[50] The Japanese view was that it was the result of incessant Allied bombing of communication lines, preventing the movement of rice to the cities.[51] Whatever the cause, most of the 1945 rice harvest was lost. Corpses were scattered about the streets and footpaths of Hanoi and other urban centres, mainly peasants who had struggled into Hanoi to beg. In the period from March to August 1945, 2,429 famine-related deaths were registered in Hanoi.[52]

The Allies had determined that France would return to govern Indochina, and French troops and administrators arrived back in Hanoi in June 1946. Between March and May, Ho had attempted to negotiate a peaceful settlement with Sainteny and the army chief, General Raoul Salan, and even travelled to Paris to facilitate matters. However, unlike the arrangements being put in place for the British Commonwealth of Nations, the French Constitution introduced by the Fourth Republic did not allow for fully independent member states within the French Union and Ho's efforts failed. In November 1946 he reacted with own constitution ignoring French claims, formed a third government and excluded, for the first time, the non-communist Viet Minh parties.[53]

In the same month, the so-called Haiphong Incident occurred in which minor hostilities on shore led to the French navy bombarding the port city and killing some 6,000 Vietnamese.[54] Clearly there could be no satisfactory settlement with the French, no smooth transition from colonial rule to constitutional independence. The provisional government withdrew from the capital and on 19 December it launched the first attack on the French in what has become known as the First Indochina War. The next three months of battles in Hanoi, Hue and other cities resulted in 43 French civilians killed and more than 500 French civilians captured, including women and children, some being imprisoned until the final Vietnamese victory at Dien Bien Phu in 1954.[55]

We are not told the number of Vietnamese casualties. But we do know that the destruction in Hanoi was massive, especially in sections of the Ancient Quarter and in the Cité universitaire area. People and neighbourhoods were shelled by tanks and damaged by door-to-door street fighting. In the Dong Xuan Market in February 1947, a hand-to-hand battle took place across five rows of butchers' tables as the Vietnamese Battalion 101

Dong Xuan Market in the Ancient Quarter in 1956. (*Anh Vo An Ninh* (Thong Tan Xa Viet Nam, Hanoi, 1990), p. 39)

tried to re-take the northern part of the Ancient Quarter. We know, too, that some of the most significant historical monuments in Hanoi and Hue were badly damaged or destroyed. The Mot Cot Pagoda was blown up by French troops as they withdrew from the city in September 1954, while the inner pavilions and courtyards of the Royal Citadel at Hue were devastated.[56] It is estimated that 21 per cent of the municipality of Hanoi's houses were completely destroyed and another 8 per cent partially destroyed, leaving the remaining 70 per cent as either lightly damaged or intact.[57] These parts of the city were a desolate sight, with rows of houses destroyed and roads full of craters.[58] In the central business and administration core, however, the main public buildings were little damaged, according to Suzanne de Saint-Exupéry writing in the Saigon magazine *Indochine Sud-Est Asiatique* in 1952.[59] But life was draining out of Hanoi in favour of Saigon. 'Too many people have left, too many students are in the army. The only activity comes from the garrison troops and, when military operations drag them away, the town suddenly become saddened like a woman abandoned by her husband.'

From February 1947 until May 1954, the French controlled Hanoi but were kept in a state of siege by Ho's forces who controlled much of the countryside. This made economic recovery and the redevelopment of essential infrastructure impossible, and the standard of living of the average Hanoi resident began the long, slow decline that continued until the 1990s. Despite the commercial accords concluded between Vichy and Tokyo, trade had been decimated during the Japanese occupation. Vietnamese imports in 1944 were only 2 per cent of what they had been in 1939, and exports only 14 per cent. Inflation was running at high levels (44 per cent in 1944). Ships avoided the northern ports for fear of attack from one side or the other, and the port of Haiphong was closed in 1944.[60]

The First Indochina War also put a final end to French planning efforts in Hanoi, including the 1942 town plan by Henri Cérutti-Maori. As reflected in French statistics, construction work during the period of the Japanese occupation was quite limited in comparison with previous periods: a mere 600 dwellings were constructed, 23 hectares of swamps were reclaimed, and seven kilometres of new roads and 14 kilometres of new sewers were laid.[61] Initially, people had fled the city, reducing the population of inner Hanoi, according to one scholar, William Turley, to perhaps as few as 10,000 by 1948–49.[62] Thereafter, people were reluctant to return due to the delay in restoring services, the destruction of homes, the lack of work, the high cost of living and the 'patriotic distaste at the idea of returning to a zone of French control'. But from around 1949, Hanoi's population began to expand rapidly, to an estimated 292,575 in 1953, including 129,861 in inner Hanoi.[63]

In 1948, the Hanoi municipal authorities took back the city's adminis-tration from the Civil Security Council and turned its attention to the number of people returning to Hanoi for resettlement.[64] The task of housing this booming population reached crisis point in the early 1950s. A. Franck, a contributor to the Hanoi newspaper *L'Entente* in March 1953, argued strongly for an extension of the city towards the river rather than towards the interior as advocated in official plans.[65] He calculated that housing development between the dyke and the river, despite all the threats from flooding, would provide convenient accommodation for 80,000 people 'in healthy conditions'. A private enterprise housing project would generate revenue for the municipality and generate two million workdays to reduce the serious unemployment and under-employment situation. Franck maintained that flood control was feasible. The municipal authorities took up this approach, apparently supported by US$2 million in United States aid.[66] Today, the banks of the river are densely covered with low-income and frequently inundated housing.

Strangely, given the continuing hostilities in and around Hanoi, cultural tourism did not altogether disappear. The municipality's Social and Cultural Service published in 1951 a tourist booklet entitled *The Curiosities of Hanoi Town* that describes a set of tourist itineraries through the 'Modern Quarters' and 'Eastern Quarters'. It noted the military presence in the town, giving it a certain allure. Ba Dinh was becoming an attractive recreational area, with its formal landscaping, proximity to West Lake, and access by tram. The Hollywood Dance Hall on the Avenue du Grand Bouddha (now Quan Thanh Street) boasted a bar, orchestra, 'taxi-girls', 'rhythm' and 'ambiance' in the evenings and a tea dance on Sunday afternoons. The El Rancho cabaret and dance hall at 84 Boulevard Carreau (Ly Thuong Kiet Street) also reflected the presence of American OSS and other military in town. Soldiers, the brochure advised, stop at the Hotel de l'Union, 85 Rue Mandarine opposite the railway station, but advertisements in the publication indicate that troops were important customers almost everywhere. 'Militaires', announced a hotel (today's Dan Chu), 'When you come to Hanoi don't forget to come and try the à la carte meals at the Hotel de la Paix, No 35 rue Paul-Bert'. Even Maison Joséphine lingerie shop at 73 Rue Paul Bert got into the act by specialising not only in ladies-wear but also military flags, insignias and decorations.

The other side of this coin was the ugly face of colonial Hanoi: the hundreds of bars, cabarets and nightclubs were commonly fronts for brothels and opium dens. Up to 1954, more than 100,000 people were forced to engage in prostitution, according to one Russian critic, I.M. Shchedrov.

> The mere mention of the Meteorological Street would evoke salacious smiles from the mercenaries of the colonial army. Here, in almost every house, there was trade in 'live goods' and the representatives of Western civilisation were not ashamed, but rather, have advertised this: there were

Top Armour-plated vehicles in front of the Hanoi Opera House. Its façade still bears the shell marks of the First Indochina War. (*La Guerre de l'Indochine en photos 1945–1954* (P.A., Paris, 1989), p. 19)

Above The last French convoy leaving for Haiphong, 1954. (Courtesy Ian Adie)

Left Ho's troops entering Hanoi, 10 October 1954. (Tap Anh, *45 Years of Vietnamese Labour Party Activities (1930–1975)* (Cuc Xuat Ban Bao Chi An Hanh, Saigon, 1975), p. 69) books published with a description of the brothels with maps showing where they were and including a special set of regulations for the brothels. During the command of the French Expeditionary Corps, there was even a special department or a special authority to look after the brothels. Opium smoking and gambling were also kept up in the city. In Hanoi in 1954, there were several hundred opium dens and many hundreds of gambling dens.[67]

Even allowing for likely bias in reporting, the sleazy side of the colonial presence was undeniable.

Eventually, the struggle with the French was resolved, not by a frontal assault on the capital city, but with the debacle at the provincial town of Dien Bien Phu, some 300 kilometres away as the crow flies. Negotiations got under way in Geneva on 8 May 1954, a day after the French had raised the white flag on their last Vietnamese battlefield, and the 'Geneva Agreements' were adopted on 21 July. They were not a peace treaty, but merely an armistice leading to the country being split again along north–south lines. In the north, the Worker's Party of Vietnam (*Dang Lao Dong Viet Nam*), the successor to the ICP,[68] had finally gained control and set about establishing an independent and socialist Democratic Republic of Vietnam, with Hanoi as the capital. The non-communist south remained allied with the West, becoming the Republic of Vietnam with its capital at Saigon. Elections across the entire country were to have been held in July 1956 but did not eventuate. The stage was set for further open conflict.

The colonial heritage: A past better forgotten?

The official heritage list in 1951 included 31 classified items. To the EFEO list of 1926 had been added nine communal houses and the two small pavilions at Chau Thieu and Bich Cau. The Director of the Department of National Heritage Conservation was now a Vietnamese senior bureaucrat, Nguyen Gia Duc. As might have be expected, once the Communists came to power, their response was to recognise sites associated with the revolution as significant to the city's cultural heritage. It followed then that in 1960, on the 30th anniversary of the foundation of the Vietnamese Communist Party, the Hanoi Cultural Service, with the support of the Department of Heritage Conservation, turned 5D Ham Long Street, 90 Tho Nhuom Street and 105 Phung Hung Street into museums.[69] The fittings and furniture were restored to how they had been in the period 1928–29. By contrast, there was little recognition given at this time to the theatre balcony from which the August Revolution had been proclaimed. It was not until 40 years later, during the refurbishment of the Opera House in 1997–99, that this revolutionary connection was officially recognised. One room – the great Mirror Hall that opens on to the balcony – was left untouched and will be meticulously cleaned and restored to how it was on 19 August 1945. Bullet holes in two of the hall's mirrors memorialise the fighting between the Viet Minh brigades and the French forces, while the theatre's exterior still bears the marks of shells launched by French tanks.

Recognition of the theatre's revolutionary significance seems to have been delayed because it had been seen primarily as a symbol of French oppression and Western theatre arts, which were regarded as decadent. Recently, French hopes of regaining a commercial and cultural footing in Vietnam led to the Chirac government providing funds for a two-year, US$20 million refurbishment to be completed in time for the Hanoi summit of the commonwealth of French-speaking countries, the Francophonie, in November 1997. The restoration work, like the original construction, used Vietnamese labour under foreign supervision and followed a philosophy of preserving the colonial appearance while upgrading the materials, improving the sound and lighting systems, and enlarging the stage.[70] Hanoi has ended up with a better entertainment facility, but what does the effort to restore this French colonial *folie de grandeur* say about the changing ideology of the Vietnamese regime, of the permanence of the Vietnamese revolution, and the processes of heritage definition and protection? It is a sign of the melting of old hostilities that the Hanoi Opera House was restored under the direction of architect Ho Thieu Tri, a Viet Kieu or Overseas Vietnamese, who left his home-town, Saigon, shortly before it was taken by the Viet Cong in 1975.

The Vietnamese Communists seemed to have successfully challenged the great meta-narrative that had history revealing and endorsing the pre-eminence of Western culture and civilisation.[71] After peace eventually returned to Vietnam and the country was reunified, the revolutionary fervour carried over into a continuing devaluation of the West's contribution to Vietnamese development – a castigation of all things Western that was, in fact, a kind of Orientalism in reverse. This, to differing degrees, is a problem for most Asian nations and one that impacts on the practice of heritage conservation in Asia generally. Most Asian nations experienced a colonial period, as well as an earlier feudal past. Official heritage definitions and planning approaches in those countries handle the resultant cultural layering in various ways, and some continue today to reject the imposed European legacy associated with colonialism. An inclusive view of heritage sees all of these layers having significance, but recognition of this has often been difficult for newly independent nations. Now, however, with growing political maturity, many Asian countries are able to reassess the significance of the Western elements and some are beginning to take steps to protect the best examples. Postcolonial societies in Asia no longer need to fight back by denying important formative stages in their past.

This is true of Vietnam and its treatment of the cultural heritage of Hanoi. In fact, the change in attitude towards the colonial heritage has been, if rather late, at least very rapid. As recently as 1990, it was clear that government ministers and senior bureaucrats responsible for the city's planning excluded (with the exception of one or two examples) the legacy of the French colonial buildings from the official definition of Hanoi's heritage. These buildings represented a period of Vietnamese subjugation best forgotten in times of independence. By 1994, however, a shift in attitudes was clearly signalled in a paper given by the Vice-Minister for Construction, Pham Sy Liem, at a UNESCO seminar in Hanoi. He announced that there was a need for research on the French and Ba Dinh quarters where the streets and houses 'bear the cachet of Europe in their building methods and architecture' and should be classified as part of Hanoi's heritage.[72]

This apparently 'counter-revolutionary' statement cut right across the orthodox arguments of Vietnamese historians and architectural historians who saw the French architectural impact as merely part of the country's colonial subjugation. One of these, Dang Thai Hoang, summed up the case: 'In the final analysis, most of the building activities of the French were only designed to keep the country militarily quiet and the population ideo-logically bankrupt.'[73] He described the construction of the Long Bien Bridge as issuing a 'nature-taming message' intended to impose 'a sense of obedience on the Vietnamese while preparing to rob their country of its natural resources'. Hébrard's town plan might have embodied a number of novel ideas being applied in Europe, but it was 'too far-fetched' in the social conditions prevailing in Hanoi at the time. Cérutti's town plan fared even less well: it was dismissed as impractical, 'more of a propaganda exercise than anything else'![74] Nguyen Quoc Thong also described the colonial town plans of Hanoi as propaganda for the superiority of French culture and railed at the French planners' neglect of the substandard outskirts of the city where labourers from rural areas were 'exploited, destitute and lived in temporary shelters'. This polarisation between centre and periphery of the town was 'the inevitable result of French colonial policies in Vietnam'.[75]

What seems to have been behind this attitude shift towards the French urban legacy? It is no doubt related to the dimming of memories and the mitigation of pain that goes with the passage of time. 'The major gain', explains Michael Schudson,

is perspective — distance can give people historical perspective on matters that may have been hard to grasp at the time they happened. With time, not only does the emotional intensity diminish but individuals can increasingly view from multiple perspectives events they originally could see only from one.[76]

The Thon Nhat Hotel
in 1990, prior to its
restoration as the
Hotel Metropole.

But it was no mere coincidence that the flow of international tourists to Vietnam had gone from a trickle in the late 1980s to a torrent by the mid-1990s and the Vietnamese government was seeing tourism as something of an economic panacea.[77] In fact, Raymond Betts, the historian of French colonial theory, was quite wrong when he declared that French imperial expansion had met with 'public apathy at best, antipathy at worst'.[78] The French have showed their intense fascination with their former colonial possessions by travelling in droves to Indochina as cultural tourists; indeed, for much of the 1990s they represented the largest single national group. Many French tourists were chasing after myths, lured by family histories, perhaps by childhood memories, or by novels and films. In the 1931 Colonial Exposition, the French had sought to attract settlers and investors to Indochina by using iconographic representations to portray Indochina in 'glossy colours and inviting terms'.[79] In the 1990s, the French sought to recapture the time and place through the cinema with offerings such as *Indochine*, *The Scent of Green Papaya* and *Dien Bien Phu*. All were made in 1992 and helped push French tourism to Vietnam to a peak in 1995.[80] Modern tourism continues, therefore, a long line of myth-making and misrepresentation about Indochina using all the techniques of advertising language, graphic design and communications media. The aim is to transform Indochina into 'an alluring and commodified object', as Norindr Panivong in his book *Phantasmatic Indochina* calls it – 'a familiar icon or sign to be desired or possessed'.

What did the French tourists hope to find? What did they find and, importantly, what did the Vietnamese want to show them? The built fabric of Hanoi still conjured up dreams of empire, of world stature as a colonial power – an advanced European society that attempted to assist a developing nation and was misunderstood for it. The villas and tree-lined boulevards, the Opera House and the works of Vildieu, Hébrard and Cérutti, all reflected positively on French culture and its transferability to the ends of the earth. Of course, Hanoi reflected on the ground the best and worst aspects of colonialism, but it was easy for the French in the 1990s to ignore the failures, or to explain them away in terms of subsequent mismanagement under the Communists. The Vietnamese, for their part, sought to focus the tourists' attention on the old core around Hoan Kiem Lake and the more monumental French buildings. The Vietnamese government preferred the top end of the tourist market, believing such tourists not only brought in most foreign revenue but were also easiest to control.[81] The joint venture investments in tourist hotels often exploited the historic character of buildings, remodelling them to suit Western levels of comfort. This meant that the heritage that was presented tended to be sanitised and the historic memories falsified.

The extensive renovation of the Metropole Hotel in the early 1990s demonstrates this effect.[82] It was one of the first major joint ventures in hotel development in Vietnam, linking the government Hanoitourism enterprise with the giant French hotel and service conglomerate, the Accor Group. The project took the hotel, described as cold and bare in Graham Greene's *The Quiet American* and even more severely run-down in the ensuing years of communism in Vietnam, and turned it into a luxury hotel, every bit as stylish as it had been in colonial days. The original 1901 exterior with the additional floor added in 1962 was maintained, and the dark timber floors in its 109 rooms were kept. Cyclos still wait outside. The 'Beaulieu' dining room retains its 1930s' art deco make-over and a few historic reminders remain here and there. Modern additions are largely hidden behind the main building – a five-storey extension and swimming pool. For most of the 1990s it was the only four-star hotel in Hanoi and its Gallic flavour attracted French and other Western tourists and business people alike. Even the reaction from the Vietnamese architectural fraternity was positive – once again showing the significant shift in attitudes to the colonial heritage that was taking place. When he visited in 1993, the Secretary-General of the Vietnamese Architects' Association, Nguyen Truc Luyen, found many factors that did credit to the hotel:

> One of the most important factors is that the Hotel still retains the features of the French construction, the ambience hasn't changed and it's easy for the familiar eyes to enjoy the beloved façade of the hotel. Once the threshold of the hotel has been crossed, right from the entrance hall, the interior conveys a real sense of the bygone days of Hanoi.[83]

Hoa Lo Prison Museum and Hanoi Centre twin towers, 1998.

But the local Vietnamese rarely enter the Metropole; it remains as separate from the people of Hanoi now as it ever was under the colonial regime.

The Hoa Lo Prison was even more obviously a symbol of French oppression. The Vietnamese had to keep it for at least two reasons: because of the colonial brutality it demonstrated, and because of the significant part it played in the revolutionary struggle. The roll call of revolutionary and later communist government figures incarcerated there includes Nguyen Thai Hoc, leader of the Yen Bay Mutiny in 1930, who was imprisoned and executed in that year. Truong Chinh, who was imprisoned in 1931–32, was luckier and later became the General-Secretary of the Vietnam Communist Party from 1941 to 1956. Le Duan was also imprisoned in 1931–32, later becoming Secretary-General of the VNCP in 1960–69 and President of the Democratic Republic of Vietnam after Ho's death in 1969. Nguyen Van Linh was imprisoned in 1930 before rising to General-Secretary in 1986. Do Muoi, who was Secretary-General from 1991 to 1997 and is still a powerful figure behind the scenes, spent 1941 and 1945 in the prison. Far from repressing the nationalist movement, this flow of key leaders through Hoa Lo made it one of the main centres for revolutionary education and the instillation of nationalist fervour. Even a revolutionary newsletter, *Lao tu tap chi* (*Prison Review*), was published monthly without discovery.

Despite the pleas of veterans from both the Vietnamese and American sides to keep the whole complex as a memorial,[84] Hoa Lo has now been reduced to the main entrance block and opened to the public as a museum. Almost all of the horror of the place has disappeared. For the Vietnamese visitor, the background is known through the public education system, if not through personal or family memories of the prison's role in earlier times. The foreign tourist is somewhat at a loss. It is possible to view several narrow cells, with their black walls and tiny window too high to see anything but a patch of grey or blue sky according to the passing seasons. A guillotine is on display. But the interpretation panels, which attempt to tell the story of French brutality towards political prisoners – even mothers with children kept behind bars – lack explanation in the major tourist languages. Moreover, the museum is antiseptically clean; the smells and cries of prisoners are gone ... Perhaps the cleanest area is where the American airmen are said to have been kept. History is being rewritten here through the changed appearance of the buildings. There is enough to remind but not completely offend French tourists, and a deliberate effort has been made to counter the expectations American tourists have of the harsh treatment meted out to their pilots. Outside, the sense of colonial oppression has been totally swept away, to be replaced, perhaps, with a new kind of economic control, for, apart from the museum, the prison has been demolished to make way for a new twin tower business complex.

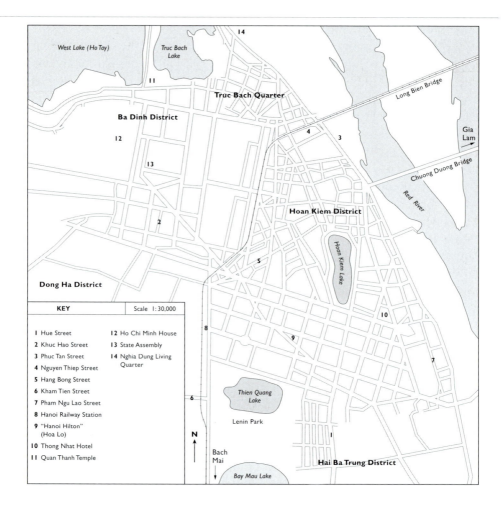

West Lake (Ho Tay)

Truc Bach Lake

14

11

Truc Bach Quarter

Long Bien Bridge

Ba Dinh District

12

13

2

4

3

Gia Lam

Chuong Duong Bridge

Hoan Kiem District

Red River

Hoan Kiem Lake

Dong Ha District

5

10

KEY	Scale 1 : 30,000

8

7

1 Hue Street
2 Khuc Hao Street
3 Phuc Tan Street
4 Nguyen Thiep Street
5 Hang Bong Street
6 Kham Tien Street
7 Pham Ngu Lao Street
8 Hanoi Railway Station
9 "Hanoi Hilton" (Hoa Lo)
10 Thong Nhat Hotel
11 Quan Thanh Temple

12 Ho Chi Minh House
13 State Assembly
14 Nghia Dung Living Quarter

9

6

Thien Quang Lake

Lenin Park

N

Bach Mai

1

Hai Ba Trung District

Bay Mau Lake

Chapter 5

Under American bombs: Hanoi during the Vietnam War

Operation Rolling Thunder and the Battle of Hanoi

On 11 August 1967 the Cau Long Bien, formerly known as the Doumer Bridge, was hit by a United States' air attack. Almost 100 tons of high explosives were used, and one bomb took out the central span. Since the bridge provided Hanoi's only link with Haiphong and the north apart from relatively primitive ferries across the Red River, it was an enormous blow to the Ho Chi Minh government in its 'American War'. It was essential to restore communications, and the bridge's central span was quickly replaced by bamboo gangplanks and later a pontoon consisting of small boats laced together. The patched bridge was reopened on 5 October, only to be hit again on the 25th and 28th and finished off completely in attacks in November and December. Real repairs on the bridge could only start after the Operation Rolling Thunder bombing campaign eased the following April, and it was back in full service by June. In the reconstruction, the steel pylons were not rebuilt. The French diplomat François de Quirielle, in his memoirs about the years 1966–69 when he was posted to Hanoi, erroneously attributed these to Eiffel.[1] The bridge was never restored and remains today a misshapen but essential component of Hanoi's heritage — a memorial to both the French colonial period and the struggle against the new 'imperialist invaders', the Americans.

During World War 2, the United States had repeatedly spoken in favour of the principle of post-war independence for colonial peoples. Tragically for the Vietnamese, this principle was lost in America's Cold War concerns about dominoes falling to communism in Europe and Asia.[2] From 1950 the United States began providing assistance to the French colonial authorities in their war with Ho's nationalist forces. Support escalated, turning into direct military intervention in the mid-1960s. This was the Second Indochina War that ran from 1955 to 1975. Only part of

The Long Bien Bridge today. It is now only used for rail and foot traffic, with motorised traffic taking the nearby Chuong Duong Bridge, built in 1983–85.

The Long Bien Bridge after the second bombardment. (François de Quirielle, *A Hanoi sous les bombes américaines. Journal d'un diplomate français (1966–1969)* (Tallendier, Paris, 1992), p. 132)

this was, in fact, the 'Vietnam War' (or 'American War' to the Vietnamese). Although the United States was sending funds and advisers from 1950 to aid the French, it was not until the Johnson Administration manufactured the so-called Gulf of Tonkin Incident in 1964 that direct intervention occurred. The President persuaded Congress to pass the Resolution of the same name, and in 1965 the first ground combat troops landed at Danang and the bombers were sent in from bases in Thailand and from aircraft carriers off the Vietnamese coast. America's direct military involvement ended with the troop withdrawal in 1973, leaving the final stage of the war to be waged between the two Vietnamese sides.

This chapter investigates the impact that this period of war had on Hanoi's cultural landscape. Apart from the Long Bien Bridge, what other surviving reminders of the period might be regarded as significant elements in Hanoi's cultural heritage? Initially, American intervention did not affect Hanoi greatly and, even when the bombing campaigns were intensified and focused on Hanoi, there seems to have been relatively little physical damage done to the city. This is contrary to popular images that Westerners then had – and still have – of Hanoi's treatment during the Vietnam War, raising complex issues of memory distortion. Much of the damage was quickly covered up, buildings were reconstructed, and the replacements were easily merged with the old under the usual layers of whitewash and mildew. A first task is to establish more exactly the extent of physical destruction to the city.

The first bombs were unleashed on Hanoi on 29 June 1966 in an American air campaign known as 'Operation Rolling Thunder'. This offensive had commenced in March 1965, the same month that troops landed near Danang, and lasted three years. This is said to have been the most frightening campaign of bombardment in history and easily the most costly. There were 300,000 sorties over North Vietnam and 860,000 tons of bombs were dropped, averaging two tons each minute for three years. Approximately 52,000 civilians were killed.[3] At first only localities near the Demilitarised Zone were targeted, but, from April 1966, all of lowland North Vietnam came under attack. Johnson and his principal civilian advisers kept a tight control over the target selection process and initially Hanoi and Haiphong were prohibited areas that pilots could overfly only with the President's specific permission.[4] However, de Quirielle recalled that bombing could be heard closing in on Hanoi by mid-April. On 12 June, an American plane was downed seven kilometres from the centre of Hanoi, and several days later another plane flew over the city, drawing response from the Vietnamese artillery below.[5] By the end of June, suburban Hanoi was under fire. Marking a turning point in hostilities, bombers flew in from Thailand and struck the oil and gas depots at Gia Lam, two kilometres from the Long Bien Bridge. This demolished the Hanoi petroleum, oil and lubricants site. International protests followed, but US General Westmoreland claimed 'the allies were winning the war'.[6]

Ho Chi Minh took up the challenge in his famous speech of 17 July 1966:

> Whether they number 500,000, a million or even more, never will the Americans break the iron will of our people. The war can last 5 years, 10 years or 20 years or more, and Hanoi, Haiphong and other cities might be destroyed, but the Vietnamese people will not be intimidated. Nothing is more precious than independence and freedom.[7]

A ring of defence installations was set up around Hanoi and Haiphong, with classical artillery augmented by Russian surface-to-air missiles (SAMs) by the end of 1966, and by MIG fighter planes in 1967, supplied by the Chinese and Russians. A number of aerodromes were constructed on the city's periphery, and anti-aircraft batteries were set up inside the city designed especially to protect the dyke systems. Hanoi was spared for the rest of the summer of 1966, although the village of Phuc Xa, five kilometres up the Red River, was hit by anti-personnel fragmentation bombs, killing 24 people and destroying the livestock and harvest.[8] Daily carpet bombing was aimed at knocking out North Vietnam's railway stations and lines, roads, bridges, radar and artillery posts. The Hanoi–Haiphong railway line and the port facilities at Haiphong were a main target of air raids originating on the aircraft carriers of the 7th Fleet in the Gulf of Tonkin or bases in Thailand. Little settlements like Phu Ly and Hai Duong along the Hanoi–Haiphong railway line were totally destroyed.

But, on 12 November 1966, President Johnson authorised the 'Rolling Thunder 52' campaign which allowed the US Air Force to bomb targets inside the Hanoi prohibited area, with the aim of knocking out power plants and port facilities. Enemy attacks on the capital resumed in December.[9] The Van Dien truck depot and army barracks eight kilometres south of Hanoi centre, the Ha Gia oil facility north of the city, and a railway switching yard only four kilometres from the city centre were blown up. Then the bombs began to hit the city proper. The busy commercial street, Hue Street, was damaged on two occasions in early December, and the 'March 8' Textile Mill in the southern suburbs was destroyed, apparently killing a first Hanoi civilian resident and wounding others.[10]

The air raids of 13–14 December were among the most violent attacks on the city and suburbs. On the Gia Lam side of the river, official buildings, workshops and two railway stations were hit again. In the Ba Dinh area, the Chinese and Rumanian embassies were struck, along with the Canadian Mission of the International Control Commission whose role it was to help monitor the 1954 Geneva peace accord arrangements. According to de Quirielle, seven bomb craters were blasted in the city, leaving an official tally of 23 dead and 62 wounded.[11] North Vietnamese official documents indicate that seven of the dead and 30 of the wounded were in a main suburban thoroughfare to the south-west, Giang Vo Street, where nine houses were destroyed.[12] Rockets hit Khuc Hao Street in Ba Dinh District and Hang Chuoi Street in the southern Hai Ba Trung District, damaging houses, and the Medicine and Pharmacy Faculty in La Thanh Ton Street. An apartment block, the Trade Union Cadres Training School and the Water Conservation Institute were hit in Tay Son Street in Dong Da District, killing five people, wounding another 11 and destroying many houses. Four people were killed in Phuc Tan Street in the Hoan Kiem District between the dyke and the river. The street was a dirt road lined with mud-walled, thatched-roof houses and there was not much of it left after the attack. An entire block of 300 houses had been obliterated,

Hanoi residents rummage through the remains of their homes in Phuc Tan Street following a US air attack, December 1966. (E. Doyle, S. Lipsman and T. Maitland (eds), *The North* (Boston Publishing Co., Boston, Mass., 1968), p. 70)

leaving only the charred remains, chimney stacks and bomb craters. The death toll was low because the residents had been in their air-raid shelters when the attack occurred.

Four others were killed and 13 houses destroyed in Nguyen Thiep Street near the Dong Xuan Market in the Ancient Quarter. This was a narrow, paved street of working-class houses made of brick and stucco with tiled roofs. The journalist Harrison Salisbury, who visited the site shortly after the attack, noted that, in a narrow lane running off the street, the Phuc Lan Pagoda had had its roof blown away. It seemed to have been used as a school but, fortunately, because all schools had been evacuated from Hanoi, it had been empty at the time of the attack. Salisbury had picked up leaflets warning residents 'Don't live near a military target!'[13]

These impacts on the city were the result of missiles, incendiary bombs, and percussion or 'wind' bombs designed to flatten buildings by exploding above them. Even though the US Air Force claimed a margin

Accidental bombing of Nguyen
Thiep Street in Hanoi's Ancient
Quarter, 14 December 1996.
(J. Morrocco, *Thunder from
Above: Air War, 1941–1968*
(Boston Publishing Co., Boston,
Mass., 1984), p. 133)

of error of only 200 metres for its dive bombers, many of the strikes on
inner Hanoi seem to have been botched attempts to hit the Long Bien
Bridge and the railway viaduct that carried the northern and Haiphong
lines through the Ancient Quarter to the Hanoi Railway Station. However,
Salisbury wondered whether they were warnings to Hanoi, showing that
the United States could hit the bridge if it wanted to, or just careless or
accidental. He seems to conclude that the first explanation fitted better:
'[T]hese were a suggestion to Hanoi of what we could do ... an example
of bombing as a psychological or propaganda weapon.'[14] He observed that
Hanoi's main electric power plant in the Truc Bach area north of the
Ancient Quarter had not been attacked; nor had the dykes whose
destruction would have led to the complete inundation of the city. 'If there
is an answer to this, it must, it seems to me, lie in the realm of psychological warfare. Or politics. Not military tactics.' The aim was to impress
on the authorities and people of Hanoi just how vulnerable they were.[15]

Following North Vietnamese and international protests about civilian casualties, Johnson curtailed the Rolling Thunder 52 program, prohibiting aircraft from traversing a ten-mile (16-kilometre) ring around Hanoi and limiting attacks to no more than three new targets a week.[16] This did not last long, however, and a decision was made in March 1967, at a meeting in Guam between Johnson and South Vietnam's leader, General Thieu, to resume the bombing of Hanoi. This led to the Battle of Hanoi in the summer of 1967 – an offensive characterised by de Quirielle as being massive, different in the choice of target, power and use of new types of bombs, and becoming more and more violent and deathly.[17] Although so far relatively spared, Hanoi knew now it would be the centre of the battle.

In the following months, enormous damage was done to air strips, the water supply plant, the electric light bulb and thermos flask factory, a dispensary near St. Joseph's Cathedral, Hue Street, industrial suburbs such as Gia Lam, the railway stations at Gia Lam and Yen Vien, and the neighbouring towns of Ha Dong and Van Dien.[18] On 8 April, Johnson approved the Truc Bach electricity plant as a target and on 19 May – Ho Chi Minh's birthday – planes aiming at the plant missed their target and badly damaged surrounding houses and the Korean and Rumanian embassies. The planes returned two days later and did their work successfully, cutting off Hanoi's electric power as well as its water supplies. The electric power station and its precinct were subjected to frequent repeat bombing through 1968 and again in 1972.[19]

There were 12 air raids on 21 May, one of the worst days Hanoi had to face. The Australian Malcolm Salmon, arriving at Gia Lam Airport on 2 May, observed the Gia Lam railway workshops and workers' flats that had been hit three days earlier. Writing later for the Australian communist newspaper *Tribune*, he described a rocket attack on Thuoc Bac Street in the Ancient Quarter. One death occurred, that of a crippled schoolteacher, Nguyen Hieu Dang, who had risked continuing to mark student work rather than struggling to the air-raid shelter for the eighth alert that day.[20] By mid-1967 the United States had officially admitted that Hanoi had been heavily and repeatedly bombed, but was still insisting that the targets were strictly military. North Vietnam, on the other hand, was claiming that most bombed areas were visibly civilian. This became a crucial international controversy: was the United States acting criminally?

Harassment continued during early 1968 with Johnson reducing the ten-mile ceiling to five miles on 3 January and removing the limit altogether on 6 February, following the surprise Tet Offensive that saw the communist forces capture key targets across central and southern Vietnam.[21] During the nights of these two months, Hanoi residents had to rush to shelters 25 times. A new set of targets was added to the bombers' list. Attempts were made to knock out the radio station, as well as the pontoon that had replaced the Long Bien Bridge. A number of bombs went astray, killing 40 civilians in a car repair workshop, razing a residential precinct on the river edge, and wiping out a catholic village in Ba Trieu District and its Gothic-style Catholic Church of the Little Flowers. At that period the village was in an outlying section of Hanoi surrounded by market gardens. According to Mary McCarthy, the well-known author of *Venice Observed* and *The Group*, who visited the bombing scene, it was 'remote from the main highway and from any discernible military target'.[22]

There were 17 alerts in the last week of March before President Johnson announced a partial halt to air attacks, ending almost three years of bombardment.[23] Johnson may have been growing apprehensive about such bombing errors; certainly he was concerned by the increasing criticism from the United Nations and America's allies. Finally, he accepted the argument that Defence Secretary Robert McNamara had been making for the previous 15 months that 'There may be a limit beyond which many Americans and much of the world will not permit the United States to go'.[24] Johnson's last important decision of the war was to announce on 1 November 1968 an immediate end to Operation Rolling Thunder and all air and naval bombardment of the North, except for contingency 'protective strikes' in support of reconnaissance flights.

Some 918 US aircraft had been lost in the campaign and 818 US airmen killed. In addition, a number of airmen ended up incarcerated as prisoners of war in the Hoa Lo Prison, the 'Hanoi Hilton'.[25] By contrast, it is estimated that some 200 Vietnamese were killed in Hanoi during Operation Rolling Thunder. [26] A whole generation of Hanoi residents was traumatised by air-raid alerts, bomb blasts, death and devastation. But this was also a story of survival, of triumph over the disaster of war.[27] How did Hanoi cope with the destruction – and the reconstruction that followed?

Surviving the bombardment: Life in the city

The geographer Kenneth Hewitt, commenting on the post-1945 physical recovery of war-torn Nagasaki, Tokyo, Frankfurt and Milan, observed that 'some scholars hold the view that the bombing was beneficial in that it allowed more rapid and rational modernisation than was the case in cities or neighbourhoods where it did not occur'.[28] He noted that such an argument 'serves to transform devastation (or construction) into neutral terms, mere processes or accidents'. The historian Jeffry Diefendorf sought to identify the 'benefits' that might be obtained from sound reconstruction practices. His key question was whether it was possible to take the opportunity of war-related reconstruction to engage in much-needed and long-desired urban environmental improvements.[29] Other questions followed: Were new streets needed and created? Were new social amenities established? What happened to heritage elements in the cultural landscape? Were new buildings, monuments and sites created that merit inclusion in today's inventory of Hanoi's heritage?

In Hanoi, these questions need to be analysed in two time periods: what was done, what was wanted, what was possible during the war itself, spanning 1965–73; and what was done after the war ended. The second period is covered in the next chapter of this book – the period of socialist reconstruction from 1975 to 1990. During the periods of air strikes, the primary need was clearly to keep the capital city functioning, repair damaged utilities, keep roofs over people's heads, and maintain a supply system for food and essential services, including air-raid warning and defence structures. After each air raid subsided, government authorities and residents quickly swung into reinstating what had been damaged as best they could. Longer-term issues of urban renewal, social amenities and city beautification had to wait. More critical were practical issues about clearing the rubble and debris, obtaining and allocating building materials, and controlling and financing the reconstruction.

Ly Thu Ho talks about the labour gangs responsible for patching up after American bombing attacks in her 1969 novel *Au milieu du carrefour* (*In the Middle of the Crossroads*).[30] Western observers commented on the speed of repairs. Malcolm Salmon described a road repair gang of 100 youths and girls in May 1967 restoring the bomb-damaged section of road from Gia Lam to Hanoi.[31] Mary McCarthy remarked how quickly the devastated villages, such as the Ba Trieu hamlet, had been levelled off and market gardens recultivated.[32] Michael Maclear referred to 'the straw world of the villages' as being 'essentially indestructible' – and the process of quick reconstruction using simple materials, once a feature of feudal Hanoi, was reintroduced into the city in response to emergency conditions.[33] In other cases, especially in more central areas such as Nguyen Thiep Street, reconstruction occurred in roughly the same style as before. This was not part of an attempt to deliberately replicate the original urban townscape for symbolic reasons, as occurred in Warsaw, Nuremberg and other war-torn European cities, but was merely due to constraints of existing knowledge about building techniques and the availability of materials.

Salmon's observation hints at the way in which labour was organised during this period to keep the city functioning. Several contributions to the book *Thu Do Ha Noi* (*Hanoi, Capital City*) also describe the labour organisation and reward systems.[34] During the war, people in Hanoi's districts and surrounding villages were mobilised to support soldiers and their needs in the battlefields and to accomplish the so-called rear-guard policies. The Youth Volunteer Brigades were set up in July 1965 by the Labour Youth Union to repair roads, bridges and communication lines.[35]

The people of Soc Son District, located at the frequently targeted intersection of National Highways 2 and 3 near Hanoi's Noi Bai Airport, not only downed numerous B-52 bombers but also contributed tens of thousands of workdays to repairing the airport, digging trenches, and building cannon and rocket emplacement mounds.

There were also labour obligation systems controlled through family register notebooks; that is, people of working age were required to work on projects decreed as important for the maintenance of the city by the authorities. This system had, in fact, begun in the 1950s. A notable example was the development of the park around Bay Mau Lake south of central Hanoi, originally part of Hébrard's scheme for the area. Work here began on 11 November 1958 and the necessary drainage, embankments and landscaping was completed with the use of 'tens of thousands of socialist working days'. The park was inaugurated on 30 May 1961 as Reunification Park but was renamed 'Lenin Park' on 19 April 1980 to commemorate the 110th anniversary of Lenin's birth.[36] As a way of mobilising the people, the most cooperative districts and villages, or organisations within them, were awarded titles such as 'hero district', 'heroes of agricultural production', 'village most determined to win the victory' or 'golden hand organisation'.[37] Sometimes the authorities conducted competitions with such titles as prize. Ancient customs were often drawn upon, such as the campaigns of 'Returning the credits and favours' (*Den On Tra Nghia*) and 'Ten guarantees' (*Muoi Bao Dam).*

McCarthy thought that 'repairing bomb damage' was the only building activity going on in the city and suburbs.[38] But who was making the planning decisions and who paid for the reconstruction activity? Under the French colonial administration, a system of building permits had been implemented by the municipal Service du Cadastre et des Domaines de Hanoi (Survey and Municipal Lands Department). Archival records indicate that following the destruction of 2,837 houses in the December 1946 hostilities and another 1,028 between 1947 and 1951, a total of 4,418 reconstruction permits were issued by the end of 1951 to private property owners.[39] But this system collapsed with the withdrawal of the French authorities in 1954 and, during the Second Indochina War, the reconstruction of houses in the cities appears to have been carried out on a 'do-it-yourself' basis. Residents simply called on their families, friends and neighbours to refill the bombed spaces with little guidance from the municipal authorities.[40]

Nevertheless, McCarthy's comment that, if damage was severe, buildings were simply condemned and habitation was forbidden indicates some official involvement, even though town planning departments in Hanoi, Haiphong and other northern cities were not effectively re-established until the 1990s. Most residential reconstruction during this

period was therefore technically 'illegal' although nevertheless sanctioned
– indeed, encouraged – by the authorities given the circumstances of war.
Private titles to land had, of course, been abolished in the Democratic
Republic of Vietnam and, where constructions spread beyond the accepted
boundary line on to footpaths or roadways, the authorities sent in bull-
dozers to demolish the offending structures. There was also considerable
rhetoric about reconstructing better cities designed to bolster public confidence in the war effort. The most famous and influential of these (even
if it referred to 'our land' rather than specifically to cities) was the
declaration in Ho Chi Minh's will and testament that:

> Our mountains will always be, our rivers will always be, our people will
> always be; The American invaders defeated, we will rebuild our land ten
> times more beautiful.[41]

Ho Chi Minh expounds on
Hanoi's development at a
meeting with city planners.
(*Nhan Dan* newspaper, Hanoi)

From the Vietnamese point of view, life in Hanoi during the bombardment would have been unendurable had it not been for their conviction that they would ultimately beat the American aggressors.[42] The national psyche was formed from a blend of Buddhist stoicism, Confucian restraint, and a patience that came from a history littered with wars, invasions and resistance movements. Most residents were evacuated under government orders after the bombing raids on Hanoi began at the end of June 1966. The aged, children, the unemployed, shopkeepers and craftsmen, and anyone else not directly contributing to the defence of the city or to essential services and production, were sent to the countryside. The evacuation program reached its peak in early 1968, by which time, according to Western correspondents, about one-third to one-half of the populations of Hanoi, Haiphong and other major cities were evacuated to rural areas.[43] Governmental offices were relocated up to 75 kilometres away; 90 per cent of industries were dismantled and scattered. The removal of schools to the countryside made for long, tiring trips for the children being evacuated, especially due to the transport chaos and interruptions during bombing raids. This had a great impact on the close-knit Vietnamese families, but reluctant parents had to comply or lose their rice rations.[44] De Quirielle recounted men cycling 50 or more kilometres to rejoin their families on Sundays.[45] Motorised travel was virtually impossible because nearly all public and private vehicles had been reassigned for military use or for evacuations. The roads, railways and bridges had been badly bombed, and travel was largely done at night and at an extremely slow pace.[46]

Those artisans and shopkeepers not evacuated to the countryside remained in their run-down tube houses, while most factory workers and labourers lived in thatched cottages along ill-kept roads and pavements.[47] Since 1954 the colonial villas, formerly occupied by officials of the colonial administration and wealthy Vietnamese, were taken over by the families of government officials and workers, usually several families crowding into each house. Much physical deterioration of the building fabric occurred due to the US bombing attacks on the city: the ground shook, plaster fell from ceilings, and water and electricity services failed. Most of these houses remained in desperate need of repair 20 years later.

No. 4, Pho Hang Bong in the Ancient Quarter was typical. It had been occupied by the Anh family since the 1940s. Originally a two-storey house, it had been levelled during the 1946 conflict with the French and rebuilt on a smaller scale in 1949. During the Vietnam War the husband was a soldier in the North Vietnamese army, operating anti-aircraft guns in Hanoi. His wife had been evacuated as a child and grew up in the jungle. During the war there were only one or two people in the house. When the sirens blew, they dived for the manhole cut into the footpath in front of the house. After the war, as evacuees returned, the house became home to numerous families and the Anh family ended up with a single room in which they lived, studied and worked. A mezzanine was added to allow several more occupants. Vibrations from the bombing had caused the roof to fall in and the ceiling was never repaired. With the economic liberalisation and the wave of redevelopment in the mid-1990s, the house has been demolished and replaced by a multi-storey building. The Anh family have apparently been displaced to the suburbs.

House at 4 Hang Bong Street, 1991.

A corner of the family room, 4 Hang Bong Street, 1991.

No major gatherings were permitted during daytime, so the life of the city began before dawn, stopped during daylight hours and resumed after dark. Churches had to follow the same time restrictions, and the few authorised shops opened between six and eight o'clock in the morning and again after six in the evening. The old colonial trams continued to operate, but convoys of trucks gathered under the shelter of trees to move off as soon as night fell. In his autobiographical novel *The Sorrow of War*, Bao Ninh has the war-weary protagonist describe the view from his house towards Thuyen Quang Lake:

> In the streets below, scattered lights shone, the light mixing with the rain. Illumination stopped at the end of the street, marking the start of the vast lake. Swinging his vision to the right he saw the dark cloud canopies low over the familiar tiled roofs of Hanoi, although hardly any of the houses emitted light. There were no cars on the street, and not a single pedestrian. At this moment the city was so calm that one could practically hear the clouds blow over the rooftops. He thought of them as part of his life being blown away in wispy sections, leaving vast, open areas of complete emptiness, as in his own life. The spirit of Hanoi is strongest by night, even stronger in the rain. Like now, when the whole town seems deserted, wet, lonely, cold, and deeply sad.[48]

The Filipino television journalist Gemma Cruz Araneta also noticed the calm that pervaded Hanoi, but puts on it a different spin. She seemed rather disappointed that the city in 1968 looked 'so awfully unwarlike'.[49]

During the daytime the city was deserted, with barred-up doors and closed shutters. Bao Ninh writes that 'Notes were left pinned on doors, others written in chalk out front. These public messages, from wives to husbands, mothers to children, served as public notice-boards'.[50] At night the street stalls and eating houses with their acetylene lights disappeared and the street lighting was dimmed. This was all a far cry from the bustling Hanoi of the pre-1940 French era. The few shops held a jumble of old, shop-worn goods of little use to anyone – wind-up phonographs, boot polish, enamelled wash bowls, bicycle chains and second-hand spark plugs. The chief source of the few available consumer goods was the state-run department store on the corner of Hoan Kiem Lake, described by a foreign visitor as 'well-run but dispiriting'.[51] Peasants sold their produce of chicken, muddy-tasting paddy fish, waterweed and other vegetables on the free market until the central markets in the Ancient Quarter were closed down in July 1966.[52] McCarthy explained that the markets were 'too dangerous an assembly point' but described peasant women continuing to sell flowers, fruit and vegetables from little stands on the footpaths.[53] Certain areas in the outskirts of Hanoi were set aside for vegetable growing to supply the city and production quotas had been allocated, but supplies were disrupted by bomber attacks and the evacuation. Rationing was introduced, with one pound of rice per person per day in the early war years but doubling later. The cloth ration was almost five metres per person per year, enough for an annual change of the shirt and trousers that had become the standard dress for both men and women.[54]

Despite these hardships, morale and discipline remained strong. Factory and office workers and even elderly persons helped in digging and camouflaging the air-raid shelters and engaged in rifle practice against aircraft. The Women's Association in Hanoi had launched a 'three responsibilities' campaign, parallel to the 'three readies' movement adapted by the youth of North Vietnam.[55] The three responsibilities were to: (1) Replace the men, freeing them for combat duties; (2) Take charge of the family, encouraging the husband and older children to leave for the front; and (3) Serve or take part in combat where necessary. The death toll was minimised by the air-raid alert system of radar and a network of loudspeakers in Hanoi and drums in the villages. This network was also used to rally crowds to jeer at captured US pilots.[56] The loudspeakers operated into the early 1990s, waking Hanoians with recorded music, and the sirens that blasted central Hanoi from the roof of the Opera House were only removed in the restoration of the late 1990s.

A network of air-raid shelters was built throughout Hanoi and in towns and villages. In Hanoi, these were initially rough brick shelters above the surface, but later trenches were dug around Hoan Kiem Lake and in other places. Finally, individual holes were dug every five to ten metres between the trees in the main streets and topped with concrete pipes and lids. Each of these was to hold several people. Individual holes were often cut into compacted earth in the surrounding villages. The people had their own mental plans about how to get to a hole near home or work. If they were caught in transit during an air raid, cyclists and pedestrians dived for cover, we are told, without panicking.[57] The well-known Vietnamese writer To Hoai also tells us that many residents became lazy and only moved to the shelters when urged to do so by the officials.[58] Many sought to overcome their fears of the bombing raids by drinking too much 'white water' (rice wine), although, To Hoai observed, many people were more worried about dying of hunger than about the more unfamiliar death caused by the bombs. This overwhelming sense of depression is also seen in the testimony of Mr Kung in Martha Hess's collection of eye-witness accounts, *Then the Americans Came: Voices from Vietnam*:

> Every village had a gong, usually made from a bomb. When they beat the gong we went down to the shelters. During the Nixon War, they beat the gong all the time. Sometimes I wouldn't go down to the shelter, but stayed behind, in bed. Odd thing, sometimes we didn't care.[59]

An air-raid bunker on the
banks of Hoan Kiem Lake.
(Harrison E. Salisbury,
*Behind the Lines – Hanoi
December 23–January 7*
(Secker & Warburg,
London, 1967))

Life for the Westerners in Hanoi was, of course, quite different but not
without its difficulties. There were, in fact, few Westerners left and almost
no European women to be seen, the wives of socialist country diplomats
rarely leaving their embassy compounds.[60] The International Commission
monitoring the Geneva Peace Agreement was housed in the Thong Nhat
Hotel (Metropole Hotel). De Quirielle provides an insight into the
expatriate community's existence during Operation Rolling Thunder.[61] He
and his wife arrived at Gia Lam Airport in January 1966 and were
installed at the French Embassy. Originally the site of a colonial distillery,
the compound comprised ten or so buildings with a staff of 15 Vietnamese
workers. The embassy was described with appreciation by a later French
diplomat, Philippe Richer, who was stationed there in 1975, as nestling
behind high walls in an imposing rectangle of greenery: enormous vines,
tall flamboyants and little tropical flowers.[62] De Quirielle and his wife,
however, found their accommodation too large for the modest receptions

they had to hold and they created a comfortable living room upstairs away from the draughty spaces of the ground floor. It all needed refurbishing: the curtains were musty and discoloured, and the carpets were stained. But they made the most of the pieces of furniture left behind by fleeing compatriots and, aided by a cabinet-maker, his wife fitted out the reception rooms with sideboards, tables and corner-stands, as well as chairs that they had recovered with materials purchased in Hong Kong. While not luxurious, it was welcoming at least. The downstairs salons were also patched up and ready for the 1968 Bastille Day celebrations. The festivities were marked, however, by the collapse of a false ceiling, eaten away by termites. Fortunately, the last guests had just departed.

Obtaining foodstuffs was a problem due to severe rationing. Rice and buffalo meat were delivered by Vietnamese officials, fresh and frozen food was flown in from Phnom Penh, and groceries and drinks came by sea from Hong Kong by way of Haiphong. But there were sometimes breaks of three or four weeks in the supplies. Foreigners, including diplomatic staff, were confined to the Hanoi urban area. De Quirielle was refused a driving licence, so used a bicycle to move around town. Special visas allowed him to make an occasional trip to Haiphong to collect imported goods or to visit Ha Long Bay. Except for walking exercise or visits to the one or two antique shops that had somehow survived the socialisation of commerce, there was little to make de Quirielle or his wife want to venture out into Hanoi. All of this created a climate that became depressingly claustrophobic after a while. Even postal connections with France and the outside world were constantly interrupted by the war. The embassy was given a special fund to send French staffers out to Hong Kong, Singapore or Phnom Penh for a couple of weeks' break. During air raids, the French and Vietnamese embassy personnel took shelter in the cramped shelter constructed by the Japanese in the grounds. In the late 1960s a Schrike fragmentation missile burst above the embassy grounds, scattering sparks and bits of steel across the buildings, lawns and paths. Worse came in October 1972 when the main embassy building was destroyed by another US bomb and Ambassador Pierre Susini, de Quirielle's successor, was killed, along with several Vietnamese staff.

Overcoming his sense of despondency about the situation in Hanoi, de Quirielle was still able to make the point proudly that the city was the masterpiece of French urbanists. He admired the way they had respected the old quarters and constructed a modern town around them, with fine tree-lined avenues bordered by elegant dwellings.[63] However, 'events had made it lose many of its attractions': roads and houses were now poorly maintained and the 'pleasure of strolls along streets with broken footpaths, leprous facades, and thrown into obscurity as soon as night fell, quickly died'. The shops offered only empty windows and counters, the restaurants had disappeared one by one, and the few cinemas showed nothing but insipid Soviet films. The theatres scarcely played anything but propaganda pieces, and the few monuments of artistic or tourist interest, such as the Mot Cot Pagoda or the Temple du Grand Bouddha (Quan Thanh Temple), were nearly always closed.

'Uncle Ho' and the American renegades

The will of Hanoians and the North Vietnamese had not been broken by Operation Rolling Thunder. The campaign was a military failure with severe consequences for the United States' international standing and for confidence and solidarity at home. The Tet Offensive in January 1968 especially eroded American support for the war. As a result, in May 1968 the United States and North Vietnam commenced negotiations in Paris towards finding a 'just and honourable peace', and on 1 November the total cessation of the bombing campaign was announced. In South Vietnam, the 'Vietnamisation' of the war began, and even as US troop numbers peaked at 543,000 in May 1969, America was preparing to withdraw.

But before this could occur, the anti-war movement back home escalated violently. A constant stream of Hanoi sympathisers began the routine of visiting North Vietnam, conducting interviews with a charming Ho Chi Minh and other leaders, then reporting back to the media and general public in America. Very often they wrote books about their impressions. These 'renegades', as Washington saw them, included popular figures such as the actor Jane Fonda, the novelist Mary McCarthy, the novelist and critic Susan Sontag, and the folk singer Joan Baez. Respected journalists such as Harrison Salisbury, associate editor of the *New York Times* and Pulitzer Prize winner, and Felix Greene of the *San Francisco Chronicle*, were included. So, too, were a mix of less well-known left-wing and social activists and churchmen like student leader David Ifshin, Canadian Rabbi Feinberg and Jesuit Daniel Berrigan. Sometimes deliberately, sometimes unintentionally, they gave a helping hand to Hanoi, providing the North Vietnamese propaganda machine with the chance to obtain advantageous international media coverage. De Quirielle noted that there were few visitors from outside until mid-1967 when the Vietnamese government saw that it was in its interest not to keep Hanoi in isolation and began to issue visas more liberally, especially to journalists and delegations from pacificist or left-wing movements.[64]

The visitors were met by official welcoming parties and were shown the discipline and courage of the Hanoi population and as much US bomb damage as possible. Mary McCarthy, one such visitor, described her welcoming party at a generator factory:

Above Visitors today
continue to be impressed
by the contrast between
Ho Chi Minh's house on
stilts and the adjacent
Governor-General's palace.

Below Audience
space beneath Ho
Chi Minh's house.

It was startling to visit a generator factory and be received, with bouquets of gladiolas, by a bevy of young women dressed in bright au-dais and with big red Cupid's bows, reminiscent of the twenties in America, painted on their lips. Assembled at the factory entrance, coloring shyly through the disks of rouge on their cheeks, they looked like bridesmaids emerging from a church.[65]

Many visitors met President Ho and could not help being impressed by this 'paragon of durability impervious to events', as Rabbi Feinberg described him.[66] Gemma Cruz Araneta, visiting in 1968, commented favourably on Ho's decision to live in the servant quarters of the French Governor-General's palace, setting a role model of self-sacrifice that the rest of North Vietnam followed.[67] Later, in May 1968, a replica of the stilt-houses from Ho's native village was built for him in the gardens behind the Governor-General's palace.[68] The North Vietnamese propaganda machine made great use of the image of 'Uncle Ho' surrounded by adoring school children in the audience space created under the house. Another renegade, historian Herbert Aptheker, was less cynical, convinced by his visit in 1966 that the meaning of 'Uncle Ho' was linked to a genuine sense of kinship in which 'every Vietnamese feels himself as being a member of the same family'.[69] For McCarthy and some of the others, inescapably, 'each departure was an adventure'.[70] Her descriptions of Hanoi are elegantly phrased. The city was, she wrote:

> ... clean but defaced and stained, reminding one of a bathtub that has been scrubbed with an abrasive powder till the finish has worn off. Outside the old French residential quarter, which includes diplomats' houses, the presidential palace and gardens, and the colonnaded Ba Dinh Assembly, the buildings have not been 'kept up' or renovated. Like the ancient elevator in the hotel, manufactured in Saigon in some other eon, and the sighing old French plumbing upstairs, shops, dwellings, and offices are survivors, veterans.

Harrison Salisbury's reports, by contrast, had been more devastating. Hitting newspaper stands around the world on Christmas Eve 1966, he described the damage witnessed only 200 metres from the Thong Nhat Hotel where he was staying, as well as in Nguyen Thiep Street and at the Chinese and Rumanian embassies in the Ba Dinh District. Salisbury minimised the impact of the bombs on Hanoi, although he did not hold back on the description of destruction in surrounding provinces where many of the targets — towns, dykes and water works — had no military significance. He urged the United States to stop bombing civilian targets and to concentrate on strategic targets such as the Long Bien Bridge and the main Hanoi electricity plant.

Salisbury's message was taken up by John Gerassi, a journalist, academic at the San Francisco State University, and member of the first investigation team sent by the International War Crimes Tribunal set up by the Bertrand Russell Peace Foundation. He wrote with moderation about his official briefing at Hanoi's town hall in January 1967 and the places bombed in 16 raids during the preceding year.[71] But for some of the visitors, there was such a burning passion to bring the 'truth' back home to Americans that the message was often overwhelmed by polemics and hyperbole. The Jesuit priest Daniel Berrigan was one of these. Having been taken to a documentary session, he reported back that he had

> ... felt like a Nazi watching films of Dachau. On and on, a record of perfidy and extermination. Leprosarium, TB hospitals, lying-in hospitals, general hospitals, medical stations. Destroyed, destroyed.[72]

Some carried their zeal into actions in Vietnam itself that many Americans regarded as treasonous. Twenty-one-year-old president of the National Students Association, David Ifshin, for instance, who went to Hanoi in 1970, spoke publicly of American war crimes against the Vietnamese and, in a broadcast later played daily by North Vietnamese authorities to their US prisoners, he urged GIs to turn against their commanders.[73] Jane Fonda visited in June 1972, staying for two months in the Thon Nhat Hotel. She pleaded on radio with the US pilots to abandon their fight and earned for herself the nickname 'Hanoi Jane'. Fonda was later featured with Ifshin on the front cover of *Life* magazine, her fist raised. President Ronald Reagan is said later to have wanted her tried for treason.

Whatever their intentions, the presence of these renegades helped to split American public opinion and to demoralise the US military. On the one hand, they helped to make Vietnam the trauma it has been for America, a trauma that kept on producing bitterness and dissension long after the Vietnam War ended. On the other hand, they helped to propel the United States into finding a negotiated solution to the war.

By the end of the 1960s, a number of the players had changed. Ho Chi Minh had died in July 1969 and, in the United States, Richard Nixon had been elected President in November 1968. Protests had spread across America, particularly after the killing of four students at Kent State University in Ohio in May 1970. In Vietnam, events were also swinging towards the Communists, with a major Spring Offensive into South Vietnam in March 1972. Nixon ordered a three-day series of B-52 strikes against Hanoi and Haiphong beginning on 5 May. This was the start of a renewed US bombardment of the North, which only finally ceased with the signing of the peace accords in January 1973. As in the early days of Operation Rolling Thunder, a no-strike zone was initially declared around Hanoi. But the private Paris talks between Secretary of State, then Henry Kissinger, and Le Duc Tho, the Vietnamese chief negotiator, were not going well and broke down on 13 December. Nixon again ordered intensification of the bombing campaign, the ferocious Christmas bombing of Hanoi and Haiphong.

Linebacker II and Christmas 1972

Officially this phase of the 1972 bombing campaign was termed 'Linebacker II'. At first, in May during the Linebacker I phase, the official directive had stated that it was 'essential that strike forces exercise care in weapons selection to minimise civilian casualties and avoid third country shipping, known or suspected POW camps, hospitals and religious shrines'.[74] However, the ten-mile no-strike ban around Hanoi was waived a month later, partly because a new breed of 'smart bombs with surgical precision' had come into action.[75] These had again struck the Long Bien Bridge, sending three more of its spans into the Red River and crippling the cross-river traffic. But the peak bombardment was Linebacker II, lasting from 18 to 30 December, with a 36-hour break for Christmas, thereby gaining the popular name of the 'Christmas Blitz'.

In these 11 days, 121 B-52 bombers dropped 100,000 bombs, with F-4s and F-111s carrying smart bombs to follow up on areas close to heavily populated targets, such as Hanoi's electricity plant, or targets missed by the B-52s. Although the official targets were the military, communications and industrial infrastructure of Hanoi and Haiphong, and despite the use of TV- and laser-guided smart bombs, a number of attacks went astray, causing civilian deaths and the destruction of prominent Hanoi landmarks and residential areas. In fact, it was estimated that in up to 90 per cent of B-52 missions, at least one bomb landed outside the designated target area.[76] The B-52s, in particular, flew high so that Vietnamese SAMs could not reach them, but a minute error in the bomb drop could produce severe damage to the wrong neighbourhood.[77] One of the most sought-after targets was Radio Hanoi, the main communication centre for the North Vietnamese Army and source of constant propaganda broadcasts by 'Hanoi Hannah'. The B-52s hit the radio station during the first few days of Linebacker II, but it required the F-4s to destroy the tiny building housing the transmitter and antennas with laser-guided bombs a few days later.[78] Other planes attacked the Yen Vien rail yard, the Hanoi and Thai Nguyen thermal power plants, and the Kinh No and Hanoi oil storage areas.[79] Four US planes were downed and 43 pilots killed or captured. Again the Vietnamese casualties are not known.

Hanoi's main railway station was one of the targets hit by Air Force F-4s carrying laser-guided bombs. As a key point in the railway communication line to communist China, it was obviously an important target and its yards, loading platforms, warehouses and support buildings,

Above Hanoi Railway Station as it was when constructed, c. 1900. (Photographic reproduction by the Bibliothèque nationale de France)

Below The rebuilt central pavilion of the Hanoi Railway Station reflects the shift from French Beaux-Arts design to the architectural ideas of the international modern movement.

as well as the main terminal building and lines and rolling stock, were either destroyed or severely damaged in the attacks.[80] The accuracy of the smart bomb in this instance seems demonstrated by the fact that it took out the central pavilion of the colonial terminal, leaving the two Beaux-Arts wings intact. This was later rebuilt in a Soviet-inspired version of the International Style using prefabricated cement blocks.

On another occasion, unfortunately, as well as knocking out the shunting yards and workshops behind the station, a load of standard gravity bombs fell short and cut a kilometre-long swathe through high-density residential and commercial Kham Tien Street, destroying 60 houses and shops, and killing 215 civilians.[81] *Newsweek* quoted the description of the scene by Agence France Presse correspondent in Hanoi, Jean LeClerc du Sablon:

Kham Tien Street
monument to the
215 people killed on
26 December 1972.

One of Hanoi's most colourful streets, Kham Thien, is a mass of ruins and a scene of desolation and mourning today in the wake of the latest series of American air raids ... [A]n entire family lay dead, their bodies pressed against each other — Nguyen Van Si, his wife, a young daughter, an adolescent boy, and a boy of 4 or 5 years grasping an infant to his chest.[82]

According to Phung Thi Tiem, head of the Kham Thien Women's Union in the late 1980s when interviewed by Martha Hess,

It was 10:20 on the evening of December 26, 1972. People had returned from work, eaten dinner, and many had already gone to bed. And then the Americans came. Many older people, women, men, and many children were killed in that bombing. They were supposed to have been evacuated, but the 24th was a Sunday and the 25th was Christmas Day. So people thought the Americans wouldn't bomb. They returned to their homes.[83]

The Bach Mai
Hospital today.

Another resident, Nguyen Van Thong, recalls that his home was destroyed:

I began to dig quickly, and found three bodies — my father, my younger brother, and my sister. My mother had been evacuated with the younger children. My older brother and sister-in-law I couldn't find. The next morning I found my brother's head. I never found my sister-in-law, nor one of my aunts. My uncle's body was found two months later, near the house. My neighbour Mr Van, his wife and five children were killed, seven people.[84]

Funeral service for Bach Mai
Hospital bombing victims.
(J. Morrocco, *Thunder from
Above: Air War, 1941–1968*
(Boston Publishing Co., Boston,
Mass., 1984), p. 158)

This was the most destructive civilian hit in this phase of the war in Hanoi. Later, another B-52 missed the railway station and obliterated three houses to the south. Almost 30 people were killed.[85] The densely populated working-class residential quarters of An Duong and Nghia Dung in Ba Dinh District were badly damaged. The embassies hit this time included those of communist Albania, Cambodia, Cuba, East Germany, as well as those of India and Egypt.

During Linebacker II, the three airfields on the outskirts of Hanoi were also chief targets. Apparently aiming at one of these, a minor airfield south of Hanoi's centre, B-52 bombers accidentally struck the Bach Mai Hospital on 21 December, creating another civilian catastrophe. It was the main hospital in North Vietnam and the principal teaching school for the Hanoi Medical College, with 1,000 beds, 350 doctors and 800 medical students.[86] It had been hit first in June, but this time the operating and consultation rooms in several wings were destroyed and the fatalities were high. The event is described by Doctor Tran Quoc Do, who was on duty that night:

> The B-52 planes sounded like the grinding of a rice mill ... The bombs got closer and closer, and then they bombed us directly. We knew they were coming, and we brought the patients and the operating rooms underground. Under where you are now sitting are the shelters. We would do emergency treatment and then send the patients to a centre in Hoa Binh, fifty, sixty kilometres from here. When the hospital was hit we were performing surgery underground and we didn't know. We came out and found half the buildings were destroyed.[87]

There are numerous versions of these events. An Indian diplomat reported that Bach Mai Hospital had been totally razed to the ground.[88] Kathleen Gough, who visited Hanoi in the mid-1970s, maintained that the pediatrics wing was hit by five bombs and the dermatology and ENT building was totally destroyed. She put the death toll at 57. According to the journalist Neil Sheehan, seven bombs fell on the cardiology department, bringing the upper floors down on to the basement, killing 11 doctors, medical students and nurses sheltering with patients in there. The dermatology department across the courtyard was harder hit, with 17 dead. By contrast, the memorial plaque at the hospital today indicates that two people were killed in June and another 27 on 22 December 1972. These were mainly young women but included an eight-year-old boy. Whatever the precise facts, the economic hardship Vietnam faced after the war was over meant that reconstruction of the hospital was not completed until December 1983. An American humanitarian group, Medical Aid for Indochina, gave US$200,000 in equipment, including a defibrillator, pacemaker, electro-cardiograph and Vietnam's first echocardiograph. Most of this equipment began to fail in the 1980s, and the hospital could not afford to replace it.

There was enormous public outrage following the Christmas blitz within the United States and internationally. Many Western countries and NATO allies opposed the US action. So far, Nixon and Kissinger had ignored the warnings of military and civilian leaders. They wanted to destroy the North's will to fight, while demonstrating to South Vietnam that the United States would remain committed to its independence.[89] Although the US military advisers thought the North Vietnamese were running out of SAMs, Nixon called off the bombing.[90] Probably he had gained the movement in the Paris peace negotiations he was after. In short, it was a 'savage, significant, strategic air war', as American aviation writer Robert Hotz summed it up in 1973. The United States portrayed it as a tactical success.[91] The North Vietnamese, however, claimed the moral victory when the bombing was cancelled, and renamed an avenue 'Duong Chien Thang B-52' (Victory over the B-52s Road). This road is now called Duong Truong Chinh and is part of the Ring Road No. 2 that cuts across Hanoi's southern suburbs.

The final tally of destruction: Hanoi in 1973

The 'traitorous' Australian journalist Wilfred Burchett, writing in November 1964, had predicted that 'the lunatic fringe in Washington' might well resort to 'the ultimate madness of bombing Hanoi, Haiphong and other towns of North Vietnam' but that this strategy would 'never bring the people of the North or the South to their knees'.[92] He was right. But it took eight years of relentless bombing of the North, from 1966 to 1973, before the United States recognised that the bombing strategy had simply stiffened Hanoi's resolve. By 1969 the fundamentals of a peace treaty were already being settled by Henry Kissinger and Le Duc Tho. The Christmas blitz brought matters to a head and the peace accord was signed in Paris on 23 January 1973. And so, a century after the French first attacked Hanoi's Royal Citadel, the foreign invaders departed.

Overall, it is estimated that about 200 people were killed in Hanoi during the Rolling Thunder Operation and 2200 (as well as 1557 wounded) during Linebacker II.[93] Most of these casualties were in suburban Hanoi. The 'American War' was short in the context of Vietnamese history, a history constantly marked by invasions, attempted invasions and periods of colonial domination. In so far as Hanoi is concerned, more physical damage appears to have been done in the anti-colonial resistance of the 1880s, the anti-Japanese struggle in the 1940s and during the anti-colonial resistance of the mid-1940s, than in the United States' bombing raids. This is explained in part by the absence, during the American War, of ground fighting in the North, whereas the street fighting between the French Expeditionary and the Viet Minh forces in 1946 left a toll of human and physical damage that surpassed anything later wreaked on the city.

Several commentators have remarked upon the civilian death toll being lower than expected. Certainly the toll of death and destruction does not match those described by Hewitt during World War 2 in Europe and East Asia.[94] That the destruction was less than in wars elsewhere in the world and at other times in Hanoi's history, or indeed less than might have been expected in this war given the intensity of the bombing raids, was due to two main reasons. First, the American military strategy was to use bombing as an instrument of coercion, withholding a larger force that could kill the enemy's capital city if he did not back down. It was essential not to 'kill the hostage' by destroying the critical assets inside the 'Hanoi donut', as one American political scientist, Fred Kaplan, subsequently put it.[95] In other words, although the US bombing campaigns might not meet the definition of 'place annihilation' given by Hewitt, it was clearly aimed at 'the disorganisation of enemy space'. It was intended to knock out military targets and to avoid civilian areas, to hit suburban rather than central areas. Secondly, the death toll was also kept to a minimum by the steps Hanoi took to counter the American strategy – the installation of an extremely effective air-raid warning system, the extensive evacuation program, and the high level of discipline among those who remained behind in the city.

In the 102 villages around the outskirts of Hanoi, the bombs had had their effect on the physical infrastructure. Although statistical data from the period is notoriously unreliable, it has been claimed by the Vietnamese that, in Hanoi's suburbs, 116 schools and 30 kindergartens and nursery schools had been bombed, along with 116 pagodas, temples and churches, 110 factories and businesses, 150 warehouses, and 53 hospitals and clinics.[96] One hundred and six neighbourhoods had been hit, as had Hanoi's dykes in 71 places. By comparison, the physical damage to the oldest parts of central Hanoi was minimal. No major public building, other than the railway station, appears to have been hit, although 15 embassies were damaged. A survey at the end of the war found that 215,000 square metres of housing had been destroyed or damaged in Hanoi's three districts (*quan*) of Hai Ba Trung, Hoan Kiem and Ba Dinh, probably in the more outlying sections.[97] According to the *Hanoi Moi* newspaper, this represented about 17,000 housing units.[98] A Soviet correspondent estimated that almost one-quarter of all the living space in metropolitan Hanoi had been wiped out. Serious as this was, by the standards of modern warfare involving aerial bombardment Hanoi had not been blasted into oblivion, as some of the Washington hawks had advocated.

In fact, the problem facing the Hanoi administration at the end of the war seems to have been more one of a rapid influx of people from the countryside requiring housing, than the massive destruction of buildings by the bombers. Hanoi's population had at first fallen from 643,000 in 1960 to an estimated 400,000 in 1967–68, before rising during the lull in bombing from November 1968 and April 1972 to 1.2 million.[99] Then, with renewed bombing from April 1972, the evacuation program resumed, eventually bringing the total number of Hanoi residents leaving the city to as many as 700,000 − that is, 60 per cent of the population of metropolitan Hanoi and 75 per cent of the population of inner Hanoi. This exodus reduced Hanoi's population to 480,000 by the end of 1972. However, the cessation in bombing in January 1973 saw not only many evacuees return to Hanoi, but also large numbers of new migrants from rural villages. By 1974, the population of the city reached 736,000 with another 632,000 in rural parts of the municipality.[100] This increased to 1.2 million by 1979, with another 1.3 million in rural areas, despite a registration system designed to tie people to their official residential district.[101] The result was acute housing shortages and considerable problems in running the city. Thrift and Forbes put it simply: Hanoi was in disarray. It was in no fit condition to be reoccupied, and the government was forced to assign state and party cadres to run urban blocks, a level of administration usually left to popular participation.[102] Administrative skills were sorely taxed, abnormal levels of corruption were reported, progress was disappointing and acknowledged publicly, and the city did not return to anything like pre-war normality until well into 1974 or 1975.

Media manipulation and memory distortion: Images of a city devastated

Given that Hanoi seems in fact to have been left substantially intact by the bombing campaigns, why did it become usual for Westerners to imagine the Vietnam War had left the city in a state of complete devastation? The reasons for these false mental images are many and complex. The countless eye-witnesses all had their own individual sets of impressions, be they Vietnamese or American, soldier or civilian. This diversity of perceptions is well put by Bao Ninh. Comparing his own soldier's experience with that of his novel's protagonist, he wrote:

> We'd dragged ourselves through the red dust, through the mud, carrying machine-guns on our shoulders, or packs on our backs. Bare-footed, on occasions. And both he and I, like the other ordinary soldiers of the war, shared one fate. We shared all the vicissitudes, the defeats and victories, the happiness and suffering, the losses and gains. But each of us had been crushed by the war in a different way.

Each of us carried in his heart a separate war which in many ways was totally different, despite our common cause. We had different memories of people we'd known and of the war itself, and we had different destinies in the post-war years.[103]

Also, at the time of the war, there were very limited facts available about the Vietnamese cities, their people and the effects of the war on them. This was little different from the paucity of English-language information available in the West about Vietnamese culture and history, a problem that led to serious misunderstandings and cultural arrogance on the part of the American political and military leaders.[104]

At a technical level, then, establishing an accurate mental image of what was happening in Hanoi was made difficult by a lack of comprehensive and reliable data. Reports of the impact of the war on life in the cities were fragmentary. There appear to have been no consolidated reports resulting from official commissions of inquiry. Moreover, the available fragments, whether from Vietnamese or American and other Western sources, are commonly charged with emotion – outrage on the part of the Vietnamese and self-justification on the part of the Americans – and were very often written to achieve a propaganda advantage. Statistics of damage inflicted on the cities, where they exist at all, are generally unreliable.

De Quirielle, commenting on the world's reliance on the official communiqués of the two adversaries or reports by journalists, noted that objectivity was not the main quality of the news being handed out. He complained, too, that journalists only stayed for a few days and gained a very superficial view of the situation.[105] He thought both sides were inflating the toll of dead and wounded, destruction of hospitals, schools, churches and houses in a propaganda war.[106] This view was contradicted, however, by Joseph Kraft who reported back to the *New Yorker* magazine in 1972 that the general impression among journalists covering the war was that the North Vietnamese government was underestimating damage for reasons of public morale. It is clear, however, that most journalists and other commentators had a poor knowledge of Hanoi and often gained false impressions of the extent of bombing damage. Telford Taylor, the former chief counsel at the Nuremberg War Crimes Trials, who visited the Bach Mai Hospital, overestimated the damage to it because he was apparently unaware of the hospital's vast scale.[107] Joseph Kraft admitted that the extent of damage was difficult for foreigners to ascertain because their movements were restricted: they were forbidden to drive and had to use government-assigned chauffeurs.[108]

Much of the American press in the 1960s reflected the passions aroused in the United States by the humiliating imprisonment of their downed pilots in the Hoa Lo. Conditions in the prison were graphically described – beds of concrete, and spiders bigger than one's fist. The nicknames of the various parts of the 'Hanoi Hilton' became widely broadcast – 'New Guys Village' for the new arrivals' cells, 'Las Vegas' for the torture rooms, and 'Camp Unity' for the meeting room the prisoners were allowed from 1971. So, too, were the names given to other prisons – 'Alcatraz' for the more recalcitrant prisoners, and 'Model Farm' for the gaol to which they were taken when inspections were expect-ed.[109] This line of reporting fed into the post-war Missing in Action (MIA) obsession and the punitive economic measures subsequently taken by the United States against Vietnam. However, as the war dragged on into the 1970s, the American prestige press such as the *New York Times* and the *Washington Post*, like leading newspapers in many Western countries, turned against the war. One-time American ambassador to Bulgaria, Martin F. Herz, and his co-writer, Leslie Ridler, saw this as part of a deliberate campaign against President Nixon and a violation of journalism's own standards and American democracy.[110] They saw the press forming part of a conspiracy in which the Hanoi government and those of other nationalities who sympathised with it had 'the virtual monopoly on all factual information'.

Of course, the reports coming out in the Soviet newspaper *Tass*, the Italian *Unità* or other communist party papers were sometimes little more than propaganda, with exaggerated accounts of the bombing raids. *Tass* described one Operation Rolling Thunder air-raid attack as lasting twice as long as did the diplomats interviewed by Harrison Salisbury.[111] Some of the American renegades wrote polemically, driven by their conviction of America's wrongdoing.[112] Others tried to relay faithfully what they saw, but either an unconscious process of selection occurred in their writing, or what they saw was controlled by their North Vietnamese minders. Susan Sontag, for instance, was taken to see the damage to provincial towns and cities, including hospitals and schools. She was rightly horrified by the statistics of civilian deaths that showed 60 per cent were women and children, but she chose to highlight her meeting with an elderly Mother Superior and two young nuns, the only survivors of a Catholic convent located south of Hanoi.[113] Some of the 'real life' situations presented to the visiting renegades and journalists now seem to have been transparently contrived. One wonders how Felix Greene, for instance, could have been so taken in by the spotless doctor he interviewed, nor we, the audience of his film *North Vietnam: A Personal Report*, by the coincidental air-raid alert that occurred just as he was conducting an interview. Who was fooling whom?

Back home in the United States or other parts of the West, newspaper readers and television viewers ended up with a jumble of information, stories and images. Often commentators made further errors in interpreting the data coming from Vietnam. Robert Hotz, for instance, covering the Hanoi bombing for *Aviation Week* on the basis of air photos released by the US military, claimed that the main Hanoi railway station was 'totally destroyed by five laser bombs without damaging buildings across the street'.[114] More often, because the reader or viewer had so little background knowledge of Vietnam, it was a case of the innocent displacement of mental images. In this process, scenes of horrific bomb destruction in other North Vietnamese towns such as Vinh, Haiphong, Nam Dinh and Ninh Binh were transposed to Hanoi. During the years 1965–73 all six major cities of North Vietnam, as well as 12 provincial capitals, 31 district capitals and 300 villages, were devastated. Of the cities, three were completely razed, while Hanoi was the least damaged. Harrison Salisbury and a few other observers opposed to the war attempted to put Hanoi's destruction into a reasonable perspective but were powerless to prevent the widespread 'belief' that Hanoi had been razed along with the rest.

One American journalist, Tammy Arbuckle, visiting in March 1973, went too far the other way, asserting that the Hanoi had hardly been touched.[115] While there may be some academic merit in comparing the death and destruction in Hanoi with the results of wars elsewhere, the misery brought to Hanoi should not be minimised. Of course, the United States could have inflicted major civilian casualties, could even have wiped out Hanoi totally if it had wished, and perhaps the damage was less substantial than expected or described, but the American bombs very clearly wreaked havoc in both human and physical terms. Much of the subsequent coverage of the Vietnam War by the media and historians and other scholars has focused on the psychological and sociological damage done to Americans. As Phil Melling and Jon Roper observed, 'America's reconstruction of its involvement in Vietnam, from "tragedy without villains" to "noble cause", has been accompanied by a profound lack of interest in the Vietnamese.'[116]

Vietnamese historians have still to provide scholarly analysis from the other side. It is important that this be done soon, because, among other things, those involved are ageing and dying. But it will also provide another basis for determining what is significant in Hanoi's cultural landscape. This would pave the way for the protection of another layer in Hanoi's history – the buildings and sites, Bach Mai Hospital and Kham Thien – to be protected as part of the city's heritage. The Long Bien Bridge, unrestored and missing its bombed spans, or the Hanoi Railway Station with its ugly rebuilt central section, are just as much tributes to the people of Hanoi during the Vietnam War as they are to the engineering and architectural skills of the French. These are places of

33 Pham Ngu Lao Street.

symbolic significance rather than artistic, architectural or engineering merit; they should be valued as reminders of a critical period in the development of modern Hanoi and Vietnam.

The last assault: Saigon, 30 April 1975

After the Americans and their allies pulled out in early 1973, the civil war in the South continued with the Democratic Republic of Vietnam backing the southern communist forces, the Viet Cong. The strategy to take the southern capital, Saigon, was planned in mid-1974 in a building in Hanoi – 33 Pham Ngu Lao Street.[117] Appropriately, the street was named after a Vietnamese general who had won repeated victories against foreign invaders, and the building had once been the French military headquarters. Many of the North Vietnamese leaders who met in 1974 had, in fact, convened here 20 years earlier. Uncle Ho was gone, of course, but they were mostly the same men, only older: Le Duan (General-Secretary of the Vietnamese Communist Party from 1960), Vo Nguyen Giap (Defence Minister), Le Duc Tho (the Paris negotiator) and Van Tien Dung (Commander of the People's Army and Giap's protégé). Their decisions were taken and coordinated with those of the Viet Cong leadership, and the war went into its end phase. The dramatic final assault on Saigon – its 'fall' or 'liberation', according to political viewpoint – occurred on 30 April 1975. The country was reunited and Hanoi was capital once again of a single, independent and communist Vietnam.

In Hanoi, there was much rejoicing. But the city and its people faced a daunting future of enormous development problems. There was much human grief and personal loss that would dissipate only slowly. The final word on the sorrows of war is evoked by this passage from Bao Ninh's novel:

> Military life in the jungles over those long years developed within him a deep, tender love for his home town. When he returned, some of that passion faded as the realities set in. It was not that Hanoi itself had changed – though yes, there had been changes – but he had changed. He had wanted to wind back the clock to his teenage days and relive those memories.
>
> But the impressions of the friendliness and uniqueness of his home town that he had generated during those trivia sessions in the jungle had been based on hopes in a situation of despair.
>
> Post-war Hanoi, in reality, was not like his jungle dreams. The streets revealed an unbroken, monotonous sorrow and suffering. There were joys, but those images blinked on and off, like cheap flashing lights in a shop window. There was a shared loneliness in poverty, and in his everyday walks he felt this mood in the stream of people he walked with.[118]

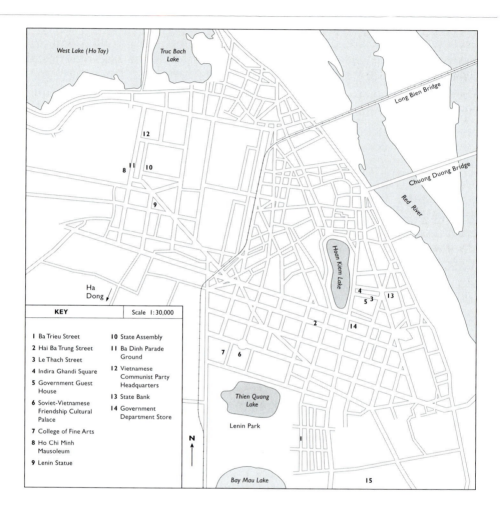

West Lake (Ho Tay)

Truc Bach Lake

Long Bien Bridge

Chuong Duong Bridge

Red River

Hoan Kiem Lake

12

11 10

8

9

Ha Dong

4

5 3

13

2

14

7 6

Thien Quang Lake

Lenin Park

1

Bay Mau Lake

15

N

KEY	Scale 1:30,000

1 Ba Trieu Street
2 Hai Ba Trung Street
3 Le Thach Street
4 Indira Ghandi Square
5 Government Guest House
6 Soviet-Vietnamese Friendship Cultural Palace
7 College of Fine Arts
8 Ho Chi Minh Mausoleum
9 Lenin Statue

10 State Assembly
11 Ba Dinh Parade Ground
12 Vietnamese Communist Party Headquarters
13 State Bank
14 Government Department Store

Chapter 6
Red River, red city:
Creating Hanoi's socialist face

Soviet–Vietnamese friendship: A new alliance

To the south of the city centre is the Soviet–Vietnamese Friendship Cultural Palace – also known as the Trade Union Cultural Palace. Soviet architects designed, and Soviet engineers helped to construct, this reinforced concrete building containing theatres, lecture halls and meeting rooms. Its design belongs to the Modern Constructivist style, the Soviet translation of international modernism, with some attempt to accommodate local building styles and artistic motifs. It was based directly on a model project for an exhibition and sporting hall developed in Moscow and replicated around the Soviet Union and its dependencies. However, the original prototype was the Moscow Palace of Labour, an important landmark for the new Soviet socialist state, that was built following an architectural design competition in 1922. It is said that the commentary by the Vesnin brothers on their entry, which ran third, became the basis of the 'form derived from function and construction' aesthetic behind Modern Constructivism.[1] The Hanoi Cultural Palace was erected on the site of the Maurice Long Museum which had been destroyed in 1945. The site was used for the People's Open Air Theatre from 1954 until it was selected to house the palace. The building was opened in the late 1980s and dedicated to the victory of the workers in their struggle for democratic reforms in the country.[2]

The presence of the landmark Cultural Palace reflects the fact that Ho Chi Minh's independent government after 1955 had moved towards reliance on the Soviet bloc rather than the United States, the West, or even its neighbour, China, with which Vietnam's relations were generally uneasy. Whether North Vietnam's dependence on the Soviets was by necessity or preference is a subject of continuing debate. However, the establishment of a socialist regime in the North – the Democratic Republic

The Soviet–Vietnamese
Friendship Cultural Palace,
a gift of the Soviet Union's
All-Union Central Trade
Union Council.

of Vietnam – in 1954 was soon followed by the formalisation of a framework for economic aid from the Soviet Union in the Economic and Technical Cooperation Agreement of May 1955. This paved the way for Soviet assistance in the reconstruction of North Vietnam.[3] It was also followed, in March 1958, by a Trade and Maritime Agreement specifying the system of exchange to be used in Soviet–Vietnamese trade.[4] Economic assistance was cut back during the 1960s and early 1970s but re-emerged after the fall of Saigon in 1975 and the establishment of the Socialist Republic of Vietnam (SRV) embracing North and South. In November 1975 the Treaty of Friendship and Cooperation was signed and this became the most important of the compacts establishing economic assistance relations between the Soviet Union and Vietnam. It made the SRV a fully-fledged member of the Soviet bloc with consequent membership of the Council for Mutual Economic Assistance (CMEA, or Comecon), the International Bank for Economic Cooperation and the Soviet-sponsored International Investment Bank. Under the treaty, the Hanoi government was permitted to run an annual trade deficit with the Soviet Union of up to 150 per cent of its exports.

Thus, Vietnam was pulled well and truly into the Soviet Union's economic orbit. According to Buu Hoan, 60 per cent of Vietnam's total foreign trade was with the Soviet Union.[5] The Soviet Union was also involved in implementing 300 projects in Vietnam of which 30 per cent were in the industrial sector. It provided all of Vietnam's fuel and lubricants, iron ore and cotton, and 95 per cent of its motor vehicles. Vietnam, in return, provided foodstuffs and industrial raw materials such as coffee, tea, rubber and tin. The Labour Cooperation Agreement of February 1981 set up a framework for Vietnamese migrant workers in the Soviet Union, and in the next eight years more than 60,000 left Vietnam to work in some 250 Soviet state enterprises.[6]

Vietnam was able to look to the Soviet Union as a model in more ways than one. The Soviet Union provided not only socialist inspiration, but, like Vietnam, it had undergone enormous human losses and physical destruction in wars against foreign powers. World War 1, the 1917 Revolution, the ensuing civil war and World War 2 had all caused significant changes to the Soviet Union's urban landscape. In the case of cities such as Novgorod, Volgograd, Minsk and Kiev, which had been razed, it was necessary to recreate them from the ground up.[7] This was clearly taken as a precedent for Hanoi's response to its own wars of independence, and Vietnam followed the Soviet Union in the way it mounted its large-scale effort to reconstruct the country's economy and human settlements.

In his recent book on Soviet urban planning, R. Antony French argues that, because no other country has experienced such a long period under the direct influence of Marxist ideology, it had been thought that the Soviet Union was 'the prime exemplar of Marxist socialist planning in all its aspects'.[8] In the field of urban planning it was held that city formation in that country was moving along a new path in line with Marxist ideology – that is, towards the creation of the 'City of Socialist Man'. The Soviet capital, Moscow, was intended to be the showcase of this revolutionary vision and a model for other Soviet cities from Stalingrad (now Volgograd) to Vladivostock. But this influence was felt much more widely, affecting urban development in all countries that came under Soviet Union tutelage, especially in the Cold War period – Vietnam, Cuba, Angola and, of course, the former satellites in Eastern Europe. Despite great cultural and environmental variation between these countries, the socialist bond imposed a common pattern of residential, commercial and industrial development. A similar socialist imprint was felt in China and countries coming under Beijing's sway. This influence was one of the major globalising tendencies of the last half-century.

As with Moscow for the Soviets, the North Vietnamese government wanted its capital city to encapsulate the vision of the new Vietnamese socialist state. Hanoi's role was to be inspirational both in ideological and economic terms. This inspirational mix was seen in the many exhibitions hosted by the national and Hanoi governments that were intended to impress the Vietnamese with the capacity and variety of production going on both in Vietnam and in brother iron curtain countries.[9] The first of these took place in 1955 when Czechoslovakia mounted its exhibition on the corner of Hai Ba Trung and Ba Trieu streets. East Germany followed, and then the Soviet Union in the former colonial Information Hall on Trang Tien Street. In early 1958 the Great Exhibition of Industry took place. Observers such as the Frenchman Gérard Tongas reported the enormous interest aroused by the pavilions showing the products of Hanoi's flourishing craft industries. More than 5,000 different products were exhibited, from simple rush mats to large modern lathes. Propaganda was everywhere in Hanoi – in wall posters, banners, and broadcasts over the public announcement system installed during the Vietnam War. These were designed to bolster public morale and to convince the residents of Hanoi that their country and city were making progress.

The published descriptions of socialist Hanoi by the North Vietnamese were usually rapturous. Looking back on 30 years of socialism in Hanoi, architect Bui Tam Trung in 1984 portrayed the achievements in the following terms:

> Except for a few rich suburbs reserved for the ruling elite, Hanoi was [until the socialist period] just a shanty town with huts and decayed slums ... lacking all sorts of facilities and healthy living conditions ... [But] over the past 30 years, we have done exactly what Uncle Ho wanted us to do:

'Hanoi must be a Socialist Capital' ... Many new buildings were constructed ... Many civic squares (public parks) were built like Lenin Park ... Slum clearance has razed all the rotting tenements and transformed them into good buildings to live in ... New roads have been built to transform the isolated areas into densely populated communities ... Now a new chapter in the development work is in the making — to do what the Minister [of the Interior] wants us to do: 'The renewal works must reflect the importance of Hanoi as a manufacturing city in a socialist regime'. That is the responsibility and the expectancy of all the Vietnamese people.[10]

Visitors from Soviet bloc countries also highlighted the good points. I.M. Shchedrov, for instance, wrote in 1961 that:

The People's power from the very first days mobilised the whole population for a struggle for better living conditions. The rubbish dumps were cleared, a campaign begun to observe the rules of personal hygiene and sanitation. Now there were around 200 pumps delivering water. By 1957, infant mortality had dropped [from around 50 per cent] to four per cent. In 1956, smallpox was stamped out. Mass unemployment was eliminated. If a significant part of the working population of Hanoi had earlier eaten only once a day, now three meals a day became normal.[11]

As we have seen, many of the Western sympathisers who visited Hanoi during the Vietnam War also wrote glowingly of the advances being made in the standard of living. By contrast, from the other side of the intellectual Cold War, Gérard Tongas damned North Vietnam as a 'communist hell'.

Transferring principles and practices: The globalisation of planning

With the growing awareness of a rapidly globalising world, many scholars and media observers in the 1990s began to take an interest in how global-isation was impacting upon national, regional and local cultures. This process of cultural globalisation is of vital concern in relation to the protection of the cultural heritage, which the United Nations and its agencies such as UNESCO recognise as a fundamental part of the identity, dignity and rights of all peoples. Countries that are signatories to the World Heritage Convention, the Hague Convention for the Protection of Cultural Property in the Event of Armed Conflict, and other associated charters and protocols, have declared their acceptance of this philosophical position. They are expected to follow through with careful stewardship of their own cultural heritage. Of course, this does not solve the question of who defines the official heritage to be protected and by what criteria and in whose interests.

One of the academics who has taken a lead in studying the roles of architecture and town planning as professional cultural practices, and of architects and town planners as agents in contributing to the globalisation of culture, is Anthony King.[12] He sees a global culture emerging largely as the product of a world political economy of capitalism as well as technological and communication innovations. But he concludes that, 'while there may be a globalising culture in relation to the built environment, it is not necessarily (and is as much likely to work against) a homogenising one'. In other words, he supports the view put by others that the forces of globalisation are just as likely to provoke a localist reaction as they are to create cultural homogeneity across the face of the earth.[13] Furthermore, there are likely to be as many cultural differences between groups within a particular national society as between nations. Finally, he claims that history is at least, if not more, useful than theory in charting the development of national, regional or international cultures and the way they become represented in the built environment.[14]

There is now an active international group of 'planning historians' who have taken on this task of plotting and explaining the global diffusion of philosophies and practices relating to the development of the built environment.[15] Stephen Ward, for example, has put forward a typology of different ways in which diffusion occurs that is useful in clarifying the processes at work in Vietnam during the Soviet period, or, indeed, during other periods when it came under external cultural in-fluences.[16] At one extreme, planning ideas are imposed in an authori-tarian manner, as in a colonial context. Such transference typically takes little care to adapt planning activities to the new, colonial environment. This was the case, as we have seen, in the early days of French colonialism in Vietnam, with a modification during the cultural-relativist Hébrard years before reverting to a more authoritarian approach under Governor-General Decoux and chief planner, Cérutti.

Another type of diffusion occurs where the local population reacts to – or 'contests' – the imposition of foreign planning philosophies and practices. This can be seen to have occurred in some colonial contexts, but is particularly the case in neo-colonial situations where more advanced nations seek to tie cultural programs to their strategies of assuring economic (and, often) political dominance over supposedly independent countries. The role of US architects in this regard is being studied by Hong Kong-based architectural historian Jeffrey Cody.[17] In this chapter, we are concerned with the linkage between the diffusion of Soviet architectural and planning ideas and the broader effort of the Soviet Union to draw Vietnam into its economic and political orbit. In fact, in Vietnam the diffusion process seems to have been mid-way between these two types. On the one hand, the Soviet architects and planners tended to impose their ideas without much modification to fit local circumstances. On the other hand, while their Vietnamese counterparts appeared to accept that the Soviet planning projects were 'gifts' and therefore to be welcomed in the form presented, there is some evidence to suggest that contestation occurred. This rarely took place explicitly in the meetings between the Soviet and Vietnamese teams in Moscow and Hanoi. Rather, the most effective contestation seems to have occurred almost surreptitiously – a polite acceptance of Soviet advice over the drawing board, but a resolute determination to implement projects their way in the end. Once again, the practice of 'bending with the wind' in order to maintain some control over cultural change was at work.

There is no doubt that, by assisting in the transfer of design principles and implementation practices to Vietnam, Soviet architects and planners played a significant part not only in helping to shape Vietnam's planning activities and its townscapes, but also in reinforcing general Soviet hegemony in Vietnam. The architectural and town planning professions had been central to the Soviet Union's post-war reconstruction and development. Since there were now hardly any private clients or land-owners in the Soviet Union, and the government and Party had become the source of all work, architects and planners were necessarily enlisted in the socialist cause. Many, of course, believed fervently in the socialist principles. Soviet architect A.T. Polyansky explains that

> Since the formation of the new state the role of the architect in the USSR has been determined out of a desire to build a socialist society by work carried out during each stage of its development and by the actual means placed at his disposal. For the first time in history, an architect's work is directed towards the realisation of creative ideas and conceptions aimed at the harmonious development of all members of society.[18]

Others no doubt felt obliged to mouth support, for there was no alternative if a livelihood was to be obtained.

The same pattern held for architects and planners in Vietnam. With the creation of a socialist state in 1954, extending to the South in 1975, art, architecture and town planning became subservient to Party policy: 'Learning from experience, our new architects must carry out the Party's resolutions, developing in our country a national and modern socialist architecture.'[19] So, starting with the platform covered with cloth, ribbons and banners from which President Ho Chi Minh read the Vietnamese Declaration of Independence on 2 September 1945, a new townscape began to be created, with icons demonstrating the brotherly links between Vietnam and the Soviet bloc countries.

This new cultural alliance had been developing for some time. In his socialistic interpretation of Vietnam's architectural history, Ngo Huy

Quynh recalls that the fledgling Vietnamese Communist Party had drafted a 'Cultural Revolution' statement at the time of the unsuccessful August 1930 uprising. This statement declared the Party's determination to make way for 'a new culture and the liberation of art and architecture from the feudal and colonial periods'.[20] However, according to Dang Thai Hoang, it was in fact only with the capital's liberation from the French in October 1954 that Hanoi could become a 'socialist capital ... [taking] a leading role in socialist construction'.[21] Architects from other socialist countries, led by the Soviet Union, assisted with the design and construction of projects, helping to demonstrate how Hanoi's architecture could be 'suitable to a country that has not passed through the capitalist period'. President Ho himself declared in an address to the Vietnamese people before the end of the conflict with the United States that 'Hanoi and Haiphong may be destroyed to the foundations, but when we achieve final victory, we will build them back even more spacious, larger and more beautiful'.[22]

So the new, socialist ideology gained a real opportunity to put its mark on the cultural landscape after 1954 in the North and 1975 in the South. Surveying 'progressive' Vietnamese architecture for Soviet Union readers, P. Prikhodko announced that 'New, hitherto unseen perspectives of development had unfolded for the architecture of the country'.[23] A Viet-namese Architects' Association was established, and an Institute of Architecture was opened to train a new era of architects and planners. In their planning and construction activities, the socialist Vietnamese authorities and educators moved away from traditional building styles and designing for religious uses. Indeed, Hoang Dao Kinh admits that there was even some destruction of temples and pagodas in the 1950s, which apparently went without protest from the architectural profession.[24] The authorities also rejected Western approaches associated with their colonial enemies and sought to borrow new ideas from the world revolutionary leader, the Soviet Union. As in the Soviet Union, urban development was centrally controlled and tied in closely to the country's five-year plans and, of course, with the course of the independence struggle.[25] Thus the plans for the period 1955–59 concentrated on economic rehabilitation, trans-formation and development in Hanoi and North Vietnam alike; while the period 1960–65 saw the start of long-term planning for Hanoi and the first major construction of accommodation, industrial and public building projects.

One of the first major buildings constructed with Soviet Union technical assistance attempted to tackle the problem of training a specialised national workforce for a modernising economy. This was the Hanoi Polytechnical Institute, built on a corner of Cérutti's abandoned *cité universitaire*, its main administrative building facing the newly created Lenin Park.[26] The Polytechnical Institute was to have had five faculties, mainly focusing on the physical sciences, engineering, mining and metallurgy. The complex was designed by a team of Soviet architects from Gyprovuz, headed by E.S. Budnik and P. Kuznetsov, and erected by Vietnamese construction organisations with technical assistance and project management by Soviet specialists. The Soviets also introduced the Vietnamese workers to innovative construction methods and provided equipment and some materials. One of the new techniques was the on-site fabrication of the concrete slabs that were to be used in the buildings, there being no industrial production of building components in Vietnam at the time. The project drew on the experience of designing the Techno-logical Institute in the Burmese capital, Rangoon, the first tertiary educational complex designed by Gyprovuz for humid, tropical climatic conditions. The Polytechnical Institute was officially opened in November

The Polytechnical
Institute located at
Bach Mai, the southern
entrance to the
'New Greater Hanoi'.

1965. Mary McCarthy visited the institute in 1968, later describing it as 'the only important new building' in Hanoi. She noted that it was finished just before the bombing raids on Hanoi began and that classes had hardly begun when they had to be transferred to the country.[27]

During the war against the United States and its allies, particularly the period from 1965 to 1972, while planning for the reconstruction and enlargement of Hanoi went on, the threat of air strikes meant little construction in fact occurred. Much of the labour and materials were diverted into the war effort. Many architectural projects and the planning of new districts started in the late 1960s and early 1970s were not finished until after the withdrawal of American troops and the signing of the Paris Peace Agreement in 1973. The American bombing campaigns had destroyed some 70 per cent of North Vietnam's factories, and large-scale industries needed time to rebuild.[28] A shortage of material goods led to a flourishing black market to fill the gaps in supply and distribution. On the other hand, some redevelopment was more quickly achieved. Handicraft and service activities soon resurfaced. New housing was constructed, although this provoked criticisms almost immediately about the poor standards of control being exercised. Much of the early effort focused on re-establishing the national infrastructure; major roads and bridges were repaired and Hanoi was again linked by rail to Danang in July 1975 and to Saigon by the end of 1976.

With the renewal of urban development activity after 1972, the Soviet influence increased. But, whereas the reconstruction of West German cities occurred with American Marshall Plan aid after World War 2, the socialist Vietnamese authorities at the end of the Vietnam War were deprived of American aid. Hanoi had repeatedly reminded the United States of its obligation under the Paris Agreement to give reconstruction aid to Vietnam, but Washington turned a deaf ear.[29] Instead, America imposed an economic embargo on Vietnam in 1978, cutting off most Western trade and investment, and refused to normalise diplomatic and cultural relations with the country. This made it inevitable that the links continued to develop within the Soviet bloc and that most of the large-scale planning, design and construction works continued to be done with 'brotherly and friendly countries', especially the Soviet Union.

Modernisation, urbanisation and industrialisation proceeded, but with great difficulty. As Bogdan Szajkowski, in his 1981 survey of Marxist governments around the world. said of Vietnam, the post-war period may be 'characterised as transition in a time of crisis'.[30] The Vietnamese approach to development was summarised by Dao Van Tap, Vice-President of Vietnam's Committee for the Social Sciences in 1980.[31] He explained that Vietnam had followed two simultaneous and interrelated policies based on the general strategy of building up the nation's urban infrastructure and urban way of life in order to increase productivity. The first policy consisted of transforming and rebuilding existing towns, while the second involved implanting evenly distributed small-sized towns in the various regions of the national territory. With regard to the reconstruction of existing bomb-damaged cities, such as Hanoi, Dao Van Tap indicated that 'the basic direction taken ... is to increase their productive activities, while gradually eliminating their "consumer town" aspect'.

Among the many factors making the implementation of these policies difficult was the dearth of architects and planners. There were only ten qualified architects working in Hanoi in the early post-independence years; all were elderly, trained by the French in the College of Fine Arts, and quite unable to come to terms with the government's demand for 'socialist architectural projects'.[32] There was, of course, a shortage of professionals and technicians generally in Vietnam after 1954, as a result of the educational policies of the French colonial administration, the interruption of training programs and the battlefield deaths of skilled personnel. Although no doubt serving the Soviet bloc's own political interests, it is nevertheless true that one of the most beneficial elements of Soviet influence in Vietnam was its effort to provide higher educational opportunities for Vietnamese men and women, and not only in the political sphere.[33] Throughout the 1955–90 period, students went in large numbers to be educated in Soviet and Eastern European universities. It is estimated that more than 3,400 Vietnamese research students, 4,800 trainees, 20,700 undergraduates and 2,000 advanced research students were educated in the Soviet Union alone, and from these numbers came 30 per cent of the professors in Hanoi's three largest universities.[34] Russian, Polish, German and Czech replaced French as second languages of North Vietnam's intellectuals. In addition, under the SRV's second five-year plan alone (1976–80), more than 62,000 technicians were trained in the Soviet bloc, including 11,000 in the Soviet Union.[35]

From the mid-1960s, a new generation of professionals and techni-cians began to emerge from the socialist colleges in Vietnam, but their experience was limited and the assistance of foreigner experts remained beneficial.[36] In the case of architecture, although Vietnam produced many of its own graduates, a small and subsequently highly influential group was trained in the Soviet Union, German Democratic Republic, Romania, Czechoslovakia, Poland and Cuba. There they learned 'much in theory as well as in practice' and brought back to Vietnam an architectural language that was in line with the needs of the socialist state.[37] Prikhodko described the work done by the first group of Vietnamese graduates at the Kiev Institute of Architecture.[38] Their final examination projects included typical Soviet-style structures – an air terminal and transport interchange for Hanoi, a Palace of Pioneers for Haiphong, a school complex to accommodate 2,800 pupils for suburban Hanoi, sports halls, swimming pools, and a boarding house for 4,000 physical fitness adherents. Prikhodko made special mention of the way in which the Vietnamese incorporated into their designs such traditional characteristics as the use of the 'flying' roof, the fusion of architecture with the landscape, especially the use of water surfaces, and the creation of microclimates by sensitive landscaping around lakes and streams.

Another main mechanism for the transfer of architectural and town planning knowledge was through the encouragement of Soviet bloc professionals to undertake missions to Vietnam and other Third World communist countries. Indeed, several Soviet architects spent long years in or made many trips to Vietnam. Among the architects, Garold Grigorievich Isakovich (1931–92) was the most influential, responsible for many of the prominent buildings and monuments of the Soviet period.[39] After graduating from the Moscow Architectural Institute in 1956, he was sent to Afghanistan in 1963–65 where he designed residential and service complexes associated with the construction of a highway across the Hindu Kush mountain range. Returning to Moscow, he worked from 1965 to 1970 in the Central Scientific Research and Project Planning Institute of Buildings of Entertainment and Sport under another prominent architect, B.S. Mezentsev. Together they designed a number of memorial structures, including the award-winning Lenin memorial in Ulyanovsk, as well as sporting grandstands and other facilities. Between 1970 and 1975, he made numerous trips to Hanoi in relation to the design and construction of the Ho Chi Minh mausoleum which, again, he designed in conjunction with Mezentsev. Isakovich was awarded the title 'Hero of Labour' in Vietnam in 1976 for this work. In the 1970s and 1980s, he was constantly engaged in designing large public buildings at home and abroad. These included the Palace of Workers' Culture in Vologda, theatres and concert halls in Beltsy, Yakutsk and Kalinin, and a cultural museum in Ufa, as well as the Soviet–Vietnamese Friendship Cultural Palace and the Ho Chi Minh Museum in Hanoi. He also collaborated with many sculptors in designing monuments such as the statue of Lenin in Hanoi. Isakovich died in Moscow in 1992.

Other Russians in Isakovich's team included Vladimir Ivanovich Reviakin, Natalia Dmitrievna Sulimova and Irina Grigorievna Zabolotskaya, while Alexander Alexandrovich Kanyghin, Karo Sergeievich Shekhoian and Sergei Ivanovich Sokolov were involved in other projects around Hanoi and Vietnam.[40] Reviakin visited Vietnam only once (1983), Kanyghin (1981–85, 1987) and Sulimova (1977, 1984) were in Vietnam twice, and Zabolotaskaya visited three times (1984, 1989, 1990). Shekhoian visited several times and worked in Haiphong as well as Hanoi. All

Isakovitch discussing the Soviet–Vietnamese Friendship Cultural Palace design with Nguyen Truc Luyen and other members of the joint Vietnamese–Soviet team. (*Lien Xo* journal, no. 9, 1984)

were graduates of the Moscow Architectural Institute, and the first three worked for the B.S. Mezentsev Central Scientific Research Institute for Standard and Experimental Planning of Sporting and Recreational Buildings in Moscow. In Hanoi, Sulimova worked on the Ho Chi Minh mausoleum and the Cultural Palace, and Reviakin and Zabolotskaya on the Ho Chi Minh Museum. Shekhoian was head of the team designing and constructing the State Palace of Pioneers and the Soviet Trade Delegation complex in Hanoi.

Kanyghin, a graduate of the Moscow Building Institute, was employed by the Soviet foreign trade organisation Technostroiexport (Technical and Building Export). It had supplied Vietnam in 1980 with two apartment-building plants that operated to Soviet technical standards and required the training of Vietnamese in their use, including the making of light concrete. Later a third plant was provided. Kanyghin worked on the new Thang Long Bridge north of Hanoi, eight blocks of flats in the satellite city of Xuan Mai, the Pha Lai thermo-electric power station, and an industrial housing estate for the Hoa Binh hydro-electric power station. He later moved on to Laos where he designed the apartments for the Soviet Embassy and trade delegation. His employing organisation also built five railway bridges, a concrete plant in Binh Son and a factory for manufacturing reinforced concrete railway sleepers.

Few of the Soviet employing bodies and none of the individuals who went to Hanoi had a great deal of previous Asian experience. Techno-stroiexport was the exception and, of course, Isakovich and Kanyghin built up considerable familiarity with Vietnam over the course of their lengthy visits. The Research Institute's previous Asian experience was in Mongolia. Reviakin had worked outside the Soviet Union previously but in Sweden and Denmark, while Kanyghin, Sulimova and Zabolotskaya had never worked outside of the Soviet Union. The only cultural preparation they had had before leaving Russia was private reading of books on Vietnamese history and culture. Only Kanyghin acquired elementary Vietnamese during his lengthy stays. The others had no knowledge of the Vietnamese language and used interpreters. Sulimova lived in the Kim Lien Foreign Experts Guest House, and Reviakin and Zabolotskaya lived at the Cuban-built Thang Loi Hotel on West Lake. They all thought the living conditions worse than in Moscow, particularly the lack of hot water, television and public transport, and some found the climate extremely trying. But they were impressed by both the traditional architecture and the French buildings. All had been pleased to take up the positions offered in Vietnam, thinking the proposed projects professionally interesting. There was an additional financial advantage of working in Vietnam in that much of their salary could be saved because of the low cost of living. Travel costs were met by the employing organisations. On the other hand, service in the Third World apparently won neither a remote allowance nor accelerated promotion.

In general, the projects made use of architectural models established previously in the Soviet Union. The Ho Chi Minh mausoleum was entirely based on Soviet technology, and Kanyghin indicated that all the projects with which he was connected were based on Soviet prototypes. The Hanoi Palace of Pioneers, for instance, was based on (and exceeded in dimensions) the Moscow Palace of Pioneers in the Lenin Hills. The Soviet–Vietnamese Friendship Cultural Palace was a standard project, although it was modified to take into account Hanoi's high water table and seismological conditions, as well as to try to reflect the traditional architectural character of Vietnam. The Vietnamese elements were apparently Isakovich's ideas. Only the Ho Chi Minh Museum seems to have no parallel in Soviet architecture and planning.

The architects, when questioned in the late 1990s, considered the designs appropriate for Vietnam. The buildings were of high quality and still suitable, they thought, although it was the Vietnamese who ultimately chose the designs from the range offered. The Vietnamese Architects' Association was the partner organisation for some of the projects, but Sulimova ventured the view that perhaps the Vietnamese did not always choose the best designs.[41] Several of the Russians gave lectures and consultations on various architectural and planning aspects, reinforcing the training that many of the Vietnamese had already had in Soviet bloc universities. In their professional relationships, the Russians were clearly in charge of the projects; the projects were gifts to Vietnam, and the Vietnamese knew and accepted the consequent relationship.

The most prominent Soviet town planner operating in Hanoi was S.I. Sokolov (b. 1940). He was an architecture graduate of the Leningrad Engineering and Construction Institute, but in Russian educational and professional structures, like the French, there is little formal distinction between urban planning and architecture. He was appointed Chief Architect of Leningrad in 1986 and later became Deputy Director of the Russian Urban Scientific Research and Planning Institute in St Petersburg (formerly Leningrad). He was made an Honoured Architect of the Russian Federation in 1992. Clearly his time in Vietnam did not retard his professional career. In fact, he travelled to Vietnam on ten occasions from 1973, visiting Hanoi, Haiphong, Hue, Ho Chi Minh City and other cities. His work on the Hanoi General Plan, which commenced in 1973, is discussed below. That Sokolov, a well-known young architect who was already the winner of numerous important architectural competitions, was selected to work in Vietnam indicates the seriousness with which the Soviet Union took its role in helping Vietnam to construct a modern urbanised and industrialised society. Vietnam decorated Sokolov with the Order of Friendship for his efforts.

Sometimes the Soviet influence was experienced indirectly, through Indochinese professionals receiving their education in China where Soviet ideas were often given a Chinese and Maoist interpretation. This was more common in the 1960s when the Soviet Union was seen to be undergoing revisionism and the Maoist line seemed purer to many in the Vietnamese regime. As a consequence, those professionals trained in the Soviet Union and Eastern Europe in the 1950s could not get good jobs in Vietnam in the 1960s because they were suspected of holding tainted ideas.[42] However, despite increased numbers of scholars and technocrats going to China for training, many continued to be trained in Soviet bloc countries. With China lapsing into the chaos of the Cultural Revolution, the Soviet influence on Vietnam's political, scientific and cultural life reasserted itself in the 1970s. Leading Hanoi architect Dr Hoang Dao Kinh, who had a Moscow education, felt that Vietnamese architects and planners did not resent the Soviet presence. It was a 'very quiet' influence, rather than overtly neo-colonial.[43]

Secretary-General of the Vietnamese Communist Party, 1991–97 and previously Minister for Construction, Do Muoi makes a point about the Hanoi Master Plan. Immediately to his left is Hanoi Chief Architect Nguyen Lan. (*Nhan Dan* newspaper archives, Hanoi)

Physical impacts on Hanoi's Old Sector

The Politburo's resolution of September 1954 emphasised the rehabilitation of Hanoi and the stabilisation of the population flow from the countryside into it. Hanoi, it proclaimed, 'must have an outstanding appearance' and this was translated into a slogan to guide architects: 'Pragmatism, economy, solidity and an artistic appearance.'[44] The principal icons inspired by such ideological rhetoric are obvious to the visitor to Vietnam and particularly Hanoi.

The most obvious is the statue of Vladimir Ilyitch Lenin opposite the Mirador Tower, west of the city centre. On a small, triangular park created on part of the ancient citadel site, the French had erected a memorial to those who had died fighting for France. But to give public recognition to the fact that the French overlords had gone and that a new ideological persuasion covered the land, the Vietnamese authorities followed socialist countries around the world in raising a statue to Lenin. The design was by Isakovich; the sculptor was A.A. Tyurenkov.[45] While Lenin statues have come tumbling down in most cities in the former Soviet camp, Hanoi's still stands, a testimony to the continuing resistance of the Vietnamese authorities to political change.

Despite Ho's dying wish that his ashes be sprinkled over the country he loved, his successors in the Party wanted a shrine to match Shchusev's mausoleum for Lenin on Moscow's Red Square.[46] Apart from the obvious socialist connection, the mausoleum as a type of funerary monument is well-established in recent East Asian history with, for example Sun Yat Sen's and Chiang Kai Shek's tombs in Nanjing and Taipei, respectively, and the Nguyen dynasty mausolea at Hue. Displaying the embalmed body of the defunct leader is not, however, part of Asian tradition, although

Above Ho Chi Minh's mausoleum on Ba Dinh Square.

Right Hanoi's Lenin statue by A.A. Tyurenkov and G.G. Isakovitch.

Below The State Assembly Building across the Ba Dinh Square parade grounds from the mausoleum.

Chairman Mao lies in state in his mausoleum in Beijing's Tiananmen Square, which was another attempt to emulate Lenin's heroic resting place.

Dang Thai Hoang describes the building of Ho Chi Minh's mausoleum as the 'architectural event that has an important political significance not only to the capital Hanoi but also the whole country'.[47] The mausoleum was placed on a key symbolic site – at the place on Ba Dinh Square where the podium had stood from which Ho had inaugurated independent North Vietnam in 1954.[48] Following the Party's 1969 decision to build a mausoleum, two competitions were conducted and at one stage 300 Vietnamese architects and engineers were working on the design. Assistance was requested from the Soviet Union and an agreement signed which gave the Soviets control over the preliminary design, labour management, organisation of the construction equipment and general direction of the project. The Vietnamese were supposedly relegated to providing most of the raw materials and the manpower. But a battle of will seems to have broken out between the Russian team, headed by architects B.S. Mezentsev and G.G. Isakovich, and the Vietnamese team headed by Vuong Quoc My and Nguyen Ngoc Chan. The Russians assumed they had the expertise and ventured to lecture the Vietnamese on what makes good 'national architecture': 'it must be majestic, symmetrical and solemn'. The Vietnamese appeared to cede to the Russians' superior experience; in fact, they quietly but stubbornly stuck to their own ideas, believing that the monument had to fit the Vietnamese Communist Party's guiding principles – 'Modern, Cultured, Dignified and Simple'. Eventually Chan's original plan seems to have prevailed with minor concessions to keep the Russians happy. The mausoleum was opened to the public in 1975.

Fifteen years later, on 18 May 1990, to mark the 100th anniversary of Ho's birth, the Ho Chi Minh Museum was opened. Designed and built between 1978 and 1990, it was built with technical assistance from Soviet and Czech architects and engineers, again under the direction of Isakovich. The Vietnamese team, led by Nguyen Truc Luyen, General Secretary of the Vietnamese Architects' Association, visited Moscow many times, usually staying for more than a month at a time.[49] The team demanded that the museum adhere to the same requirements of being 'Modern, Cultured, Dignified and Simple'.[50] The second and third criteria required that the architectural concept and design incorporate elements of Vietnamese national building and that it not be a 'stylisation'.[51] Strangely, these requirements were translated into a modern concrete structure representing a highly stylised lotus flower raised on a slender stem. At meetings in Hanoi, the Russian side had to defend their project on various levels and the results of the discussions were regularly reported to Le Duan, Secretary-General of the Vietnamese Communist Party. Many thought that it might be the last gift from the Soviet Union to the SRV.[52]

The Ho Chi Minh
Museum sits
uncomfortably next to
the Mot Cot Pagoda.

Juxtaposition of the
Soviet–Vietnamese
Friendship Cultural
Palace and a small
Sino-Vietnamese
pagoda-like building.

It possibly was, since Soviet economic aid was cut off at the end of that year and the Soviet Union itself disintegrated shortly afterwards.

The Soviet Union had financed the team of architects for the monumental Soviet–Vietnamese Friendship Cultural Palace, again headed by Isakovich.[53] While the architecture of most Soviet-inspired buildings constructed during the period 1955–90 owed little to the local culture, here, as previously noted, some attempt was made to modify the plan to fit Hanoi's climatic conditions. Broad sprawling awnings were added to shield against the sunshine and rains, and the main lobby area is a wide hallway cutting across the building that allows for through ventilation. Melnikov claims that the Soviet architects sought to introduce some local architectural characteristics into the design in order to make it blend in with surrounding structures, a difficult task given the diversity of traditional and colonial styles in the area.[54] Colonnades were constructed along the façades to break up the walls, since long continuous façades are out of character. The traditional sweeping tiled roof is transformed into a broad horizontal cornice of anodised aluminium sheets that top the main building. The roof supports forming the colonnade flair out at the base to emphasise the gracefulness that characterises much Vietnamese traditional architecture. The decorative detailing is restrained and includes some Vietnamese national motifs.

In this respect, the work of the Soviet architects picked up Ernest Hébrard's approach of incorporating elements of the local traditional art and architecture into new buildings. Of course, even if the effort was fairly token, it was nevertheless brave in that it opposed the conventional architectural Soviet thinking that, since socialism was an international movement, its Modern Constructivist style should transcend national boundaries. Any emphasis on local architectural traditions was best kept in check. A.V. Ryabushin shows this attitude to have survived among Russian architects into the 1980s: while they were 'aware of and appreciate the cultural significance of tradition', socialist architects were, however, opposed to 'the extremities of historicism and nationalism in architecture'.

> We are creating [he wrote] the architecture of the new world, the architecture of the future with all its historical documentation and roots. Architecture should form a link between periods of time in order to keep the thread of historic succession going from the national past, through the dynamic present in[to] the created future ... This is what could be called the highly humanistic calling of architecture.[55]

Numerous new administrative buildings in the Soviet version of the International Style were built in the 1970s and 1980s. These are generally marked by uninspired design, poor materials and, worse, disastrous siting decisions, having been unsympathetically constructed alongside, behind or in front of significant buildings of earlier times and architectural styles. This contrasts with the first public buildings — administrative head offices, meeting halls and schools — built by the socialist regime after 1955 in that the earlier buildings continued to follow French architectural principles, tended to be lower in scale, and therefore had less impact on their precincts. The Ministry of Construction headquarters in Le Dai Hanh Street and the head offices of the General Bureau of Forestry, Statistics Bureau and Ministry of Industry are typical of this early transitional period.

Suburban Hanoi: The microrayon as planning tool

The French had given low priority to the new suburbs and outlying villages and their urban functions. By comparison, in the period 1955–90, the suburbs engaged most of Hanoi's construction activity. This matched redevelopment priorities within the Soviet Union where the provision of good-quality housing for all citizens was seen as the most important

The Government Guest
House in Le Thach Street,
wedged between the
classical revival Resident's
Palace and the Post Office.

responsibility architects had to uphold.[56] Indeed, in retrospect, architectural historians rank this as one of the key characteristics of socialist architecture in the Soviet Union.[57] The work of alleviating the Soviet Union's dire housing shortage after World War 2 only started in the latter half of the 1950s. Ryabushin traced progress of the housing construction program.[58] It consisted of providing 'Mass housing, cultural and other amenities for the main fabric of an area ... Small well-appointed flats ... constructed to standard plans using industrial methods on an ever increasing scale'. By the early 1970s, over 95 per cent of Soviet housing and 80 per cent of cultural and other amenities had been built to standard plans. Writing in the mid-1980s, Ryabushin noted that 'There are now ten types of flats with a different number of rooms' and that some variation in outer appearance of apartment blocks had occurred since the late 1970s. Nevertheless his verdict was that

> The policy of standardising and industrialising the construction of dwellings has, in the main, been totally successful and the important task of providing people with comfortable accommodation has actually been accomplished over a very short space of time.

Vietnam followed in the Soviets' footsteps. The new housing provided by the Vietnamese government was almost entirely in medium-rise apartment blocks, minimising the use of land and infrastructure costs. From a distance, these pre-fabricated concrete slab buildings could be in Moscow, Beijing, or even New York or Melbourne; closer up, the poverty of materials and workmanship becomes apparent. At first, progress was slow in Hanoi, and Dang Thai Hoang estimated only 5,000 apartments were built between 1955 and 1960.[59] In the Ancient Quarter, Soviet-style flats were erected in Hang Tre Street. Further out, low-rise housing was constructed between 1955 and 1960 in new estates at An Duong, Phuc Xa, Mai Hong and Dai La. In the next three years, 1961–63, Hanoi succeeded in building 99,700 square metres of accommodation but this satisfied only one-sixth of the demand. Hoang maintained that more would have been provided 'if the U.S. imperialists had not fought a war of destruction in the north'.[60]

In the early 1960s the first new estates were developed at Nguyen Cong Tru, using a combination of traditional hand labour and Hanoi's first mechanical cranes, and at Kim Lien, the city's initial experiment in pre-fabricated residential buildings.[61] The housing was basic in its design and amenities. On the Nguyen Cong Tru estate, which housed 4,200 people, each block was divided in two by a staircase. On either side, four or five families each had a living room measuring 10 to 24 square metres, depending on number of family members, but shared the same kitchen, toilets and bathrooms. The average space allocated per person by the housing authority was, in theory, four square metres; in practice, it deteriorated over time to about half that area.

At Kim Lien, on a 40-hectare site, five pre-fabricated multi-storey blocks were originally erected, increasing to 22 in the final estate. According to Hoang, because the demand for housing was great, generally little attention was paid to the visual appeal of the apartment blocks at this time, and Hanoi had no specialists in this type of architecture. Worse, inadequate attention was paid to issues such as ventilation and natural lighting, the materials used were of inferior quality and the workmanship was poorly monitored. As a result, maintenance problems quickly emerged. At Kim Lien, where much of the housing was intended for staff members of various national and municipal enterprises, the buildings were above average in quality and comprised two rooms, kitchen and bathroom. However, this did not prevent many of the apartments soon becoming shared by two families, with a consequent decline in levels of privacy and cleanliness.[62] Density problems continued to escalate here, and throughout Hanoi, and were not helped by the imposition of the United States-led trade and investment embargo from 1975 to 1994.

Early residential housing estate at Nguyen Cong Tru in the Hai Ba Trung District. The open spaces between apartment blocks have become encumbered with storage sheds and yards.

Pre-fabricated apartment blocks at Kim Lien, close to the Bach Mai Hospital.

S.I. Sokolov's PhD dissertation was on the topic 'The Orientation and Movement of Microrayon Residents'. This concept — the microrayon — was the fundamental basis of new housing provision in the Soviet Union and was also followed in socialist Vietnam. Literally the 'micro-region', the Vietnamese usually translate the term as 'living quarter'. In the West we would normally equate it to 'housing estate', although the notion goes beyond housing to include the full range of services needed by a residential community. In fact, the microrayon as a residential planning concept has Western capitalist origins in the 1920s' neighbourhood planning of the American Clarence Perry, and therefore shares the same pedigree with post-World War 2 public housing estates in the United States, Europe and Australia.[63]

As summarised by the Vietnamese architect Han Tat Ngan in 1994, the Perry model was based on three principles.[64] The first was the provision of shops and other commercial services at the centre of the residential unit, allowing customers to choose commodities according to their likes and needs, and generating competition between suppliers. The second principle was the provision of educational and cultural establishments sufficient for the residential unit and, again, in a central location. Thirdly, the transport network was clearly graded, with main roads on the periphery of the unit carrying all types of vehicles, while the roads within the unit were for light traffic. But Han Tat Ngan emphasised the socialistic gloss that the Soviets had put on the concept:

> The USSR model of residential quarter that has been implemented in both Eastern Europe and Vietnam has some basic contrasts with C. Perry's neighbourhood unit ... stemming [as the Soviet model does] from an economic subsidy system in which commodities are distributed equally among people who have no right to make a choice. They live in a 'pocket' provided with everything necessary for their survival (food, clothes ...).[65]

Using a formula that related accommodation space, facilities and infrastructure to population size, these largely self-contained 'living quarters' attempted to put into practice the notion of equality that was at the heart of socialist ideology. In Vietnam, the formula was based on 60,000 to 70,000 people; that is, the number of residents that an area would require to support a viable senior high school. Once the formula was calculated, the living quarters were replicated about suburban Hanoi.

The Soviet planner's standard attack on urban problems had another prong: the reduction of centre-city concentration through the construction of satellite cities. Again, Vietnamese planners followed suit, constructing several new towns in the late 1960s and early 1970s. Two near Hanoi stand out — Xuan Hoa and Xuan Mai — built by the Ministry of Construction at the time when Do Muoi was minister in charge. These were laid out with geometrical street patterns, broad central axes and abundant open space. The housing was in long, five-storey residential buildings, an expansion on the architectural ideas used in Hanoi's living quarters.

Industrial development was also a high priority for communist Vietnam. Beresford noted that the North Vietnamese government from 1955, and especially after 1961, shared the view with most other socialist governments that industrial self-reliance was desirable.[66] Within five years of liberation, state-run industrial enterprises in engineering, chemicals, building materials

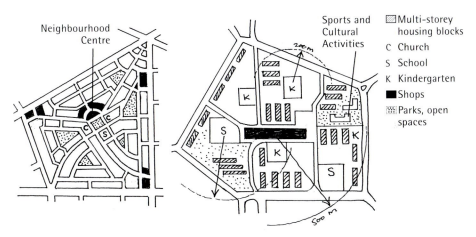

Above Clarence Perry's neighbourhood unit (left) and its Soviet modification. (After Han Tat Ngan, 'The residential quarter reconsidered', *Kien Truc*, no. 2, 1994, pp. 22–23)

Below Shopping centre and apartment blocks in the Xuan Hoa satellite city north-west of Hanoi.

and light industries had been set up, labour and materials harnessed, and a system of factories created in the capital's eastern, southern and western suburbs. In 1957 the opening of the Hanoi Engineering Plant, later renamed the Machine Tool Plant No. 1, at Thuong Dinh in the western suburbs, was regarded as a landmark development, a 'symbol of this historic [industrialisation] effort' and the result of Soviet aid.[67] The machine tool factory was constructed using ferro-concrete and brick on the site of a French officer's mansion destroyed in the fighting of 1946. Dang Thai Hoang described its interior as creating 'an industrial atmosphere, a beauty made by the framework system, conveyor belts and machinery layout. An introspective beauty ... '. This praise of beauty-in-function is almost pure international modernism in spirit, only spoiled by the admission that there were still serious problems in designing buildings suitable for the tropical climate.[68] Also at Thuong Dinh, rubber, soap, tobacco processing and other light industries were established.

The general industrial strategy was wrecked by war after 1965, with much bomb damage and the physical dismantling and decentralisation of factories. Nevertheless, in Thuong Dinh other light industrial activities were added after 1965, such as shoe and clothing manufacturing and car repairs. To the south, industrial zones sprang up at Vinh Tuy, Thanh Tri, Minh Khai and Van Dien, while in the north-west, Thuy Phuong industrial estate was created. Across the Red River in the Gia Lam District, industrial centres were established in the mid-1960s at Cau Duong, Yen Vien and Dong Anh with plywood, match, concrete and other factories built with the help of Czechoslovakia and other Soviet bloc countries. These new industrial areas were constructed, like the new housing estates, with pre-fabricated parts and minimal attention to environmental or aesthetic niceties. They remain today poorly integrated into the urban infrastructure and their pollution impacts negatively on surrounding residential areas.

Two planning schemes

The Soviet influence on Hanoi's townscape went beyond the design of individual buildings and housing estates to the planning of whole districts and cities. Here Soviet planning approaches reinforced in many ways the earlier French colonial experience. Soviet urban planning under Stalin had enjoyed close links with French *urbanisme* with its emphasis on formal design. In their determination to make of Moscow a model socialist city, Soviet planners had drawn inspiration from Haussmann's nineteenth-century approach to urban renewal and development and proceeded to carve out boulevards and avenues, create parks and squares, and contrive urban foci and vistas. The breadth and rapid implementation of such nineteenth-century capitalist ideas in the Soviet Union was, given the ideological rhetoric, quite astonishing.[69] Soviet town planning ideas were also very much the same from Leningrad to Tashkent: the simultaneous development of functional zones; the wide esplanades as the structural

A shopping centre on Nguyen Trai Road. The design and materials act like a heat bank, making conditions breathlessly hot in Hanoi's summer.

Opposite page
Cigarette factory on a Nguyen Trai Road industrial estate towards Ha Dong.

backbones of urban areas; the large residential districts formed in co-ordination with new town centres; and the large-scale geometric designs.[70]

But the Soviet planning approach was very rigid by comparison with the West, largely because of the centralisation of decision-making and allocation of productive forces. Even in the 1980s, although moving from sectoral management of the economy to a more regional and integrated approach, the Soviet Union was still a generation behind the West. Physical planning had assumed a dominant role in Soviet development thinking; that is, the drawing up of comprehensive plans for specific areas of land (regions, urban areas, smaller urban zones and precincts) and basing them in legislation, regulations, policies and procedures. This provides a 'relatively stable form of long term planning and design'.[71] Unfortunately, the world of the Soviet bloc and Vietnam in the last 15 years has been changing too rapidly for such a slow, painstaking approach to work. Once a physical plan is developed and legislated, it is too inflexible to cope with the speed of today's developments.

Between 1955 and 1965 the city planners, helped by Soviet bloc experts, began to study Hanoi's planning problems and needs. One of the first experts appears to have been Professor P. Zaremba from Poland, who paid a working visit to Hanoi in 1960 and presented a 'suggestive plan' that had the city expanding westwards with West Lake becoming the new geographical centre.[72] This may have been incorporated in the rough plan called the 'Zone Plan for Hanoi Construction' that was presented to President Ho and went on public exhibition in 1960.[73] The 'Zone Plan' seems to have led to the first comprehensive master plan for Hanoi, which was completed by the Soviet architect I.A. Antyonov in 1962, in association with Vietnamese architects, some of whom were the first graduates of the Planning Department of the Hanoi Polytechnical University. The government apparently adopted the master plan in 1965. In it, Hanoi was like a paper fan with the colonial city as the centre and five radial growth directions and three main ring roads. It aimed to revitalise the Ancient Quarter as a commercial area but promoted development to the west of West Lake, to the south-west, and to the east in Gia Lam across the Red River. A new city centre would extend from Hoan Kiem around West Lake and incorporate the Ba Dinh area. Detailed planning for the area between the two lakes showed the penchant of the time to develop radiating roads aligned with key buildings to create striking vistas – the Haussmannian model still. A railway network around the river and two bridges to the south of the existing Long Bien Bridge and two to the north were planned.

The plan was not implemented due mainly to the war and aerial blitzes between 1965 and 1972. The planners were temporarily diverted into thinking about new town schemes, notably based on Vinh Yen and

Suoi Hai, that would decentralise the capital city's functions and provide a better strategic pattern for Vietnam in times of foreign aggression. Nevertheless, the 1965 plan created an important model for later plans, notably in seeing expansion of the commercial centre around West Lake.

In 1973 the Soviets were again called upon to lend their expertise, on this occasion in drawing up a new town plan — named the 'Leningrad Plan', since it was undertaken by a team from the Leningrad Institute of Urban Research and Planning, headed by S.I. Sokolov.[74] Although the Leningrad Institute already had considerable experience in the development of city master plans, this was for cities in Siberia and Kazakhstan and the Hanoi master plan represented its first effort in tropical Asia. Hanoi can receive up to 200 millimetres of rain in an hour during the monsoon season; in summer, it is hot (45°C), humid (90 per cent) and extremely uncomfortable; in winter, the temperature falls to 5°C, and it is cloudy and damp. As Sokolov acknowledged in an interview with journalist A. Kucher of the *Leningrad Pravda*, this was

> ... our first experiment in planning large cities in a tropical zone. The difficulties? There were many of them. Firstly, climatic; secondly topographical: the city is built on a practically flat location. The question arose: How should we dispose of the abundant rainfall? ... [and] What about the transport problem?[75]

Kucher described the planning of Hanoi as 'one more symbol of the indestructible Soviet–Vietnamese friendship'. However, even though Vietnamese planners were involved in the process, the project recommendations were fantastic, having been based on an inadequate understanding of Hanoi's history and demography, and totally divorced from both the local culture and the economic realities of an impoverished government. A new city centre was to be built on the southern and south-western banks of the West Lake with radial boulevards, green spaces, high-rise public buildings and pedestrian overpasses. Standard Soviet planning techniques were used, such as the planning of residential communities as microrayons. Five industrial districts were planned, each with its own specialisation. As in the earlier plan, growth was to be channelled to the north-west, west, south-west and across the river to Gia Lam and beyond.

Although the aim was to take the railway lines and most automobile traffic out of the old town, much of the transport plan misfired. A ring railway and a new airport at Noi Bai were planned, but only the latter was constructed.[76] A major highway planned to run from it to the city centre, cutting the historic old sector in two, was fortunately aborted. The population predictions for the year 2000 on which the plan was based were unrealistic, as was the prediction that Hanoi's area would need to expand three times. As a result, the Noi Bai Airport stands in open countryside, an unnecessary 65-kilometre drive from the city centre. The Vietnamese government approved the first stage of the plan in 1976, no doubt in the first heady days of peace and unity; it was finally approved in 1984.[77] The Thang Long Bridge, a massive structure with road and railway traffic on separate levels, was constructed between 1979 and 1985 with Soviet design and financial support. Linking the Tu Liem District in Hanoi's northern suburbs to the Dong Anh District on the Red River's left bank, it speeds the trip to Noi Bai and allows Hanoi to expand northwards. The projected volume of bridge traffic was 6,000 vehicles per day; when first opened, the traffic amounted to only half that figure. This was fortunate, since the highway ended abruptly when it reached Hanoi's inner areas and the traffic had to filter out into the existing network of narrow, crowded streets.

The 'Leningrad Plan'. (After S.I. Sokolov, 'Town on the Red River: In Leningrad a general plan has been formulated for the development of the capital of Vietnam', *Leningradskaya Panorama*, no. 8, August 1983, pp. 26–29)

Opposite page 'Leningrad Plan' sketches of the new central business district. (After S.I. Sokolov, 'Town on the Red River: In Leningrad a general plan has been formulated for the development of the capital of Vietnam', *Leningradskaya Panorama*, no. 8, August 1983, pp. 26–29)

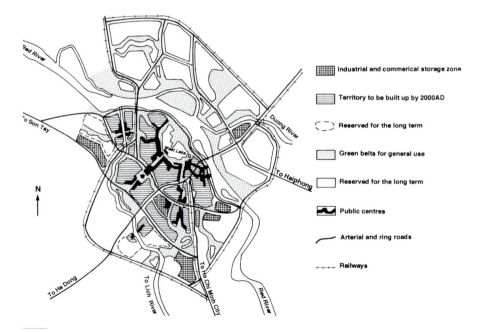

Industrial and commerical storage zone

Territory to be built up by 2000AD

Reserved for the long term

Green belts for general use

Reserved for the long term

Public centres

Arterial and ring roads

Railways

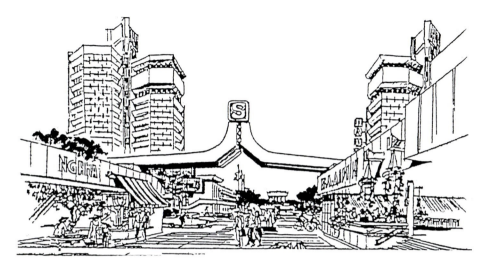

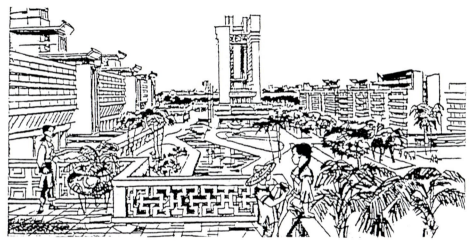

Today, in retrospect, it is clear that the optimism underlying the plan was ill-founded. The Vietnamese government and the Hanoi People's Committee remained concerned with restraining the flow of country folk into Hanoi and wanted the city to grow more slowly and under their tight control. By the 1990s, Vietnam's planners and architects were beginning to completely rethink the basic principles of their town and regional planning efforts.

Ba Dinh Square: The heart of the nation

The Ba Dinh Square precinct demonstrates better than any other part of Hanoi the way in which the built environment is a manifestation of the changing ideologies that underpin successive political regimes. As we have seen, the area was initially part of the Royal Citadel area before being first redesigned by the French in the first decades of the twentieth century and then becoming the focus of Ernest Hébrard's grandiose plans to create a governmental centre for the French Indochinese Union. The area gradually assumed a monumental aspect with the erection of the Governor-General's palace and ministry buildings. The proposed French Indochina Union parliament and Hébrard's plan for broad radiating streets along Haussmannian lines did not come to fruition before Vietnam was engulfed in its so-called wars of liberation. Under Vietnam's socialist regime, the Ba Dinh Quarter was again reshaped to reflect the new political ideology and now houses a new set of streets and squares, street names, official buildings and socialist icons.

Because it was the national capital, the stylistic choices made by government-employed architects and planners in the post-war period were often aimed at impressing with a monumentalism designed to reflect the power of the state and its ideology. The most prominent of these constructions is Ho Chi Minh's mausoleum at the apex of Hébrard's three grand boulevards, the very point at which the French had planned the entrance to the new Governor-General's palace. Other socialist monuments are the parade square, the Ho Chi Minh Museum, the Lenin statue, the State Assembly, the headquarters of the Vietnamese Communist Party and former Soviet bloc embassies. This redesign of Ba Dinh Square was consistent with the socialist principles established in the Soviet Union. Kudriavtsev and Krivov inform us that after World War 2 the design of the square became one of the most prestigious aspects of architectural practice in the Soviet Union.[78] Certainly a central square focusing on a dead heroic leader's mausoleum and acting as a political rallying point had become a standard feature of socialist capital city planning and could be found in Moscow (Red Square), Beijing (Tiananmen Square) and Sofia (Georgi Dmitrov Square).

Changes in the official definition of Hanoi's cultural heritage also reflect

Hébrard's redesign of Ba Dinh Quarter as the new
governmental district, approved by Governor-General
Merlin in 1924. (After E. Hébrard, 'Lurbanisme en
Indochine', *L'Architecture*, vol. 41, no. 2, 1928, pp. 33–48)

Socialist Ba Dinh Square.

1   Ho Chi Minh Mausoleum
2   Central Committee, Communist Party of Vietnam
3   National Assembly and State Council
4   War Memorial
5   State Planning Committee
6   Ministry of Defence
7   Mirador Tower and Army Museum
8   Lenin Statue
9   Chinese Embassy
10 Russian Embassy
11 Ministry of Foreign Affairs
12 Ho Chi Minh Museum
13 State Reception Building (former Governor-General's Palace
14 Ho Chi Minh's House Museum
15 Mot Cot Pagoda
16 Van Mieu
▨ Ba Dinh Square (Parade Ground)

the ideological scene. As outlined in Chapter 5, after 1954 certain buildings and sites associated with the nationalist movement were raised to the status of historic icons. But Vietnam was also socialist, and the official line on architectural merit and heritage significance now followed Party directives. Rather than drawing on indigenous Asian forms, Vietnamese architects in the period 1955–90 followed the models set by the Soviets for the international communist world. Even where some local traits crept into the design, they were deliberately restrained. Thus, 7 Thuyen Quang Street by architects Luyen, Tiep and Duc was hailed by Ngo Huy Quynh as typical of the 'first step in identifying the national style'; 'with fresh touches, it was obviously the result of the revolutionary movement ... [in accordance with] the "Fundamentals of Cultural Revolution"'.[79]

Other townscape changes reflecting the ideological change included the renaming of streets and buildings to honour revolutionary leaders, past and present. 'Street names are not always significant,' wrote David Marr in his study of Vietnamese anti-colonialism.

> Nevertheless, when hundreds of thousands of persons chose to fight and — inevitably — to die in struggle against a colonial ruler, particularly one that has the temerity to name Vietnamese streets after such 'great colonisers', as La Grandier [sic], Paul Bert, and Gallieni, then one may surmise that the renaming of streets upon independence will carry deep symbolic value.[80]

Thus, some names were altered by the non-communist Tran Trong Kim government in 1945, only to be altered again by Ho's regime in the 1950s. Rue Henri Rivière became Pho Ngo Quyen, Boulevard Gambetta became Pho Tran Hung Dao, Boulevard Amiral Courbet became Pho Ly

Thai To. Paul Bert Square became Indira Gandhi Square to acknowledge her pro-Soviet Union leanings, and the Hôtel Métropole became, as we have already seen, the Thong Nhat or Reunification Hotel.

For a while this seemed the way forward. However, by the early 1990s, Vietnam's architects and planners were beginning to question the artistic orthodoxies of the socialist period. This partly flowed from the general unease that had developed through the 1980s about the value of the Soviet–Vietnamese economic and cultural connections. Despite its extent, Soviet aid to Vietnam was now generally seen as inefficient and often directed in ways that did not meet Vietnam's needs. The extremely heavy reliance on distant Soviet bloc markets was also increasingly seen as problematic. By the mid-1980s, Vietnam had amassed debts estimated at US$4 billion to the Soviet Union and Eastern Europe.[81] Growing dissatisfaction was being felt on the Soviet side, too. Under the fourth five-year plan (1986–90), the Soviet Union had agreed to provide US$14.5 billion in aid to Vietnam, with the East Europeans contributing another 20–30 per cent on top of that.[82] But Soviet observers were virtually unanimous in agreeing that the aid had become both ineffective and wasteful and that it should be reduced. The Soviet economy could no longer stand a Vietnamese civil debt of almost 10 million roubles.[83]

Hanoi, the national capital, was in trouble. The Hanoi resident could see all around that the city's environmental patrimony was in a state of decay that, without an injection of large amounts of capital, would probably have been terminal. The poverty was overpowering. When Gabriel Thien Than, a *Viet kieu* (overseas Vietnamese), returned to Hanoi in the early 1980s, he found an 'ascetic capital':

> It is the poverty which hits you as soon as you arrive in Hanoi. In the streets, crowds of thin bodies and emaciated faces perambulated on foot or on bicycles. In this rather sad and old-fashioned town, an impression of being at the end of the world overwhelms you. Foreigners are so few and the humidity in the atmosphere seems to slow everything down.[84]

The once fashionable Rue Paul Bert was now an extremely depressed Trang Tien Street; the private shops and cafés had gone, replaced by the State Department Store – a 'palais de la désolation' according to Claude Palazzoli.[85] Population densities in the Ancient Quarter had become extreme – a mere 1.5 square metres per person – and people were feeling that life was scarcely better now than during the war when at least they had their revolutionary ardour to cheer them. In the streets of Vietnam's major cities Russians had become objects of derision, regarded in Hanoi as 'boorish and clumsily arrogant'[86] or, in Ho Chi Minh City, as Americans without dollars.[87]

By the mid-1980s it was becoming clear to Vietnamese leaders that the centrally controlled economic system was not performing well; indeed, with inflation running at 700 per cent annually, it was on the verge of collapse. Pressures to liberalise the state's economic organisation came to a head at the Sixth Party Congress in Hanoi in 1986 and emerged as the new *doi moi* (renovation) policy. The death of Le Duan in July 1986, followed by the retirement from office of 'old guard' leaders such as Truong Chinh, Pham Dong and Le Duc Tho, and the accession of the reformist Nguyen Van Linh to the Secretary-General position, also hastened the implementation of new economic policies and the questioning of ties with the Soviet Union. The January 1991 decision by the Soviet Union to cut military and economic aid to Vietnam meant that Vietnam would have to pay for Soviet imports in convertible currency and at world prices. In June 1991 the Soviet Union disbanded the CMEA economic bloc whose member states collectively took 80 per cent of Vietnam's imports.[88] Finally, after 35 years, the Soviet Union officially withdrew from Vietnam: the period of Soviet socialist influence on Vietnamese urban development was over.

Godard's Department Store at the corner of Rue Paul Bert and Boulevard Dong Khanh, c. 1910.

By the start of the 1990s, political scientists Ramesh Thakur and Carlyle Thayer were able to assert that 'No influential Asian regards or advocates the Soviet Union as a suitable model for the developing countries of Asia'.[89] The period of Soviet influence on Hanoi's cultural landscape was over. In April 1992, another change in Hanoi's environment marked the even broader and more fundamental transition that began in 1986 and gained pace in the 1990s. The Vietnamese Communist Party agreed to remove the enormous portrait of Ho Chi Minh from the top of the State Bank in central Hanoi where it had stood for two decades. This symbolised for all to see not only the dismantling of the Soviet bloc connection, but a major shift in Vietnam's entire socialist orientation. As Vietnam began to open up to Western thinking (economic, if not yet political), once again old symbols started to give way to the new, and Hanoi's urban environment began to undergo yet another politically driven transformation.

The State Department
Store at the corner
of Pho Trang Tien
and Pho Hang Bai,
1991.

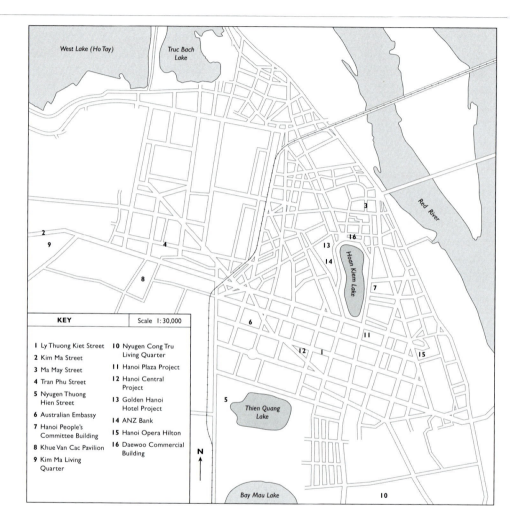

West Lake (Ho Tay)

Truc Bach Lake

Red River

Hoan Kiem Lake

Thien Quang Lake

Bay Mau Lake

KEY	Scale 1:30,000

1 Ly Thuong Kiet Street
2 Kim Ma Street
3 Ma May Street
4 Tran Phu Street
5 Nyugen Thuong Hien Street
6 Australian Embassy
7 Hanoi People's Committee Building
8 Khue Van Cac Pavilion
9 Kim Ma Living Quarter
10 Nyugen Cong Tru Living Quarter
11 Hanoi Plaza Project
12 Hanoi Central Project
13 Golden Hanoi Hotel Project
14 ANZ Bank
15 Hanoi Opera Hilton
16 Daewoo Commercial Building

N

Opposite page
Recycling a French
colonial villa as the
Australian Embassy
office annexe in 1990.

Chapter 7
Doi moi and the return of capitalism: Hanoi in the 1990s

The battle lost?

In 1990, the Australian Embassy consisted of a single building – a colonial villa in Ly Thuong Kiet Street, in the French Quarter near the United Nations Development Program office. The Vietnamese government had allocated the building at the expense of the 60 or so former residents who were summarily displaced. In very poor repair, the villa was restored by David Abotomey, an Australian builder-conservationist, in order to provide offices downstairs and an elegant residence upstairs for the Ambassador. During the early 1990s, the building could not cope with the demands generated by the rapidly increasing trade, business and cultural

relations between Australia and Vietnam,[1] and so the villa to the left was obtained for an office annexe and the villa to the right for a larger ambassadorial residence. This led to more population displacement. An apartment block for embassy staff was erected in the rear courtyard. By the mid-1990s the complex was again found to be inadequate and the Australian government negotiated to obtain part of the land formerly allocated to the Russians in the western suburbs at Van Phuc, past the new embassy area developing behind Kim Ma Street. In April 1997 a new embassy compound designed by Australian Construction Services and constructed by Leighton Holdings was opened. The original embassy buildings in Ly Thuong Kiet Street have been kept as downtown offices.

This story encapsulates Vietnam's changing international relations during the post-*doi moi* period, notably the dismantling of the Soviet connection, and the new courting of Western and other sources of capital. Indeed, during the early and mid-1990s, Western Prime Ministers and senior ministers flowed through Hanoi on an almost weekly basis, hoping to open the way for trade links and investment opportunities. By contrast, the first official visit by a Russian Prime Minister did not eventuate until Victor Chernomyrdin's tour in November 1997, seven years after the Soviet Union officially pulled out of Vietnam. But the Australian Embassy story also shows a move towards Western capitalist ideas about development, planning, architectural and heritage conservation – ideas such as the adaptive re-use of historic buildings, the upward reappraisal of the French colonial impact on Hanoi's built environment, the privatisation of architectural activities, and governmental withdrawal from public housing provision.

At the time of the Sixth Party Congress in 1986 and the introduction of the *doi moi* policies, Vietnam was gripped by severe economic malaise. This stagnation had effectively eliminated the redevelopment pressures experienced in the West since 1945 and more recently in other Asian cities, so that Hanoi's Old Sector remained largely intact. The survival of Hanoi's built heritage is perhaps, therefore, one of the very few benefits to come out of a disastrous half-century of economic depression, wars, crushing poverty, lack of foreign investment and rigid, centralised government. On the other hand, these factors had created another threat to the historic fabric, the threat of physical deterioration due to a lack of building maintenance. Problems of physical decay, such as leaking roofs, unstable masonry, rotting timberwork, damaged spouting and downpipes, and rising damp, needed (indeed, still need) to be addressed urgently throughout the Old Sector, as do the inadequacy of bathroom, toilet and kitchen facilities, water supply and other infrastructure elements. These problems could, of course, be overcome and the buildings reinstated by conservation work but this would require significant expenditure of funds.

The Vietnamese Architects' Association estimated in 1991 that over 100,000 people were living in temporary shelters.[2] The narrow tube houses, originally designed for a single extended family, now held four or five families; French villas accommodated up to 120 people each. As we have seen, public housing along modified Soviet architectural lines made some attempt to provide accommodation but was of poor standard and quickly became dilapidated; these apartment blocks also now accommodate far more residents than was originally intended. But, also in the early 1990s, a shortage of housing and hotel accommodation for visiting businessmen and tourists emerged, as well as of good-quality office space. This pushed up property rentals and increased pressures to redevelop historic central areas. By 1995, rentals had soared to the levels of Paris, London, Singapore and New York − approaching US$600 per square metre per annum.[3] In such a context, it was difficult to resist the pro-development argument, and the Vietnamese and Hanoi authorities seemed to accept the claim that the city needed many more high-rise buildings in order to bring land and rental prices down.[4]

Following the introduction of a new housing policy in 1985 that came into effect in 1989, the government largely withdrew from the provision of public housing in favour of the construction and renovation of apartment buildings and houses by the private market.[5] This policy shift also allowed the sale of public housing. The authorities began to sell off the apartments in the Soviet-period housing estates and to concentrate on satisfying the foreign investment and rental demand. But another result of this dramatic policy change − one that impacted particularly on the built fabric of the Ancient Quarter − was a private construction boom. The Hanoi planning authorities were caught off guard and Hanoi began to experience redevelopment by both foreign and local investors without having in place any effective system of control.[6]

With the Vietnamese government allocating properties to Western ambassadorial and commercial organisations, the impact on inner Hanoi residents grew. Those displaced were relocated in the suburbs, their established networks severed and their access to employment often reduced. The *Vietnam Investment Review* reported in 1993 that the Hanoi authorities were planning to evict 1,000 Vietnamese families from 150 French colonial villas that it owned in central Hanoi in order to put the properties on the rental market.[7] Included among those to be displaced were former officials and military heroes who had been given accommodation as a reward for services rendered to the country. Another 2,000 families were also to be relocated later to make way for modern apartment buildings for foreigners. More recently, in June 1998, another decision was taken to sell 398 state-owned villas to private individuals.[8] Again, these were villas that had been confiscated by the revolutionary government when it came to power in 1954.

To those Vietnamese who had fought under the socialist banner, this totally new type of thinking was indeed shocking, seeming to negate everything that the struggle of the previous half-century had been about. Several prominent intellectuals were prepared to speak out. This led Professor Dang Thai Hoang, writing in the Hanoi newspaper *Nhan Dan* in 1994, to caution against

> ... foreigners coming to our country [who] have only the goal of seeking out and obtaining profitable interests. What will become of the stability of our living environment? Even a number of foreign culture experts and architects of good will are very concerned about our circumstances. Is sitting back and waiting for the outcomes of foreign-influenced urban planning and construction and the aftermaths of land dealing a way to improve the urban image of Hanoi? We need to assess the issue in a less optimistic way.[9]

These developers were profit-oriented, of course, and so seeking to construct buildings in harmony with the Vietnamese cultural heritage was of very secondary, if any, importance.

Other Vietnamese as well as Western commentators noted the irony that, what the bombs could not achieve, capitalist economics seemed to be doing with impunity – indeed, with the active backing of the socialist state. It seemed that Vietnamese society would be defeated and the traditional built environments destroyed after all. Hanoi historian Nguyen Vinh Phuc, whose opinion carried weight with the Hanoi People's Committee, raised the warning:

> The time-honoured capital Hanoi is again besieged. Over its history of more than one thousand years, it has survived many foreign invasions including the American B52 air raids twenty years ago. Nowadays it has to confront a new peril: the dollar invasion of foreign investors who want to devour the estates of Hanoi piece by piece.[10]

In short, 1986 represented another discontinuity in Vietnamese history, another sharp change in direction in many ways no less dramatic than 1883 when the French arrived. Although almost a century apart, these two years saw Vietnam being brought into the Western global system – in 1883 through incorporation within France's global colonial empire, and in 1986 into an economic world dominated by the United States and Japan and integrated by means of new information technologies. Initially, the establishment of direct economic relations with the United States was held back by the trade and investment embargo and the pariah status Vietnam acquired in the 1980s as a result of its invasion of Cambodia. But several Western nations, such as Sweden and Finland, had rejected the embargo and continued to inject aid into the country. In Hanoi, this took the form of funding and technical assistance for hospitals, schools and water supply infrastructure. In time this led to a shift in balance away from socialist bloc aid to Western aid. By the mid-1980s, Australia, France and Britain had resumed bi-lateral humanitarian aid and, by the early 1990s, development aid. Although officially continuing to back the embargo, Japan was clearly developing business interests as well as providing aid in the form of technical assistance. Eventually, in February 1994, the United States abandoned the embargo.[11] This cleared the way for American investment and a radical restructuring of the Vietnamese economy in the context of a mixture of private and public forces.

In terms of the built environment and cultural heritage of Vietnam's cities, the economic liberalisation ushered in by *doi moi* was a mixed blessing. On the one hand, it attracted investment in property maintenance and introduced approaches to building and area conservation that were more in line with practices in the West. But, on the other hand, the massive redevelopment pressure it generated threatened many heritage sites, buildings and monuments. In Hanoi, the agents of redevelopment were investors and developers, both foreign and local. Foreign investment had the French Quarter as its main target, because the colonial villas were adaptable to commercial needs and the building blocks there were larger and better suited to redevelopment than those elsewhere. The impact of local investment was most pronounced in the Ancient Quarter.

Changing ideology, changing heritage

This transition in state ideology, the severing of the relationship with Russia (formerly the Soviet Union), the growing links with the West, and the dimming of revolutionary memories and fervour were combining to produce yet another major shift in the way the urban heritage was conceived in Hanoi. In particular, the relative significance of the revolutionary and Soviet heritage was being downgraded, while the growth of international tourism to Vietnam gave a new economic value to certain cultural heritage features of interest to the main foreign tourist groups. In addition, foreign investment was making possible the construction of modern high-rise commercial buildings, while the emergence of a middle class in Vietnam with resources to invest in new buildings was leading to the development of a new and distinctive local style (ironically called 'European style') in architecture. We were starting to witness the creation of Hanoi's future urban heritage – a new cultural layer that, like those that went before it, reflected the ideological conditions that had made its creation possible.

With the perceived failure of Soviet socialism and the collapse of international communism, there was a wholesale rejection of the town planning and architecture of the period by Hanoi's politicians, planners and the public. The impact of the shift on Hanoi's architecture, town planning and heritage definition in the late 1980s and 1990s can be tracked through the pages of the Vietnamese Architects' Association journal, *Kien Truc.* Conversations with Hanoi planners and architects reinforce the general picture of the 1986 *doi moi* liberalisation leading to the socialist design dogmas being challenged, the earlier architectural and planning efforts of the French being reappraised, and contemporary Western approaches being adopted (and adapted). The general feeling seemed to be that Soviet-style buildings and precincts should be replaced. To some extent there was an intergenerational element in this process of rejection in which new groups of professionals were seeking to gain jobs by ousting the incumbents on the grounds of changing design paradigms. There was also an attraction to the postmodern architectural ideas that were by then flowing more freely into Vietnam. But neither of these factors would have come into play without the basic ideological shift in governmental thinking.

At first, the criticisms of Soviet-period practice were carefully couched within the Marxist–Leninist intellectual framework.[12] But by the early 1990s, leading architects gradually became more outspoken. Dang Thai Hoang regretted, for instance, that some of the ugliest buildings were erected during the socialist period in the most beautiful sections of Hanoi.[13] He singled out for particular criticism the Hanoi People's Committee Building (Town Hall) designed by Nguyen Tien Thuan:

> Usually a mayor's office should represent the beauty of a city, but this building lacks the national identity and must be ranked at the bottom of the ladder compared with Chua Mot Cot and Van Mieu. We feel like strangers in front of its big cubic blocks.

And, says Hoang, the interior was even worse.

Here the municipal authorities in the 1980s had attempted to define, for the people, which elements of the existing urban environment were to be regarded as symbolically significant and treasured as part of the city's 'heritage'. In line with the general disdain felt by the socialist authorities at the national level for the French colonial quarters, their villas and boulevards, the Hanoi People's Committee knocked down the former Louis XVth-style town hall. They replaced it with the modern block that towers today over Hoan Kiem Lake, clashing with the surrounding French colonial buildings. The building is now sometimes referred to as 'the guillotine' because the design of the unfriendly entrance looks like a guillotine blade about to fall — a loop back to those very colonial days whose memory the People's Committee was trying to destroy.

The Hanoi People's
Committee Building
towers above the
tree-line beside
Hoan Kiem Lake.

Other civic buildings that have been referred to as 'Stalinist monstrosities' are the Soviet–Vietnamese Friendship Cultural Palace and the Ho Chi Minh Museum. General Secretary of the Vietnamese Architects' Association, Nguyen Truc Luyen, was harsh in his revaluation of the larger reinforced concrete structures of the 1980s.[14] He particularly attacked the Ho Chi Minh Museum for its 'heavy feel' and lack of refinement. While a few professionals could still be found who continued to espouse the use of architectural and planning policies based on 'sound socialist principles',[15] most architects and planners were adopting a more flexible, professional outlook. They were now prepared to strike a balance between Western and indigenous architectural forms in order to develop a distinctive Vietnamese style, to achieve first-class architecture in harmonious townscapes and to protect heritage precincts.[16]

The *Kien Truc* editorial writers also expressed concern about how Hanoi's ancient lakes, such as the Van Chuong opposite the Van Mieu Pagoda, were being eaten up by the encircling houses and polluted by household wastes. Another main target of rebuke was the glass curtain-wall office buildings – part of the 1970s' and 1980s' array of architectural techniques – appearing in precincts characterised by traditional and colonial buildings.

Criticism mounted, too, against the town planning that had occurred during the Soviet period. The Director of the National Institute of Urban and Rural Planning (NIURP) in the early 1990s, Nguyen Ngoc Khoi, and the Hanoi People's Committee Chief Architect since 1993,[17] Nguyen Lan,

A 1990s' attempt to pastiche the iconic Khue Van Cac Pavilion. The materials and strong horizontal lines of its glass curtain-wall fail to respect the Ancient Quarter's design character.

both wrote critically of the Soviet master plan and the methods used to develop it. It was too spread out, and involved too much demolition and too much high-rise construction. Furthermore, it only envisaged the use of government funds in the urban development process, rather than those of the citizens themselves or of foreign investors.[18] Pham Han went further, using the term 'rural urbanisation' to describe the results of planning in Hanoi since 1954: new residential zones compartmentalised into separate housing estates which look in on themselves like rural villages rather than opening out to be part of the greater Hanoi.[19] *Kien Truc* editorials supported his damnation of declining building and infrastructure standards, crumbling pre-fabricated apartment blocks and rusting above-ground sewerage pipes.[20]

Once regarded proudly as one of the great socialistic planning concepts, the microrayon also came in for a battering. It had even been thought that these new housing 'micro-regions' in Hanoi could serve as a model for similar workers' housing developments in industrial Nam Dinh and other cities.[21] And, indeed, these new areas were an important component of the concerted effort under the socialist national and municipal governments to provide shelter and jobs for the majority of Vietnamese. However, Western observers were aghast at the living conditions and state of dereliction of these housing estates. Claude Palazzoli, who visited Hanoi for the first time in 1971, was one of these, describing his shocked reaction in his book *Le Viet Nam entre deux mythes*:

> The tired spectacle of the public housing estates lined up in Beijing or Moscow style gave an idea of what the new Hanoi could become and the housing blocks already built around its perimeter, intended for workers, officials, even foreign experts or diplomats, provided a disquieting foretaste of it. Moreover, no-one would risk predicting a life of more than a few years for the horrible and leprous buildings concerned, which, rising here and there out of the mud, had the praiseworthy goal of providing decent housing for the people but had been built with a total misunderstanding of the most elementary laws of architectonics and town planning.[22]

In the late 1980s, local architects had begun to join in this criticism, but, rather than rejecting the concept totally, contributors to *Kien Truc* initially tried to put a case for adjusting the microrayon model to make it more 'creative and flexible'. Unless this was done, they nevertheless conceded, the model should be abandoned altogether in favour of 'the model in which houses are built contiguously along the roadsides'. In other words, such critics were returning to the traditional model of urban settlement that, for all its dilapidation, poor sanitation and lack of open space, was still so evidently attractive to residents in the old streets of Hanoi.[23]

Tired Soviet-period walk-up flats in the Kim Ma living quarter, 1991.

Soviet-style apartment blocks now stand empty and derelict in the Xuan Hoa satellite town north-west of Hanoi, 1995.

Further out, the ambitious satellite experiments at Xuan Mai and Xuan Hoa were an even greater failure. Budgetary problems had meant that the infrastructure plans were never fully realised and the people selected to live there felt abandoned in their sterile dormitories and cut off from the bustling life they had known previously. By the mid-1990s, Xuan Mai had become empty and was being demolished; Xuan Hoa was still occupied. The Prime Minister of the day, Vo Van Kiet, published a plan to turn Xuan Hoa into a university town, making the most of its attractive hilly terrain close to Dai Lai Lake. This appears to have met with sufficient resistance from the Hanoi educational institutions involved and the town had been partly vacated. By contrast, surrounding the new town was a linear private enterprise village whose houses and shops were flourishing. A similar plan was put forward for Xuan Mai, with an outdoor architectural park displaying typical houses of Vietnam's ethnic minorities alongside a National University campus.

Similarly, many of the industrial buildings proved to be inappropriately designed for Hanoi's climatic conditions. A Russian guest at the celebration to mark the 'triumphal commissioning' of the Machine Tool Plant No. 1 thought that 'The equipment, ventilation in the workshops and, finally, the delighted smiles of the workers in their dark blue overalls spoke for themselves'.[24] It was 'a joyous occasion for the Hanoiese', this being the first machine building factory in the country. But the design faults soon began to appear.[25] The roof design impeded the dispersal of heat from the manufacturing process, and the ferro-concrete construction materials acted like a heat bank, retaining heat for long periods and making the workers in the factory suffer. The plant's impact on the surrounding environment was equally problematic, with waste from the plant polluting the atmosphere and blowing across nearby residential areas. Inadequate attention had been given to providing vegetation buffers around this, and other, factories.

While this reappraisal of Hanoi's Soviet-period architecture and planning was going on, the earlier planning efforts by the French were experiencing improved popularity. By the mid-1990s, Nguyen Ba Dang, Director of the Ministry of Construction's Architectural Research Institute, had recognised the experimental nature of French colonial planning, describing it as marking the start of modern Hanoi.[26] He noted, too, that the urban environment in the French colonial quarters was in better condition than that of other parts of the city. 'In general, the colonial Quarter of Hanoi is a precious architectural composition,' he concluded, 'and it's worthwhile to explore possible solutions to preserve it.' International tourism to Vietnam, with the largest national group in the 1990s being the French,[27] reinforced the interest in the colonial buildings and quarters, adding an economic rationale for their protection.

Discover the culture and beauty of Vietnam from just $1,199.

With Viva! Holidays you can now explore the French colonial architecture and natural beauty of Vietnam. Your package includes return economy airfares, transfers and 7 nights accommodation at the International Hotel, plus a Viva! travel bag and ticket wallet. Conditions do apply and you have to depart by August 30, 1995. For bookings and information, contact your nearest licensed or AFTA travel agent, Qantas Travel Centre or call Qantas in Melbourne on 805 0124 or 008 813 996.

QANTAS
THE AUSTRALIAN AIRLINE

QXH 2785/MEL Lic No. 2TA 003 005. *Price is based on per person share twin from Sydney, Melbourne, Brisbane & Adelaide. Valid for outbound travel to 30 August, 1995, except for 28 June, 1995 ($1,299). Price is subject to change without notice.

With the country opening up to international tourism from 1990, Hanoitourism and other Vietnamese government-owned tourism companies favoured group tours by relatively affluent Westerners, rather than individual and economy travellers such as backpackers.[28] It was believed that the affluent tourist groups expected to find Western-style hotels and tourism services. A consequence has been the provision of bland hotels largely lacking in Vietnamese distinctiveness. Even in the new Hoa Lo Museum, a focus on cleanliness, which is seen as meeting Western requirements, has led to greater falsification of the historical environment than necessary. It would have been better to focus on

The Bong Sen Hotel, formerly the Kim Lien Foreign Experts Guest House.

adopting the best international practice in museum interpretation. However, the growth of tourism provided new uses for some historic buildings that had been struggling to maintain viability. The Bong Sen Hotel is a case in point. It was previously the Kim Lien Foreign Experts Guest House, where the Russian architect Natalia Dmitrievna Sulimova lived when she was working in Hanoi. Again, such recycling – or adaptive re-use – falsifies the historical evidence, but this is better than losing the buildings altogether.

In contrast to the many characterless modern hotels constructed in the 1990s, the development of modern housing was strong on local style. Where residents of Hanoi's Ancient Quarter or surrounding suburbs had acquired some capital and had eagerly replaced or modernised their dilapidated houses, the impact tended to reinforce the localisation rather than globalisation of architectural design. Although referred to as the 'European Style', in fact every architectural influence known in Vietnam was being combined in true postmodern spirit to create fanciful façades and frivolous roof-lines that served little purpose except to signal the economic status of the owners. Some Vietnamese architects refused to accept responsibility for this fashion. One young Hanoi architect, Nguyen Hoang Viet, in fact saw it as a case of the architects being overruled by

New middle-class house in 'European Style' on the main Red River dyke at Yen Phu.

Attractive entrance and green spaces at the Nguyen Cong Tru living quarter.

owners whose 'lack of basic knowledge and understanding of culture in general and architecture in particular ... leads them to ridiculous decisions'.[29] But this is too harsh a judgment. The style is certainly distinctive, and, like other Hanoi styles before it, is a product of its historical and geographical context – in this case, an exuberant reaction to the preceding 40 years of austerity.

To reject all architecture and planning associated with the Soviet period would also be too harsh. The Soviet impact on Vietnamese cities stands as a manifestation on the ground of an important stage in the country's movement towards postcolonial independence and post-war rehabilitation. Some monuments, buildings and precincts also have heritage value as excellent examples of the various architectural and planning styles of the time. The Soviet–Vietnamese Friendship Cultural Palace is one such building of major heritage significance. But many other lesser buildings have a continuing usefulness, especially given the shortage of funds for new building construction and less obvious heritage value. For example, the Nguyen Cong Tru living quarter taken as a whole has heritage significance as one of the first and better attempts to create a new urban environment according to socialist principles. While most 1960s' apartment blocks, or 'tiger cages' as they are nicknamed, are unpleasant to live in, being unbearably hot in summer and cold in winter, and are in very poor physical condition, Nguyen Cong Tru is of superior quality.[30] Something of the original vision is reflected in the generous open spaces, tree planting and architectural details of doorways. On the other hand, the walk-up flats have deteriorated badly, with some indiscriminate practice of adding new rooms and sheds, detracting from the visual appearance.

An inclusive approach to heritage definition recognises the importance of all the cultural layers that make up the urban landscape. The story of Hanoi's evolution is reflected in the bipolarity of the feudal city, the oppression represented in the colonial imposed city, the destruction of World War 2 and the two wars of independence, the attempt to achieve a socialist vision and, now, the changes flowing from *doi moi*. Just as Hanoi's politicians, planners and public are now able to embrace the French colonial as part of their heritage, so, too, they will come in time to reinstate the best of the Soviet period. The key lies in the notion of inclusiveness – a notion that is currently gaining attention internationally, as evidenced by the establishment of an ICOMOS International Scientific Committee in 1999 to focus on 'the shared heritage'.

However, 'heritage value' is not generally attributed in such a rational and even-handed manner. It is the symbolic meaning given to buildings, monuments and sites that effectively defines their urban heritage value, and symbolic value depends on subjective, emotive and often plainly ideological considerations. It depends, too, on the highly complex process of societal 'remembering' — a process characterised by instability of memory (fading with temporal distance from the circumstance being remembered) as well as of meaning (shifting with the evolving value systems of the society and individuals within it). In postcolonial Hanoi, memories of past events and environments are imperfect, being selective and fraught with misconceptions and prejudices.

It is common for positive values to be deliberately given to places in order to elevate certain memories for ideological ends. That is, they serve the needs of the prevailing political and social elite. This is Roland Robertson's 'wilful nostalgia' referred to in Chapter 1. But increasingly, histories are being reinvented to serve the commercial needs of the tourism industry. In Vietnam, international tourism has become a major agency of cultural globalisation, placing a 'heritage value' — really an economic value — on certain memories relating particularly to the pre-colonial and colonial past and leading to the same sort of heritage packaging that the tourism industry creates everywhere in the world. This, of course, has a positive side: it means that the tourism industry starts to put pressure on the authorities to resist tearing down heritage build-ings and monuments on sites that might be redeveloped. Moreover, government funds begin to flow more generously into the maintenance and restoration of heritage attractions. In 1998, for instance, with an eye to propping up the faltering numbers of international tourists, the Hanoi People's Committee dedicated around US$1 million to restoration works on the Hoa Lo Prison, the Van Pond at the Van Mieu, the Dong Thay mound, the ancient citadel of Hanoi and the former capital at Co Loa.[31] The Vietnam Oil and Gas Corporation, a state-owned enterprise, decided in 1999 to invest US$1.4 million in a project to restore over the next two years the Quoc Tu Giam (National School), an ancient Confucian lecture hall in the Van Mieu complex.[32] This is believed to be a first sponsorship of a major restoration project by a Vietnamese company.

So it is that both forms of distortion, ideological and economic, are generating a significant landscape impact — a thoroughly contemporary impact that selects certain environmental features for respect and preservation and casts others aside for neglect and demolition. In the case of the Soviet places, it is the latter, negative process that is operative: any positive values are in danger of being swept away and the buildings, monuments and sites from the Soviet period are threatened. Perhaps it is simply too soon for Vietnamese to see the merits of protecting selected Soviet places. It is, after all, less than a decade since the official view of the built heritage of Vietnamese cities excluded the French colonial impacts. However, according to Hoang Dao Kinh, the Soviet period in Hanoi is not yet distant enough for Vietnamese architects and planners to view it objectively.[33] The recent past always suffers from this problem. It is too close to view dispassionately, and the monuments, buildings and sites from that period are commonly ascribed minimal heritage value, being written off simply as old-fashioned or representing ideological values that are themselves in the process of being rejected.

Whose sense of place? Who decides?

Intense contestation occurred in the 1990s about what precisely constituted Hanoi's significant cultural heritage and the extent that it should be protected from change. That such contestation occurred – and increasingly in the public domain – was an inevitable and desirable consequence of *doi moi*, the opening up of Hanoi to foreign investment, the growing local accumulation of wealth and building redevelopment, and the fragmentation of society into groups with different interests and needs. We have seen how those who accepted that Hanoi has a heritage worth protecting were modifying their definition of the components of that heritage. But there were also now key actors – both in government and among foreign and local investors – who denied the need to save any heritage features at all in their pursuit of modern development. For conservationists there was, then, a challenge to convince these actors that Hanoi's heritage was so significant that it demanded special protection. For Hanoi's urban managers – the Hanoi People's Committee, its Chief Architect's Office and other agencies – the task was to find new ways to handle these divergent opinions within the context of planning and development policy-making and implementation procedures. How much should be protected? How could an effective heritage protection and modern development be achieved in a balanced manner that satisfied all parties?

Many developers saw conservation and conservationists as major obstacles to Hanoi's modern development. The Australian architect Peter Purcell, for instance, argued in 1994 that 'They have brought a lot of development to a grinding halt. It's not what Hanoi needs'; 'They want to turn the city into an architectural zoo, for whose pleasure I am not sure. Certainly not the Vietnamese.'[34] Purcell was at the time involved in the troubled 24-storey twin-tower Hanoi Plaza project on the Government Department Store site, one of the most sensitive locations on the south-eastern corner of Hoan Kiem Lake. Originally a Hong Kong joint venture project, it had gone through another two foreign joint venture partners before John Holland, a Thailand-based company, signed on to complete the project. After the intervention of the former Prime Minister, Vo Van Kiet, the architects were required to keep the historic façade and to set the towers back on a podium that matched the height of neighbouring buildings. However, the façade was later totally demolished on public safety grounds and the site remains vacant.[35]

This was one of a handful of high-rise hotel and office projects by Hong Kong, Singaporean, Australian and other foreign investors that stand out for their dramatic effects on key heritage buildings and sites around Hoan Kiem and in the French Quarter. The 24-storey twin-tower hotel, conference centre and office project, built by a Vietnamese– Singaporean joint venture company on the site of the Hoa Lo Prison, has already been mentioned. One of the most intrusive projects has been the Golden Hanoi Hotel, again on the banks of Hoan Kiem where it will impinge upon key vistas of the lake, its two islands, the 1843 Ngoc Son Temple and nearby floating restaurant. Originally designed to be 11 storeys high in an area where technically a five-storey height limit prevails, the project remains incomplete.

Here the conservationists have indeed been instrumental in delaying construction and forcing the project to be redesigned. The Goldino–Haneco joint venture between Hong Kong-based developers and Vietnamese counterparts commenced construction in 1996 despite warnings from local and foreign planners at the proposal stage that the building would have a serious visual impact on the lake and cut it off from the adjacent neighbourhoods.[36] But when construction reached the third storey, a general outcry broke out. According to the monthly magazine *Xua vang Nay* (*Past and Present*), more than 100 newspaper, television and radio items on the issue appeared in 1996, making it one of the ten most controversial stories of the year. It would appear that the developers exceeded the construction permit issued by the Hanoi People's Committee and that the permit itself did not conform to the five-storey official height and the density regulations for the Hoan Kiem Precinct. After protests in the media, the People's Committee eventually demanded a halt to construction. The developers responded that they would claim US$30 million in compensation if the building did not proceed. This stand-off appears to have drawn the direct intervention of Prime Minister Vo Van Kiet who, visiting the Vietnamese Architects' Association, agreed that 'if the issue is affirmed absolutely correct, then it is a very serious offence'.[37]

Official protests by a number of professional associations – notably the Vietnamese Architects' Association and the Vietnamese Association of Historical Science – captured the public outrage and challenged the legitimacy of actions by both Hanoi planning authorities and the foreign developers. One of the principal complaints of the protesters was that the developers had taken 'our people's cultural standard lightly ... Indeed, "the more conceding we are, the more forward the foreign bosses are". It is because they are concerned with the end of sheer profit only, disregarding the sentiment and cultural traditions of our capital, disrespecting the Vietnamese public opinion and law.' The Prime Minister eventually halted the building works and insisted on the renegotiation of the Hong Kong developers' building permit.

The Golden Hanoi Hotel
site on the north-west
bank of Hoan Kiem Lake
in 1992.

Although falling short of an organised popular protest movement, the representations made by the professional associations appear to have achieved a major victory, showing that informed public opinion, even in a communist state such as Vietnam, could successfully force top-level intervention to protect the local heritage. This was a foretaste of what could be expected in Hanoi as *doi moi* encouraged the development of an affluent middle class that was no longer prepared to remain quiet when it disapproved of official planning blunders or the destruction of key elements of the city's historical environment by private companies. Almost concurrently, in May 1996, in the village of Kim No on the outskirts of Hanoi, another general outcry about planning decisions erupted into a series of angry demonstrations. In this case, the issue was the approval given to the South Korean Daewoo conglomerate to turn paddy fields into a 128-hectare luxury golf course for foreigners. These events marked an important political change – the start of serious community involvement in setting direction of change in the city and another step towards the emergence of civil society in Vietnam.

By contrast, some private investment in property maintenance and new development in Hanoi proceeded more sensitively, attempting to find new uses for old structures, to blend new building fabric with old, and to restore historic façades and interiors. The various embassies in the Ba Dinh and

French Quarter provide excellent role models in this respect. Among commercial enterprises, the ANZ Bank's adaptive re-use effort made a positive contribution to maintaining the historic buildings around Hoan Kiem Lake. New developments along Trang Tien Street were required to respect the general streetscape by maintaining a podium and setting back high-rise towers. And at the end of Trang Tien Street, the Hanoi Opera Hilton was a major example of a serious effort being made to fit a new architectural project into its heritage context. On a site previously used as a petrol station next to the restored Opera House, French architects Eric de Chambure and Philippe Pascal deliberately set out in 1992 to demonstrate that a contemporary tower could be successfully built next to a historic landmark. The semi-circular design makes the structure look smaller than it is − 11 storeys and 269 rooms, the second-largest hotel in Hanoi. Neoclassical touches also mean that 'the hotel's architecture speaks to the Opera House but does not compete with it'.[38] Public opinion in Hanoi has been favourable, and the building is seen as enhancing the city's character.

It is not only foreign investment that presented threats to Hanoi's heritage. Contestation in fact also raged in the mixed commercial–residential precincts of the Ancient Quarter where many small resident investors took little notice of the planning rules or the historical character of the area. Often their 'overnight renovations', as Ngo Quang called them,[39] meant demolishing the old house on a Friday night so that the planning inspector, on returning to work on Monday morning, found only an empty block − or perhaps even the foundations laid for a new building. Very frequently no building permit had been obtained. Bribery of petty officials seems to have been rife, and the occasional fines were too low to have had any impact upon illegal building activity. The Deputy Director of the Hanoi municipal construction department, Trinh Hong Trieu, openly admitted in 1991 that the current regulations existed mainly on paper: 'Often when people apply for a building licence, they have already built the house according to their wishes. After they're caught, they have to pay fines, but it's so low that they're willing to pay it.'[40] Throughout the 1990s, even after the establishment of a Chief Architect's Office in Hanoi charged with drawing up and enforcing planning regulations for the city, private individuals continued to demolish, remodel or reconstruct without official approval.

Of course, it is understandable that the residents of Hanoi should be seeking to remedy substandard and crowded housing conditions as quickly as possible. In the mid-1990s it was estimated that 50 per cent of Ancient Quarter households were still sharing a kitchen, 95 per cent a toilet, and 100 per cent the courtyard and corridor.[41] But while it is impossible to begrudge the Vietnamese their rising standards of living, much of the investment in fact went into the redevelopment of sites for conversion to

Above Application by the
ANZ Bank of a Western
adaptive re-use approach to
heritage protection added
both economic and prestige
value to this colonial villa.

Below The Hanoi Hilton
Opera wraps around the
Opera House. Built at a cost
of US$60 million by the
first American hotel chain
to operate in Vietnam, it
was opened in 1999.

non-residential uses, such as mini-hotels for foreign tourists, or bars and offices. In these cases, the investment process was doing nothing to improve the overall housing conditions for local Ancient Quarter residents but was part of a process leading to the formation of a new property-owning middle class. Much of the physical change being wrought in the city was for short-term private gain and was short-sighted in terms of the broader community needs. Hanoi economist Nguyen Quy Lan summed up the situation: 'The only law here is supply and demand.'[42]

In short, the most difficult group of investors the planners had to deal with were in many ways the Vietnamese residents of the old city. Cao Xuan Huong, Deputy Secretary-General of the Vietnamese Architects' Association, summarised the planner's dilemma: 'The liberalisation of Vietnam's economy, begun in 1986, has put cash into the hands of once-impoverished residents [and the] Old Quarter is being destroyed.'[43] By the mid-1990s the Chairman of the Hanoi People's Committee, Hoang Van Ngien, who has been described as Vietnam's first businessman mayor, expressed concern that 'the ancient city is being destroyed'.[44] Nghien wanted to avoid Hanoi becoming 'another Bangkok', or even another Ho Chi Minh City.

The public utterances of Hanoi's Chief Architect, Professor Nguyen Lan, remained equivocal, reflecting the highly delicate balancing act that his role demands. In particular, he was concerned about the locational choices made in many joint venture developments, especially around the Hoan Kiem and West lakes, which were approved before he came into office:

> ... many new buildings have appeared around Ho Tay [West Lake] which is populated by poor residents. We have to ring the alarm because these constructions did not follow our planning policies and are encroaching on the flower-growing plots ... The traditional An Ninh suburb next to the [Cuban-built] Thang Loi Hotel is being cheekily converted to urban use with the appearance of tall buildings the height of the Thang Loi. The tourist industry on the other hand is trying to lure visitors by filling in the charming lake in front of the Kim Lien pagoda ... These buildings are indeed adding their own beauty to the area, but do we really want such grandiose constructions in this traditional environment?[45]

Developments were also encroaching on to the main section of West Lake. Fergus T. Maclaren reported in 1994 that West Lake had already decreased in size by one-fifth since the 1970s.[46] Other lakes such as Giang Vo and Ba Mau were suffering the same fate, destroying one of the acclaimed distinctive characteristics of traditional Vietnamese environmental planning – the marriage of architecture and water features. By 1999, one-quarter of the 40 lakes existing in Hanoi ten years earlier had completely disappeared, filled in by unscrupulous developers who illegally dumped rubbish and rubble into them to provide foundations for housing.[47]

Luxury housing developments cut
off the Kim Lien Pagoda from its
traditional West Lake setting.

But the pro-conservation point of view had begun to be more loudly voiced in political, planning and architectural circles. Pham Sy Liem, Vice-Minister for Construction, set a new tone in 1994 when he called for the acceleration of conservation plans, combined with a population transfer program.[48] He advocated the construction of a range of new, well-serviced suburbs that would attract residents away from the Old Sector and allow the area to be upgraded physically as well as the heritage features to be protected. Former Prime Minister Vo Van Kiet frequently spoke out in favour of protecting the best of Hanoi's architectural heritage. For instance, addressing cultural and artistic organisations in Hanoi in 1992, the Prime Minister focused attention on the role of architects and planners in post-*doi moi* Vietnam.[49] The government, he asserted, should have

> ... a policy on architecture and laws to aid urban planners right now because, with the present free market economy, all citizens and all organisations are encouraged to take part in urban renewal and in building activities. Effective management is therefore a necessity if we are to maintain harmony and good cooperation between various bodies at all levels ... We desperately need zoning laws to protect our national identity in architecture. The zoning laws will help prevent the hotchpotch erection of ugly buildings and also regulate what kind of construction can be carried out to protect our culture in general and our national identity in architecture in particular.

However, the statements and actions of senior politicians also showed the same mix of concerns expressed by the Chief Architect — support on the one hand for protecting Hanoi's heritage, and fear on the other hand that it will impede new development. In fact, the threat of investors leaving town, moving their activities to Ho Chi Minh City or Guangzhou, often seems to have caused their actions to belie their public statements of support for the heritage. By 1998, investor flight was already occurring as a result of the Asian financial crisis and Vietnam's general inability to put in place the legislative and administrative frameworks that foreign (especially American) investors said they needed.[50] It was feared that heritage or other environmental controls would be seen as the last straw. It is said that the former Prime Minister was wont to intervene in the Chief Architect's Office decision-making, telephoning the Chief Architect late into the night to demand special relaxation of planning restrictions for major investors. The conclusion to draw from this is that a large question mark hangs over the degree of commitment to heritage conservation that existed at the highest levels in Hanoi. Yet, if heritage conservation is to be successful, top-level support is critical.

The views of Westerners visiting or working in Hanoi were also mixed. Numerous ambassadors, academics, architects and tourists, especially in the early 1990s, extolled the beauty and historic significance of this city that appeared frozen in time due to the absence of redevelopment pressures during the half-century of war, American embargo and Soviet socialist influence. John Mant, Sydney lawyer and urban planner, for example, saw Hanoi having

> ... many of the qualities which cities around the world have lost and are trying to recapture: the sense of continuity with the past, a bustling street life, easy and cheap access for huge numbers of people, and streets unpolluted by fumes of motor vehicles. The scale of the buildings, their relationship to one another and to the streets, trees and lakes have a pleasing visual effect at the same time as creating an exciting but pedestrian friendly environment.[51]

But many of these same Westerners also appreciated that change is inevitable and even desirable, and they were uncomfortable in supporting a heritage campaign to preserve quaint but decrepit shop-houses and villas when they knew they can easily catch a plane to their high-quality lifestyles back home.

Heritage planning in the 1990s: National & international interventions

Gradually, heritage conservation became part of the Hanoi planning agenda. Over the 1990s, many national and international planning interventions were made, but by the end of the decade little appeared to have been accomplished. The first high-rise towers rose above the trees of the French Quarter by 1996. Medium-rise mini-hotels broke the streetscapes, and old shopfronts gave way to glitzy new ones in the Ancient Quarter. The narrow streets were already proving incapable of carrying the motocycles, cars and taxis now being driven through the area, and the infrastructure of water, gas, electricity and sewerage mains barely coped with the rocketing demand. But what should and could government have done to protect Hanoi's cultural heritage in this new post-*doi moi* context? It is easy to say that a proper plan balancing heritage protection with modernisation and redevelopment would have been much more likely to achieve the desired results than the lack of effective planning controls that existed. But the planning system, and the planners in it, had to come to terms with the new market environment in which they now had to operate, as, too, did the politicians who controlled the decision-making processes at the national level and in the Hanoi People's Committee.

Numerous attempts were made by international organisations to help the Hanoi planners adjust to the new context. The first of these was the UNESCO report on the Old Sector in 1990.[52] UNESCO's interest in Hanoi, as in its other campaign areas, was based on the view that the proper management of cultural resources offered a wide range of benefits to the local citizens and to the country and world generally. Protection of Hanoi's Old Sector was thus seen as a way of helping to arrest the decline in that city's cultural environment and to ensure that links with the nation's past were maintained. Socially, it would help to improve living conditions by the physical upgrading of the urban environment, as well as by the increased employment that would be generated through restoration and reconstruction activities. In light of experience elsewhere, UNESCO expected that many of these activities would support a revival of traditional Vietnamese arts and crafts. On the economic front, a heritage protection program in Hanoi's Old Sector would strengthen the basis for a tourism industry with potential to generate substantial amounts of foreign revenue for the local and national economies.

UNESCO's 1990 intervention focused global and local attention both on the existence of an urban heritage of considerable world significance in Hanoi's Old Sector and on the need for heritage protection regulations to be put in place before international investment activities built up. This put the Vietnamese and Hanoi authorities in a difficult situation, since they were eager to show themselves to be pro-investment but also in favour of cultural maintenance. This ambiguity in governmental stance continued throughout the decade, leading as we have seen to an unclear degree of commitment to heritage protection at times. But eventually the heritage protection issue was taken up by the Hanoi People's Committee in revisions to the Hanoi Master Plan, special sets of regulations for the Ancient Quarter and the broader 'Hanoi Planning and Development

Control' Project funded by AusAID and carried out jointly with the Chief Architect's Office.[53]

The master planning process that had originated with the French and been reinforced by the Soviets continued to operate. A *Master Plan Hanoi 2010* was approved in December 1993. Under this plan, the main directions of new growth were to the south and across the Red River towards the Noi Bai Airport. The commercial centre was to be focused in the area immediately north and south of Hoan Kiem Lake (that is, the Ancient Quarter and the inner section of the French Quarter), while the political and administrative functions would be further concentrated in the Ba Dinh Quarter. Success in integrating heritage protection into the planning of Hanoi depended very much on the kind of strategy adopted in the Master Plan. It seems to have been recognised that a 'New World' city form with a high-rise central business district, or even the modified structure of Bangkok or Jakarta with their more disjointed and dispersed CBD functions, would intensify the threats to heritage buildings and precincts. A controlled city profile, by contrast, would allow a balance to be struck between heritage protection and commercial high-rise development by enforcing strict building height and heritage regulations in the Old Sector and encouraging the modern high-rise construction in carefully defined peripheral zones.

In the mid-1990s there were hopeful signs that such a 'Paris model' was being treated seriously in Hanoi. Already there was the beginning of a modern hotel zone on the West Lake several kilometres north of the Old Sector. Areas in Hai Ba Trung District, to the south of the French Quarter, also offered scope for high-rise redevelopment. At the November 1993 Friends of Hanoi Workshop, Nguyen Ngoc Khoi, then Director of the NIURP, unveiled his organisation's preliminary proposals for the Ancient City area.[54] Some elements have since been implemented, including the use of the two main north–south thoroughfares as one-way roads. But the key idea of retaining streetscape façades and redeveloping the interiors of street blocks has progressed little. Nevertheless, in 1999, Dr Nguyen Ba Dang, Director of the Ministry of Construction's Architectural Research Institute, was still arguing that high-rise towers should only be built in suburban districts and should not be allowed to dominate the 'architecture and personalities' of the ancient streets of the historic core.[55] He conceded, however, that high-rises in the inner city are convenient structures, often with high architectural merit, and useful landmarks for the people and tourists.[56] The question is not whether to prevent redevelopment, but where it should be allowed to occur.

The Master Plan was adjusted in mid-1998 to establish planning controls for the 20,000-hectare Hanoi New Town north of the Red River. This new satellite area was intended to deflect development pressures away from the existing built-up area of Hanoi, including the historic core, in line with prime ministerial requirements that the population of Hanoi proper be held to 2.5 million; that is, not much greater that its present size. The project was approved by Prime Minister Phan Van Khai in 1998[57] and is being developed by the South Korean Daewoo conglomerate and the Hanoi People's Committee. While the project reflects the new global investment context in which Vietnam now operates, attracting funds for the implementation stage from a variety of capitalist sources, the approach still largely follows the conventional pattern of centralised decision-making, top-down direction, and emphasis on rigid definition of zones and controls.

Will this strategy of deflecting development pressures away from the centre work? The experience of the Xuan Hoa and Xuan Mai satellites does not give great cause for optimism. But the general strategy of developing new peripheral areas to the north-west has been a constant feature of Hanoi planning for several decades. In the mid-1990s, Ha Van Que, Assistant to the Chief Architect, confirmed that the Chief Architect's Office was trying to encourage developers to build in selected outlying areas, especially in Van Phuc and beyond West Lake, in order to conserve the architectural flavour of central Hanoi.[58] The Australian architect Peter Purcell argued on the other hand that 'There's no point in putting buildings in rice paddies because no one is going to show up'.[59] It will be another ten years or so before we will see whether the Hanoi New Town meets its growth targets and successfully attracts pressures from the historic centre.

Professor Nguyen Lan appears to have been acutely conscious of the Hanoi planning system's shortcomings and, spurred on, it is said, by the Prime Minister's ultimatum in the wake of the dyke scandal to get the system working effectively, actively sought international assistance. Because much of the earlier socialist planning theory and practice had been rendered obsolete by *doi moi*, the Chief Architect's Office was enthusiastic about learning about Western architectural and planning approaches. It has worked closely with various international teams of experts, including the Australian AusAID team, transport planners from Japan and housing experts from Sweden. Advice has also been sought from other international sources, especially Singapore. In a context where Vietnam is seeking to liberalise its economy and improve standards of living, the Singaporean development model is, of course, highly attractive. That it is an Asian model adds to its appeal. Moreover, Singapore offers a contrast to Bangkok, which is held up as the Asian city whose development path should not be followed. The high degree of central control over the development and planning processes in Singapore fits well with Vietnamese Communist Party thinking, and Singapore

Dong Anh West District in
the Hanoi New Town. The
artist portrays an
international blandness
rather than the
distinctiveness of the
Vietnamese context.

appears to have produced a modern, efficient city. The downside, to many observers as well as to many potential international tourists, is that the city has been over-sanitised and that there is little cultural heritage left that is distinctly Singaporean.

On the basis of its own analyses and the advice of foreign experts, the Hanoi People's Committee, through the Chief Architect's Office, took a major step to protect the cultural heritage of the Ancient Quarter when, in April 1992, it decided to incorporate heritage matters in the Hanoi Master Plan. Following approval by the National Council of Ministers, in August 1993 the *Regulations on Construction Management and Conservation of the Old Quarter of Hanoi* were promulgated.[60] These provided a level of planning detail missing in the 1984 *Ordinance on Protection and Usage of Historical, Cultural and Famous Places* and were described by the Chief Architect as the first real step in protecting the cultural townscape of the Ancient Quarter.[61] Under the Regulations, the boundaries of the Old

Quarter were temporarily defined until more definitive identification studies were completed. Within this area, a system of construction and conservation was to be established which, while allowing infrastructures to be modernised, maintained the characteristics of the road networks with their traditional names, protected the artistic architectural works, and preserved and restored classified relics. It was intended that a number of sections of old streets and works would be restored and upgraded in accordance with the typical characteristics of the area. Other parts of the area could be renovated or redeveloped in line with the provisions of the Regulations. All private developers were required to apply for construction or demolition permits. Illegal, polluting or otherwise inappropriate buildings were to be moved out of the area. Owners of classified buildings were to receive financial assistance for repairing and restoring works, while occupants of such buildings, should they need to be removed under the Old Quarter restoration plans, were to be compensated.

The August 1993 Regulations were followed in March 1995 by the Ministry of Construction's *Decision No. 70*, which gave approval to a plan to both protect and develop the Ancient Quarter – to maintain the historic character and essential sense of place, while allowing modernisation of living spaces.[62] It set a height limit of three storeys for buildings with a street frontage and four storeys for other buildings, and it required the use of tiled roofs and façade materials that maintained the Quarter's traditional harmony. About the same time, the Ministry of Construction established the National Architectural Research Institute under Dr Nguyen Ba Dang to provide better training and research in architectural and urban design issues.[63] The Ministry's previous studies had largely been limited to analysing the existing conditions of buildings in old Hanoi rather than identifying their historical significance. No complete list of significant buildings or statement of criteria had been drawn up. Dr Dang's team set to work on these tasks, extending the analysis beyond traditional pagodas and temples to take in shop-houses and churches and demonstrating that *doi moi* represents not only an economic liberalisation but also an opening up to contemporary Western ideas of urban planning and heritage definition.[64]

Another Master Plan adjustment that occurred in mid-1998 introduced preservation policies for metropolitan Hanoi and placed the requirement on future developments of 'effectively blending construction styles'.[65] A steering committee headed by the Deputy Prime Minister Ngo Xuan Loc and the People's Committee Chairman, Hoang Van Nghien, was established. A Hanoi Ancient Quarter Management Board was also set up by the Hanoi People's Committee and was headed by the Committee's Vice-Chairman, Luu Minh Tri. In June 1999 the Hanoi People's Committee adopted the board's more complete set of interim regulations for the management, construction, preservation and upgrading of buildings in the Ancient Quarter.[66] The regulation defined the Ancient Quarter as comprising 76 old streets covering an area of approximately 100 hectares, and authorised the restoration and renovation of shop-houses, pagodas and churches.[67] The new rules also sought to encourage the improvement of living conditions through the renovation of building interiors and upgrading of local infrastructure. The regulation permitted the construction of buildings with street frontages to a height of three storeys, and for those located in the interiors of street blocks a height of four storeys. This was a reduction on the previous heights allowed and it is yet to be seen whether compliance by local investors can be obtained.

The enforcement of regulations is clearly the key to any effective planning in Hanoi and heritage protection cannot proceed without it, a point that has been made consistently since the first UNESCO report in 1990. But enforcement has been almost impossible to achieve. Trinh Duy Luan believes that much new construction in Hanoi is out of line with the Master Plan and cites an unnamed expert's view that up to 70 per cent of recently built houses have been erected without any permission.[68] However, there are other bureaucratic problems that have slowed the introduction of meaningful controls. The continuing reliance on the master-planning approach is targeted by Lawrie Wilson, the AusAID team's principal statutory planner, who has described Hanoi's plan-ning structure as 'a dinosaur'.[69] Planning in Vietnamese thinking still essentially means 'economic planning', and urban planning remains large-ly a design and construction coordination exercise conducted in a con-tinuing context of government monopoly and central command. New policy directions, laws and regulations still flow from the top-down as they did under the old pre-*doi moi* era. The national and municipal governments and the Ministry of Construction are still reluctant to step aside and allow the private sector a free hand. Against this, the Director of NIURP, Dr Le Hong Ke, justifies the continued dependence on master planning and strong government intervention on the grounds that 'My country is a socialist country ... We must find a compromise in order to accommodate the two systems [market and socialist]'.[70]

Wilson believes the planning system at the present time is not working effectively because the Chief Architect's Office staff are not equipped to make it work.[71] 'The Vietnamese are good architects and engineers,' says Wilson, 'but they were trained in the Eastern bloc countries 20 or 30 years ago. They have never experienced a situation where they're confronted by a property developer who's motivated by profit and therefore wants to exploit a property to its utmost.' They are also not paid enough, so it is not in their interests to perform quickly or even well. He believes the key issues are well understood at the National Assembly level, but the bureaucracy is too vast and too entrenched in malpractice, and too many officials see change as a threat to their personal situation. But there is also little sense of ministerial or departmental responsibility, so that individual officers must take the blame personally for mistakes. In the planning arena, this means that officials at the work-face often avoid making decisions and often turn a blind eye (or take a bribe) when construction permit infringements occur.

In addition, there has been constant debate involved in achieving a balance between planning for Hanoi as the national capital and Hanoi as a large city with responsibilities to its residents. While a totally legitimate argument, this has complicated the work of the Chief Architect's Office even further. The Vietnamese Communist Party intervenes on major issues, as does the Prime Minister's Office. Where differences of opinion occur between the national bodies and the Hanoi People's Committee or its departments, the national bodies are likely to win out.[72] The Chief Architect's Office is in a clearly difficult position, unable so far, for reasons largely beyond its control, to implement an effective planning system and yet blamed by senior politicians for failing to achieve the implementation goals set by the National Assembly.[73]

On the other hand, being the national capital means that, at times of national celebration, restoration funds are made available for those elements of the cultural heritage that support the prevailing ideology. The 990th and, especially, the 1,000th birthday of the capital city in the years 2000 and 2010 are two such occasions. The Hanoi Department of Culture and Information has planned displays of national pride that include the restoration of a number of historical monuments. All of these are from the pre-colonial period – relics of the ancient citadel such as the Bac Mon (Cua Bac, or North Gate), the Doan Mon (Doan Gate) and the Hau Lau (Back Castle), the Van Mieu and the Quoc Tu Giam.[74] A Hanoi Museum will be constructed on part of the citadel site and a monument raised to the Ngoc Hoi victory over the Chinese invaders. Other cultural activities include the making of a film about Ly Thai To's 'Decree to Transfer the Royal Capital' to Hanoi and a wood carving of 'Thang Long with Ancient Streets'. This still reflects the same narrow definition of the city's cultural heritage held by the Party and State. The social, economic and cultural changes affecting Vietnamese society cannot be ignored for much longer. How will they impact on the philosophy and practice of cultural heritage conservation in this *ville millenaire*?

Medium-rise international
centre near Hanoi's opera
house: a risky balance of
past and present.

Chapter 8
Creeping pluralism:
Hanoi faces the new millennium

Globalisation and 'foreign social evils'

The economic restructuring unleashed in 1986 found its geographical focus in Vietnam's cities, but now urban development began to take place in the context of a private market in real estate and construction.[1] This profound ideological change has led, according to one's political stance, to a new set of triumphs or a new set of disasters – or, indeed, to some of each. The changing pace and the widening scope of change soon became obvious to both the citizenry and to external commentators: work practices and leisure possibilities, the composition of education curricula, the choice of available consumer goods, aesthetic tastes – all were being dramatically affected. The propaganda hoardings and advertising billboards around the city were early visual signs of change. The socialist wall posters featuring Ho Chi Minh and idealised figures of the worker, peasant and soldier disappeared. New boards went up above temples, pagodas and shop-houses for Pepsi, Fujicolor, Kenwood and Konica. For a while during 1995, the socialist icons at either end of the Chinese- and Soviet Union-funded Thanh Long Bridge over the Red River were matched by that archetypical symbol of consumerism – the Coca-Cola advertisement, on towering red panels attached to the main stanchions. Surveys (themselves a new feature) began to indicate that most Hanoi residents believed *doi moi* had brought considerable improvement in their living standards.[2] However, some Vietnamese are becoming increasingly concerned by the fragmentation of society and especially by the growing polarisation they see between the affluent and poor members of society.

Economic liberalisation and the opening up to global capital represented a fundamental ideological shift. However, while Marx has gone, Lenin remains: the Vietnamese Communist Party still dominates the political scene and Vietnam remains a single-party state. This has created a situation in Vietnam – wittily referred to as 'Market-Leninism' – in which economic liberalisation sits uneasily alongside a still-rigid and highly centralised political system. Many Vietnam experts doubt that the resulting tension can be sustained in the long run as people grow used to enjoying economic freedom and seek to achieve a more democratic political system. Indeed, the 1990s already witnessed a number of important changes in this direction.[3] The country's social structures and political institutions have begun to change in response to the global spread of industrial and communication technologies, and to the value of wage labour and the goods produced being set by the marketplace. A creeping pluralism is occurring. This includes the re-emergence of a Vietnamese middle class, many of which have become involved in property development and dealing. The economic strength of the new middle class is seen in the estimates that the average Hanoi household had savings in 1999 of over 23 million Vietnamese dong (approaching US$2,000) and that idle household savings in Hanoi totalled more than three times the city's budget for infrastructure construction.[4] Religion, too, has revived, with Buddhist and Christian places of worship being better attended and the religious institutions wealthier and more significant as players in Vietnamese society and politics. This has led to the restoration and renovation of many churches, pagodas and temples in Hanoi. It is also true, however, that the population generally has become more focused on consumer materialism than was ever before possible in Vietnam.

Many in Vietnam oppose this growing materialism, consumerism and social polarisation; others fear that too-rapid social and cultural change will lead to political instability. This has led since the mid-1990s to a 'foreign social evils' campaign, waged by conservative elements in the national and municipal authorities intent upon removing foreign cultural influences that they blamed for undermining Vietnamese traditional values. A public debate emerged as early as 1993 about the growing moral vacuum in Vietnam, with criticism directed at Western cultural influences in particular, which they branded as 'cultural pollution'.[5] This seems to have led to a renewed emphasis on traditional songs and dances on the government-run Vietnamese television. However, the concern about 'foreign social evils' peaked in the run-up to the Eighth Party Congress in June 1996. These evils included problems such as drugs, violent and pornographic video-tapes, prostitution and gambling, but extended to the use of English in street advertisements and the influence of the Western media and music industry. In Hanoi and Ho Chi Minh City, hundreds of nightclubs, bars and brothels were closed or severely restricted, and videos, calendars, books and playing cards deemed unsuitable were publicly burned. Although the extent to which some of these problems stem from Western rather than Vietnamese or Asian regional sources is in

An Ancient Quarter
temple now used as
a shop, reflecting
the shift towards a
more materialistic
culture.

fact unclear,[6] conservative politicians have sheeted the blame to *doi moi* and the opening up of Vietnam to Western capitalism. Clearly there is a tension between, on the one hand, economic reform, 'openness', foreign investment and international tourism, and, on the other hand, the maintenance of political stability and 'cultural purity'.[7] It is unfortunate that a by-product of the 'foreign social evils' campaign may have even been the re-stoking of old suspicions about the motives of Western interventions in Vietnam across a much wider field, including, perhaps, urban development and heritage protection.

The fear of globalisation is one context in which the 'foreign social evils' campaign in Vietnam needs to be seen. Globalisation is said to be undermining the traditions at the heart of the Vietnamese culture. This is as true in Vietnam as it is in other developing countries, and especially affects the young. In Vietnam, as elsewhere, there is a growing public realisation not only of the richness of the cultural heritage, but also of its vulnerability and of the need for governments to protect the heritage in order to protect the sense of local identity. Indeed, this shifting attitude has begun to crystallise at the international level in a movement towards recognising that, to use UNESCO's words, 'cultural rights are, no less than other human rights, an expression and requirement of human dignity'.[8] But the translation of this fear of globalisation into the strident public campaign that it became in the mid-1990s seems to come from another, more political and local context. This is the anxiety held by the Vietnamese Communist Party (or at least the conservatives within it) that it was starting to lose its hold over the Vietnamese people. The temptation to use aspects of Vietnam's and Hanoi's traditional culture as a prop to maintaining traditional social values and, by extension, the existing political system, was overwhelming.

The growing globalising forces felt in societies around the world might seem to augur the demise of place as a basis for community identity. Indeed, some social scientists now proclaim that places are no longer clear supports for meaningful identities. In particular, as Doreen Massey noted, the new information technologies are replacing 'places as areas with boundaries' by 'articulated networks of social relations and understandings'.[9] These new relationships form a cyberspace that transcends social and political arrangements based on physical space, such as nation states. According to Carter, Donald and Squires, 'This is seen nowhere more clearly than in the contemporary city ... [where] the distinct history and heritage of certain places becomes increasingly difficult to maintain ...'[10] What is surprising, then, is the resurgence of interest in cultural identity, both as an intellectual and a political project. Sociologists like Roland Robertson make the generalisation that globalisation is paradoxically provoking a 'localist' response.[11] This reaction takes many forms and has many causes. Hobsbawm's linking of history, heritage and nationalistic politics explains many cases. But much of it also stems from the fear on the part of governments and elite groups that they stand to lose their position of power in the new shake-up of loyalties that globalisation is prompting.

Social fragmentation and cultural heritage

The Vietnamese experience reveals the continuing desire of political regimes to manipulate the cultural affairs of the citizenry in their own interests. Whether this will act as a powerful brake on the globalisation of culture in anything but the short run is doubtful, especially given Vietnam's desperate need for Western investment, the major economic benefits brought by Western tourists, and the emergence of a Vietnamese middle class with discretionary spending power. In fact, despite the foreign social evils campaign, cultural globalisation continues. The people's psychology is changing, especially that of the younger generation born since the reunification of North and South and now representing more than half of the total population. Many are moving away from the rigid conformity to social mores demanded by Confucianism and the Party, and embracing individualism, materialism and consumerism with gusto. The Party can no longer rely on appeals to Ho Chi Minh's charisma or nationalism as the basis of legitimacy and respect.[12] Western culture, especially American, has an allure – even down to the Kentucky Fried Chicken store that opened in 1999, the first international fast-food outlet in Hanoi. The intangible heritage of traditional music, songs and dance is losing its appeal to the young, who now clearly prefer to switch on to Western music – or rather 'Westernised' music, since much of it comes from Hong Kong, Taiwan and other parts of Asia and often has a peculiarly non-American lilt.

What does this globalisation, creeping pluralism and popularity of Western culture mean for the collective memories, the intangible heritage of the sense of shared history and the sense of belonging to the Vietnamese community? Will it be possible to protect Hanoi's local identity faced with the globalising forces? On current indications, it seems that the official definition of the city's cultural heritage, with its emphasis on ancient Sino-Vietnamese features, will increasingly diverge from the popular view that is being transformed by globalising cultural forces. Does this mean that the State and its heritage planning and protection agencies will come under pressure to follow this shift in popular attitudes? If so, is it inevitable that some heritage features will be discarded in future as no longer relevant to current needs and interests? Many societies around the world have found ways to handle this same tension, learning to operate at both global and

On a fast track to
affluence? Hanoi
teenagers head
towards the Daewoo
business and hotel
tower on Cau Giay
Street.

local levels simultaneously by separating the cultural domains of the family and local community from that of business and the world. The Scandinavians and Dutch in Europe and the Chinese in South-east Asia have flourished on this formula for centuries. In the postmodern West, the increasing fragmentation of society is reflected in a growing diversity of tastes in dress, music, art and architecture. Different memories and mementoes of the past appeal to and are cherished by different sections of the general public. Rather than see a widening gap appear between official and popular definitions of cultural heritage, government planning and conservation agencies in the West have taken on a broader concept of 'the heritage' in order to encompass the diversity of views and interests.

Will the Vietnamese move in these directions – towards the separation of global and local domains, and towards a more encompassing definition of the heritage? Will official definitions of Vietnamese cultural heritage become more diversified and inclusive, seeking to embrace what is regarded as significant to the many and various fragments of society? This is an important issue, of course, not only in Vietnam – an issue that must be faced by all societies if the cultural heritage is to survive as a living and meaningful entity rather than being reduced to a few national (really nationalistic) monuments and tourist theme parks. We can expect that the cultural heritage of Vietnam and Hanoi will continue to shift in the new millennium. There is a critical role here for scholars in cultural heritage studies to identify those traces of the past that have continuing or new significance and should be protected. Scholars can also take a longer view of what is significant than the average citizen or public authority is likely to do. In particular, they can help us to realise that arguments to destroy heritage features and redevelop heritage sites are often based on a short-term fall in favour due, in some cases, to intergenerational hostility or, in other cases, to changes in the prevailing ideology of the political elite.

Clearly, the different features of Hanoi mean different things to different people. This deceptively simple statement has profound implications for planners and conservationists and for any attempt to identify the sense of place that makes Hanoi distinctive. There can be no single 'sense of place' but as many as there are people who live in or visit the city. Nevertheless, the search for a city's sense of place is a common one, driven by the desire to go beyond mere physical description of buildings and sites to come closer to how they fit together to create an overall ambience. In the scholarly arena, it is a frequent theme of urban historians, architects, planners and heritage specialists. Out in the broader community the matter is less simple, with contestation about what the 'sense of place' or the 'local identity' should embrace and how this should be translated into planning regulations affecting property rights. Democratic societies have the structural potential through public

The 1984 *Ordinance on Protection and Usage of Historical, Cultural and Famous Places* listed 80 sites for the whole of Hanoi. It covered the earliest places of worship, sites related to the patriotic movement leading to independence and the socialist revolution, and French colonial buildings incorporating local building characteristics that suit the climate and acknowledge the indigenous culture.[21] By 1994 the Hanoi People's Committee claimed that Hanoi had 1,320 'relics of cultural history', of which 337 had been classified by the State.[22] This is an extensive list, but there remain four additional elements that might be considered for inclusion. First, the extensive stock of art deco buildings in the Hai Ba Trung District has so far been largely ignored. Potentially, this is one of the most significant collections of inter-war residential and commercial buildings remaining in Asia. Secondly, surrounding Hanoi, the ancient dykes that have protected Hanoi from Red River floods for a thousand years are probably the most essential element of the city's heritage and yet modern housing has been allowed to encroach upon them. Thirdly, consideration should be given to including the best of the Soviet-period buildings. Finally, in line with Western practice since the 1960s, the Vietnamese authorities should give increased attention to area protection rather than focusing on individual buildings and monuments. This is being done in the Ancient Quarter; the approach needs to be extended to other sections of inner Hanoi.

But these are my views. While I have come to know and love Hanoi in the course of many visits, it is in the final analysis not my city. In a postcolonial world, it is unacceptable for the so-called foreign experts to impose their ideas about heritage significance or planning regulations on to the indigenous population. It is appropriate only to explain the situations confronted elsewhere in the world and lay out the possible options for the Vietnamese actors in the development arena to evaluate. It is for the Vietnamese – politicians, planners, entrepreneurs and residents – to make the choices that will create a new Hanoi for the new millennium. It would be nice to think that the Vietnamese will sort this out for themselves in a democratic fashion and that somehow the Hanoi general citizenry might have a say in determining the future of their city. Some Vietnamese have been calling for greater public participation in planning. One such voice is that of Professor Hoang Dao Kinh, who, as long ago as 1994, argued that:

> The work of conservation and of revaluation of Hanoi's architectural heritage requires the active participation of all Hanoians, of all socioeconomic groups. Community groups need to be set up to lobby in favour of the protection of Hanoi's architectural heritage ... [and] to act as counterbalance to the management bodies and urban program planning. Only such an action will be able to preserve ancient and unique Hanoi.[23]

Art deco house in Nguyen Thuong Hien Street in the Bay Mau Quarter

Soviet-period elementary school of the Kim Ma-Giang Vo living quarter.

The story of the Golden Hanoi Hotel shows that greater public involvement in planning and ownership of the results is becoming possible.

In the end, no matter how imperfect we may think the mechanisms for listening to the public are, Hanoi's politicians and planners must drive their own road. A few optimistic signs of greater commitment to heritage protection have been noted recently and it is hoped that this new mood will outlive the current lull in development pressures. The Vietnamese in Hanoi still need to answer the key questions: What policy priority should be given to heritage protection? How should they treat the symbols of past regimes, particularly the French colonial vestiges? How much should be protected, and how purist should the preservation approach be? Should an attempt be made to protect traditional lifestyles as well as physical structures? And Westerners need to avoid falling into an Orientalist position of advocating the preservation of Hanoi's exotic townscapes knowing they can quickly return home to the comforts of their modern homes. In Hanoi, and other Vietnamese cities, it is essential that the need for modernisation be recognised. Heritage protection should not mean confining Hanoians to continuing sub-standard living conditions. There is a balance to be struck between maintaining links with the past and making way for a brighter future. The challenge that faces planners in Hanoi is to learn to listen to all interested parties, to articulate a vision of the city that keeps the best of the past alongside new development, to win public and political commitment to that vision, and to take firm steps to enforce it. In this way, they will not only protect the essential under-pinnings of Hanoi's urban identity but proceed to create new high-quality environments – a new post-*doi moi* cultural layer, Hanoi's heritage of the future.

NOTES

Chapter 1: Ideology, memory and heritage significance

1   The reasons for this failure are summarised in William Logan, 'Heritage planning in post-*doi moi* Hanoi: The national and international contributions', *Journal of the American Planning Association,* vol. 61, no. 3, Summer 1995, pp. 328–43.

2   L'Association Les Amis du Patrimoine Architectural du Vietnam, *Hanoi Ville et Memoire* (Conseil Régional, d'Île-de-France, Paris, [1993]).

3   See William S. Logan, 'The Angel of Dien Bien Phu: Making the Australia–Vietnam Relationship 1955–95', in M. McGillivray and G. Smith (eds), *Australia and Asia* (Oxford University Press, Melbourne, 1997), pp. 178–202.

4   Penelope Woolf, 'Symbol of the Second Empire: Cultural Politics and the Paris Opera House', in Denis Cosgrove and Stephen Daniels (eds), *The Iconography of Landscape* (Cambridge University Press, Cambridge, UK, 1988), pp. 214–35.

5   The Vietnamese commonly refer to this as the 'American War'. The war is difficult to date: it grew slowly out of the French effort to retake Indochina after World War 2, with US ground troops landing from 1965 and peaking in 1969, and it ended as an almost purely civil war between communists and non-communists after the withdrawal of the United States and its allies in 1973. Hostilities ceased with the communist capture of Saigon in April 1975.

6   Gough Whitlam, *Abiding Interests* (University of Queensland Press, St Lucia, Qld, 1997), pp. 58–59.

7   Alan Balfour, *Berlin: The Politics of Order, 1737–1989* (Rizzoli, New York, 1990) p. 11.

8   M. Christine Boyer, *The City of Collective Memory: Its Historical Imagery and Architectural Entertainments* (The MIT Press, Cambridge, Mass., 1994), p. 205.

9   Roland Robertson, *Globalisation: Social Theory and Global Culture* (Sage, London, 1992), p. 146.

10 Paul Connerton, *How Societies Remember* (Cambridge University Press, Cambridge, UK, 1989), p. 1.

11 Marc Askew, 'Bangkok: Transformation of the Thai City', in M. Askew and W.S. Logan (eds), *Cultural Identity and Urban Change in Southeast Asia: Interpretative Essays* (Deakin University Press, Geelong, Vic.), pp. 85–116.

12 Panivong Norindr, *Phantasmatic Indochina: French Colonial Ideology in Architecture, Film, and Literature* (Duke University Press, Durham, NC and London, 1996), p. 1.

13   M. Kammen, 'Some Patterns and Meanings of Memory Distortion in American History', in Daniel L. Schacter (ed), *Memory Distortion: How Minds, Brains, and Societies Construct the Past* (Harvard University Press, Cambridge, Mass., 1995), pp. 329–45.

14   In Wang Gungwu (ed), *Community and Nation: China, Southeast Asia and Australia* (Allen & Unwin, Sydney, revised edn, 1992), p. 62.

15   Denis Cosgrove, 'The myth and the stones of Venice: An historical geography of a symbolic landscape', *Journal of Historical Geography*, vol. 8, no. 2, 1982, pp. 145–69.

16   Eric Hobsbawm, *On History* (Weidenfeld & Nicolson, London, 1997), p. 5.

17   Michael Schudson, 'Dynamics of Distortion in Collective Memory', in Schacter (ed), op. cit., p. 359.

18   A.R.H. Baker, 'Introduction: The Identifying of Spaces and Places', in D. Vanneste (ed), *Space and Place: Mirrors of Social and Cultural Identities?* Acta Geographica Lovaniensia, vol. 35 (Catholic University of Louvain, Louvain, Belgium, 1996), pp. 1–2.

19   This can be seen, for instance, in the development of the 'Forum UNESCO: University and Heritage' network since 1996 and in the appearance of the *International Journal of Heritage Studies.*

20   André Masson, *Hanoi pendant la période héroique (1973–1888)* (Librairie Orientaliste Paul Gueuthner, Paris, 1929; translated by Jack A. Yaeger, and edited and abridged by Daniel F. Doeppers as *The Transformation of Hanoi 1873–1888,* Wisconsin Papers on Southeast Asia No. 8, Center for Southeast Asian Studies, University of Wisconsin – Madison, Madison, Wisc., 1983; revised edn, 1987).

Chapter 2: Thang Long, the ascending dragon: Pre-colonial Hanoi and the Chinese imprint

1   Vo Van Tuong (*Vietnam's Famous Pagodas.* CD-Rom, Tin Viet, Hanoi, 1996) puts its construction in the Early Le dynasty (AD 980–1009).

2   Ibid.

3   Bernard Philippe Groslier, *Indochine. Carrefour des arts* (Editions Albin Michel, Paris, 1961), p. 39. The Champa kingdom lasted from the third to the seventeenth century.

4   D.G.E. Hall, *A History of Southeast Asia* (St Martin's Press, New York, 4th edn, 1981), p. 215.

5   Nguyen Manh Cuong. 'Buddhist architecture in the evolutionary process of national history', *Kien Truc*, no. 2, 1988, pp. 33–39 (in Vietnamese).

6   Chu Quang Tru, 'Towers in the Ly dynasty: The nation's first multi-storeyed structures', *Kien Truc*, no. 2, 1988, pp. 28–32 (in Vietnamese).

7   Dao Hung, 'From the city of the rising dragon to the city on this side of the river', *Vietnam Courier*, no. 10, 1982, pp. 8–11.

8   Nguyen Khac Kham, 'Introduction to Vietnamese culture: Vietnamese and Chinese cultures', *Vietnam Magazine*, vol. 3, no. 7, 1973, pp. 12–16.

9   John K. Whitmore, 'The Vietnamese Confucian scholar's view of his country's early history', in Kenneth Hall and John K. Whitmore, 'Explorations in early Southeast Asian history: The origins of Southeast Asian statecraft', *Michigan Papers on South and Southeast Asia,* no. 11, 1979, pp. 193–203.

10   Ibid., p. 199.

11   Ralph Smith, *Viet-Nam and the West* (Heinemann, London, 1968), p. 81.

12   Alexander B. Woodside, *Vietnam and the Chinese Model: A Comparative Study of Vietnamese and Chinese Government in the First Half of the Nineteenth Century* (Harvard University Press, Cambridge, Mass., 1988), p. 28. Also see Nguyen Manh Cuong, op. cit.

13   Vo Van Tuong, op. cit.

14 Charles F. Keyes, *The Golden Peninsula: Culture and Adaptation in Mainland Southeast Asia* (Macmillan Publishing Co., New York, 1977), p. 259. See also Anthony D. King, *Colonial Urban Development: Culture, Social Power and Environment* (Routledge and Kegan Paul, London, 1976).

15 R. O'Connor, *A Theory of Indigenous Southeast Asian Urbanism* (Institute of Southeast Asian Studies, Singapore, 1983).

16 Keyes, op. cit., pp. 260–62.

17 O'Connor, op. cit., p. 4.

18 T.G. McGee, *The Southeast Asian City* (G. Bell and Sons, London, 1969), pp. 30–31.

19 Robert Redfield and M. Singer, 'The cultural roles of cities', *Economic Development and Cultural Change*, vol. 3, 1954, pp. 53–73.

20 Marc Askew and William S. Logan, *Cultural Identity and Urban Change in Southeast Asia: Interpretative Essays* (Deakin University Press, Geelong, Vic., 1994), p. 5.

21 Dao Hung, op. cit., p. 8.

22 According to Dao Hung (op. cit., p. 11), the city was called Dong Kinh during the reign of the Later Le kings, giving rise to the name for the northern part of Vietnam, Tongking or Tonkin. See Dao Hung, op. cit., p. 11.

23 Hoa Bang, 'The Temple of Literature and the National Academy: A Cultural Centre in Thang Long', in Nguyen Khac Vien (ed), *Vietnamese Studies: Hanoi from the Origins to the Nineteenth Century* (Xunhasaba, Hanoi, 1977), pp. 113–29.

24 Hanoi People's Committee, 'Recommendations sur la restauration et la réhabilitation du site culturel Temple de la Littérature – Collège national à Hanoi', Paper presented to the UNESCO International Seminar 'Urban Policy and the Protection of the Architectural Heritage of Vietnam', Hanoi and Hue, 29 March–2 April 1994, p. 1 (in French).

25 J. Hejzlar, *The Art of Vietnam* (Hamlyn Books, London, 1973), p. 59.

26 Smith, op. cit., p. 18.

27 *Van Mieu Quoc Tu Giam. Temple of Literature School for the Sons of the Nation Hanoi, Vietnam. A Walking Tour* (The Gioi Publishers, Hanoi, 1994), p. 6; Hoang Ni Tiep, 'The architecture of Hanoi today and tomorrow', *USSR Journal of Architecture*, nos 7–8, 1982, pp. 34–36 (in Russian); Dao Hung, op. cit., p. 10.

28 Tran Lam Bien, 'Some debatable issues concerning traditional Vietnamese architecture', *Kien Truc*, vol. 34, no. 4, 1991, pp. 43–46 (in Vietnamese).

29 Ibid.

30 Hejzlar, op. cit., pp. 61–62.

31 Smith, op. cit., pp. 18–21.

32 Groslier, op. cit., pp. 40–41.

33 William J. Duiker, *China and Vietnam: The Roots of Conflict* (Institute of East Asian Studies, University of California Press, Berkeley, Calif., 1986), p. 2.

34 Smith, op. cit., p. 7.

35 Ainslee T. Embree (ed), *Encyclopedia of Asian History* (Charles Scribner's Sons, New York, 1988), p. 32.

36 Dao Hung, op. cit., p. 8.

37 Nguyen Luong Bich, 'Hanoi from the Eleventh to the End of the Nineteenth Century', in Tran Huy Lieu (ed), *History of Hanoi* (History Institute, Hanoi, 1960), pp. 13–90.

38 Louis Bézacier, 'Conception du plan des anciennes citadelles-capitales du Nord Vietnam', *Journal Asiatique*, no. 140, 1952, pp. 185–95; p. 190. Georges Azambre, 'Les origines de Ha-noi', *Bulletin de la Société des Etudes Indochinoises (BSEI)*, New Series, vol. 33, no. 3, 3rd trimester, 1958, pp. 261–300.

39 Smith, op. cit., pp. 23–24.

40 *Van Mieu Quoc Tu Giam. Temple of Literature School for the Sons of the Nation Hanoi, Vietnam. A Walking Tour*, op. cit., p. 7.

41 Quoted in Tran Quoc Vuong and Nguyen Vinh Long, 'Hanoi: From Prehistory to the 19th Century', in Nguyen Khac Vien (ed), *Vietnamese Studies: Hanoi from the Origins to the Nineteenth Century* (Xunhasaba, Hanoi, 1977), pp. 9–57.

42 Ngo Duc Tho, *Complete Works of History of Great Vietnam* (Social Sciences Publishing House, Hanoi, 1993), vol. II, p. 241 (in Vietnamese).

43 Hoang Ni Tiep, op. cit.

44 It was razed to the ground in 1257, 1284 and 1287 by the Mongols under the Kublai Khan dynasty; between 1371 and 1378 it was taken four times and destroyed twice by the Cham; the Chinese sacked it in 1407; and it was destroyed in 1516 and 1592 as the result of inter-clan warfare. (See Azambre, op. cit., p. 290; and Nguyen Luong Bich, op. cit.)

45 Le Loi called the citadel Dong Do (Eastern Capital).

46 Dao Hung, op. cit., p. 9.

47 Nguyen Luong Bich, op. cit.

48 Samuel Baron, 'A Description of the Kingdom of Tonqueen', in Churchill (ed), *A Collection of Voyages and Travels* (Churchill, London, 1732), vol. 6. Quoted in Azambre, op. cit., p. 269.

49 Quoted in Azambre, op. cit., p. 271.

50 Nguyen Duc Nhuan, 'Do the urban and regional management policies of socialist Vietnam reflect the patterns of the ancient Mandarin bureaucracy?', *International Journal of Urban and Regional Research*, vol. 8, no. 1, 1984, pp. 73–79.

51 Christian Pédélahore, 'Constituent elements of Hanoi city (19th–20th centuries)', *Vietnamese Studies*, 12 (New Series), 1986, pp. 105–59.

52 Phuong Anh, 'Glimpses of Old Hanoi', *Vietnam Courier*, no. 10, 1982, pp. 13–17.

53 Dao Hung, op. cit., p. 10.

54 Quoted in Dao Hung, op. cit., p. 11.

55 Azambre, op. cit., p. 271. Also G. Azambre, 'Hanoi: Notes de géographie urbaine', *Bulletin de la Société des Etudes Indochinoises*, New Series, vol. 30, no. 4, 4th trimester, 1955, pp. 356–63.

56 William Dampier, *A Voyage to Tonking in 1688*, translated as 'Un voyage au Tonkin en 1688', *Revue Indochinoise*, 2nd semester, 1914, pp. 906–23. Quoted in Dao Hung, op. cit., p. 11.

57 Woodside, op. cit., p. 31.

58 Azambre, 1958, op. cit., p. 273.

59 Azambre, 1955, op. cit., p. 361.

60 Quoted in Azambre, 1958, op. cit., p. 269.

61 Dang Thai Hoang, *Hanoi's Architecture in the Nineteenth and Twentieth Centuries* (Nha Xuat Ban Xay Dung, Hanoi, 1985), p. 14.

62 Nguyen Duc Nhuan, op. cit., p. 78. Civilians were also banned from wearing clothes of the royal colour yellow or shoes of the aristocratic type known as *hai*.

63 Azambre, 1958, op. cit., p. 281; Dang Thai Hoang, op. cit.; Ngo Huy Quynh, *Understanding Vietnamese Architecture* (Nha Xuat Ban Xay Dung, Hanoi, 1991, 2 vols), vol. 2, p. 166 (in Vietnamese).

64 Jacques Dumarcay, *The Palaces of South-East Asia, Architecture and Customs* (translated by Michael Smithies, Oxford University Press, Singapore, 1991).

65 Alain Viaro, 'Le compartiment chinois est-il chinois?', *Cahiers de la recharche architecturale*, nos 27–28, 1st trimester, 1992, pp. 139–50.

66 Woodside, op. cit., p. 13.

67 H.H.E. Loofs, 'Recent Archaeological Discoveries in Vietnam and their Influence on Vietnamese Nationalism', Paper presented to the Asian Studies Association of Australia Conference, University of NSW, Sydney, 1978, p. 2.

68 Ibid., p. 3.
69 Woodside, op. cit., p. 23.
70 Smith, op. cit., pp. 30–31.
71 Ibid., pp. 40–42. The payment of tribute to China ended with the 1858 Treaty of Tientsin between China and France under which China acknowledged French control over Vietnam.
72 C.A. Bain, *Vietnam: The Roots of Conflict* (Prentice-Hall, Englewood Cliffs, NJ, 1967), p. 39.
73 Loofs, op. cit., pp. 4–5.
74 Woodside, op. cit., pp. 21, 45. Ngo Vinh Long (*Vietnamese Women in Society and Revolution*, Vietnam Resource Center, Cambridge, Mass., 1974, vol. 1: 'The French Colonial Period', p. 8) explains that the situation became more complicated under the Nguyen when two law codes in effect co-existed – the Le Dynasty Law Code, which had been accepted as customary practice; and the Gia Long Law Code, which was far more conservative and restrictive with regard to women. Under the Gia Long Code, daughters had no rights to inheritance; however, in practice, the Nyugen officials generally followed the customary law. Nevertheless, Ngo Vinh Long concludes that there were many cases of women being deprived of their rights.
75 Edward L. Farmer, et al., *Comparative History of Civilisations in Asia* (Addison-Wesley Publishing Co., Reading, Mass., c. 1977), vol. 1, p. 207.
76 Nguyen Quang Nhac and Nguyen Nang Dac, *Vietnamese Architecture* (The Vietnam Council on Foreign Relations, [Paris], n.d.).
77 Tran Ham Tan and Nguyen Ba Chi, *Den Hai Ba Trung* (Imprimerie Thoi Su, Hanoi, 1948) (in Vietnamese).
78 Nguyen Vinh Phuc, *Hanoi Past and Present* (The Gioi Publishers, Hanoi, 1996), pp. 232–35.
79 Tran Ham Tan and Nguyen Ba Chi, op. cit.
80 Fonds d'Archives de la Mairie-Résidence, Service du Cadastre et des Domaines de Hanoi; file 698.
81 Ibid.
82 Tran Ham Tan and Nguyen Ba Chi, *La Pagode de l'Ile de Jade* (Imprimerie Thoi Su, Hanoi, 1948) (in Vietnamese). There had been a small temple on the island since the Le dynasty and, in fact, the name of the island and pagoda date from that period. See also Vu Tam Lang Vu Tam Lang, 'Den Ngoc Son, Ha Noi', *Kien Truc*, vol. 26, no. 4, 1989, pp. 35–36 (in Vietnamese), and Dang Thai Hoang, op. cit.
83 As retold by the French archaeologist Georges Dumoutier, who was active in Tonkin in the 1880s. (See *Tonkin du sud* (Comité de l'Asie française, Paris, 1907), pp. 12–13.)
84 These are the words of the Russian architect E.V. Pereladova ('Some special features of landscape architecture in Vietnam', *Construction and Architecture*, no. 10, pp. 158–64 (in Russian).
85 Thap Rua is seen as the turtle's head, while Ngoc Son is the turtle's body (Tran Ham Tan and Nguyen Ba Chi, op. cit., p. 4).
86 Tran Lam Bien, op. cit.
87 Woodside, op. cit., p. 9.
88 Ibid., p. 36.
89 Truong Vinh Ky, in P.J. Honey (ed), *Voyage to Tongking in the Year at Hoi (by Truong Vinh Ky, 1876)* (School of Oriental and African Studies, University of London, London, 1982), p. 91. Also Dao Hung, op. cit., p. 11. The Vauban walls were constructed as part of French aid to Gia Long. Both French material and expert personnel were provided (Nguyen Quang Nhac and Nguyen Nang Dac, op. cit., p. 13). Vauban walls were also built in Thanh Hoa (1804), Hue (1805) and other Vietnamese towns over the next 30 years (Groslier, op. cit., p. 232).

90 David G. Marr, *Vietnamese Anticolonialism, 1885–1925* (University of California Press, Berkeley, Calif., 1971), p. 23.

91 Tran Quoc Vuong and Nguyen Vinh Long, op. cit., p. 54.

92 Azambre, 1958, op. cit., p. 279.

93 Its official title was *Laws and Decrees of the Empire of Hoan-Viet*. See ibid., p. 300. Azambre characterises the code as 'less an adaptation than a transposition of the Chinese legislation of the Manchu dynasty'.

94 The square was by far the most common ground plan for planned capitals in East Asia, according to Peter J.M. Nas (in P.J.M. Nas (ed), *Urban Symbolism* (E.J. Brill, Leiden, 1993), pp. 1–20.

95 Smith, op. cit., p. 46. Also see Embree, op. cit., p. 32.

96 Benedict Anderson, *Imagined Communities. Reflections of the Origin and Spread of Nationalism* (Verso, London, revised edn, 1991), p. 157.

97 Smith, op. cit., p. 48.

98 For example, in 1406 the Ming emperor had ordered Chinese general Chu Nang to destroy all Vietnamese books and monuments, and the majority of palaces, citadels and cities built in the Ly and Tran dynasties were destroyed (Ngo Huy Quynh, op. cit., vol. 1, pp. 7–8).

99 Woodside, op. cit., pp. 120–21.

100 Jonathan Porter, *Macau: The Imaginary City. Culture and Society, 1557 to the Present* (Westview Press, Boulder, Colo., 1996), p. 27.

101 Truong Vinh Ky, in Honey, op. cit., p. 72.

102 André Masson, *Hanoi pendant la période héroique (1973–1888)* (Librairie Orientaliste Paul Gueuthner, Paris, 1929; translated by Jack A. Yaeger, and edited and abridged by Daniel F. Doeppers as *The Transformation of Hanoi 1873–1888*, Wisconsin Papers on Southeast Asia No. 8, Center for Southeast Asian Studies, University of Wisconsin – Madison, Madison, Wisc., 1983; revised edn, 1987, p. 43).

103 As expressed by Groslier, op. cit., p. 232. See also Loofs, op. cit., p. 3.

104 Dam Trong Phuong, 'Conservation of the Valuable Heritage of Our Hanoi', Paper presented to the Friends of Hanoi Workshop, Hanoi, November 1993 (in Vietnamese).

105 Nguyen Vinh Cat, 'Old Quarters of Hanoi: An S.O.S.', Paper presented to the Friends of Hanoi Workshop, Hanoi, November 1993, p. 3 (in Vietnamese).

106 Masson, op. cit., pp. 46–47.

107 The Cua O Quan Chuong (Quan Chuong Gate) dates from 1749 and was initially called the Porte du Mandarinat or Porte du village Dong-Ha by the French. It was later called Porte Jean Dupuis after the French trader whose foray into Tonkin in 1880 to stake a commercial claim was indemnified by the French government and used as provocation for French military intervention in 1883.

108 H.E. Larsen (ed), *Nara Conference on Authenticity in relation to the World Heritage Convention, November 1–6, 1994, Nara, Japan* (Tapir Publishers, Tronheim, Norway, in association with the UNESCO World Heritage Centre, Tokyo; the Japan Agency for Cultural Affairs, Tokyo; ICRROM, Rome; and ICOMOS, Paris, 1995).

109 Note that, in the last decade, UNESCO and ICOMOS have broadened their outlook by shifting the emphasis from 'site' to 'place' and from 'authenticity' to 'significance'. This is seen, for instance, in the 1999 revision of the Australia ICOMOS *Burra Charter*, a local interpretation of the *Venice Charter*.

119 *Van Mieu Quoc Tu Giam*, op. cit., p. 8.

111 Ibid., pp. 23 and 38.

112 The history of the stelae shelters is unclear. In some accounts, four shelters appear to have existed in the seventeenth century with another four being erected by the Trinh lords in the following century. All eight seem to have been destroyed in the political

conflicts of around 1780 and the stelae were scattered. However, Hoa Bang (op. cit., p. 117) says ten porches were erected in 1484 and destroyed in 1768, a year of great ferment. According to this version, in 1863, in Tu Duc's reign, the mandarin responsible for tax administration in Hanoi, Le Huu Thanh, used monies subscribed by scholars, notables and the general populace to restore the shelters. Two others were built between 1889 and 1907 under the French, but all fell into ruin in the following decades. In the 1960s the stelae were buried in sand and surrounded by a thick concrete wall to protect them from the danger of bombing (*Van Mieu Quoc Tu Giam*, op. cit., p. 23).

Chapter 3: Hanoi: Building a capital for French Indochina

2   Sylviane Leprun and Gilles Aubry, *Interfaces culturelles et project architectural: 'L'architecture à l'exportation'. Phase 1: 1887–1914. Constitution de bases de données* (unpublished report, BRA, MELTM, Ecole d'Architecture Paris-la-Villette, Paris, 1991), p. 54.

2   André Masson, *Hanoi pendant la période héroique (1973–1888)* (Librairie Orientaliste Paul Gueuthner, Paris, 1929; translated by Jack A. Yaeger, edited and abridged by Daniel F. Doeppers, as *The Transformation of Hanoi 1873–1888,* Wisconsin Papers on Southeast Asia No. 8, Center for Southeast Asian Studies, University of Wisconsin – Madison, Madison, Wisc., 1983; revised edn, 1987), pp. 33, 44. See also Hugh Clifford, *Further India, Being the Story of Exploration from the Earliest Times in Burma, Malaya, Siam and Indochina* (Lawrence and Butler, London, 1902), p. 306.

3   Greg Lockhart, *Nation in Arms: The Origins of the People's Army of Vietnam* (Allen & Unwin, Sydney, 1989), p. 30.

4   Truong Vinh Ky, in P.J. Honey (ed), *Voyage to Tongking in the Year At Hoi (by Truong Vinh Ky, 1876)* (School of Oriental and African Studies, University of London, London, 1982), p. 72.

5   Le Vice-Amiral de Marolles, *La Dernière Campagne du Commandant Rivière 1881–1883. Souvenirs du Vice-Amiral de Marolles* (Librairie Plon, Paris, 5th edn, 1932), p. 10. Also Masson, op. cit., p. 65.

6   A third concession and consul were established at the port of Qui Nhon.

7   Le Vice-Amiral de Marolles, op. cit., p. 10.

8   Masson, op. cit., pp. 67–68.

9   Le Vice-Amiral de Marolles, op. cit., p. 81.

10 Charles Meyer, *Les Français en Indochine, 1860–1910* (Hachette, Paris, 1985), pp. 163, 165.

11 Le Vice-Amiral de Marolles, op. cit., p. 65. The French Christian mission in Hanoi had been attacked in May 1883.

12 Ibid., p. 94.

13 Nguyen Quoc Thong, 'Morphological changes in the spatial planning of Hanoi under French colonialism', *Kien Truc*, vol. 31, no. 2, 1988, pp. 40–49 (in Vietnamese).

14 Quoted in Dang Thai Hoang, *Hanoi's Architecture in the Nineteenth and Twentieth Centuries* (Nha Xuat Ban Xay Dung, Hanoi, 1985, 2 vols), p. 8 (in Vietnamese).

15 Fonds des Amiraux et du Gouverneur-Général, Centre des Archives d'Outre-Mer, Aix-en-Provence, file F.110/11,693. *Cession du camp des lettrés à Hanoi pour l'installation de ses troupes; copie de la convention de cession (un plan adjoint). 1875.*

16 Dang Thai Hoang, op. cit., p. 24.

17 Fonds du Résident-Supérieur du Tonkin, National Archives Centre No. 1, Hanoi; file 5370.

18 Georges Dumoutier, *Les pagodes de Hanoi. Étude d'archéologie et d'épigraphie annamites* (Schneider, Hanoi, 1887); cited in Masson, op. cit., p. 74.

19   Lucien de Reinach, *Lettres d'Indochine 1893–1899* (Imprimerie L. Walter, Paris, n.d.),
     p. 22.
20   Ibid., p. 25.
21   Fonds du Gouverneur-Général, Dépôt des Archives d'Outre-Mer, Aix-en-Provence; file
     6347.
22   Documentary sources give a variety of dates for the cathedral's construction. The most
     accurate statement appears to be that of Dr Nguyen Ba Dang, Director of the
     Architectural Research Centre, who gives the construction period as 1883–91 ('Projects to
     be Conserved in the French Quarter', unpublished paper, Architectural Research Centre,
     Hanoi Institute of Architecture, Hanoi, n.d. (in Vietnamese)). Vildieu may have been
     involved, but the cathedral is in neo-Gothic rather than his usual neoclassical style.
23   Paul Doumer, *Situation de l'Indochine (1897–1901). Rapport au Conseil Supérieur de
     l'Indochine (Session extraordinaire de février 1902)* (F.-H. Schneider, Hanoi, 1902), p. 2.
24   Ibid., pp. 3–4.
25   *Les Grands Dossiers de 'L'Illustration'. L'Indochine: Histoire d'un siècle 1843–1944* (Le Livre de
     Paris, Paris, 1987), p. 116.
26   P. Doumer, *L'Indo-Chine française (Souvenirs)* (Vuibert et Nony Editeurs, Paris, 2nd edn,
     1905), p. 26. This is confirmed by Thang Quang, 'The Paul Doumer project and the
     longest bridge in Vietnam: A history of the Long Bien bridge', *The Sunday Vung Tau*, no.
     19, 1991, pp. 4–5, 9 (in Vietnamese).
27   Dang Thai Hoang, op. cit., p. 23.
28   Laurent Weill, 'Travaux publics et colonisation: l'Entreprise Eiffel et la mise en valeur du
     Vietnam (1889–1965)', Paper presented to the Euroviet International Colloquium
     'Vietnam: Sources and Approaches', University of Provence, 1995, p. 6.
29   Ibid., p. 4.
30   Craftsmen under the Nguyen dynasty had had to hide their skills for fear of being
     forcefully transferred to work in the royal workshops in Hue. The French had sought the
     advice of the Tong Doc — the highest Vietnamese bureaucrat in Hanoi, directly
     supervised by the Resident — but decided they were unattractive. Ironically, French
     neglect of the handicraft industries allowed them to blossom freely over the ensuing
     decades.
31   Bernard B. Fall, *The Two Viet-Nams: A Political and Military Analysis* (Frederick A. Praeger,
     New York, revised edn, 1964), pp. 27–30.
32   Ralph Smith, *Vietnam and the West* (Heinemann, London, 1968), p. 55.
33   William J. Duiker, *Vietnam: Nation in Revolution* (Westview Press, Boulder, Colo., 1983),
     p. 29.
34   Jean Noury, *L'Indochine en cartes postales. Avant l'hourigan 1900–1920* (Publi-fusion Editeur,
     Paris, 1992), p. 7.
35   See, for instance, Richard Bernstein, *Fragile Glory: A Portrait of France and the French* (The
     Bodley Head, London, 1991), p. 15.
36   Pham Cao Duong, *Vietnamese Peasants under French Domination, 1861–1945* (Centre for
     Southeast Asia Studies Monograph Series No. 24, University of California, Berkeley, Calif.,
     1985), p. 136.
37   Chantal Descours-Gatin, *Quand l'opium finançait la colonisation en Indochine. L'élaboration de
     la régie générale de l'opium (1860 à 1914)* (Editions Harmattan, Paris, 1992), p. 180.
38   Doumer, op. cit., p. 160. In fact, Yunnan supplied 80 per cent of Tonkin's opium, mostly
     the cheap and medium qualities, while the best quality came from India.
39   Descours-Gatin, op. cit., pp. 22–23.
40   See, for instance, Henry Brenier and Henri Russier, *L'Indochine français* (Armand Colin,
     Paris, 1911), p. 19. Also, Bernard Philippe Groslier, *Indochine. Carrefour des arts* (Editions
     Albin Michel, Paris, 1961), p. 232.

41 Quoted in M. Christine Boyer, *The City of Collective Memory: Its Historical Imagery and Architectural Entertainments* (MIT Press, Cambridge, Mass., 1994), p. 251.

42 Lockhart, op. cit., p. 32.

43 Le Vice-Amiral de Marolles, op. cit., pp. 19–20.

44 Phung Thia, *Hanoi, its Heritage Sites and Landmarks* (Ministry of Information and Cultural Affairs, Hanoi, n.d.) (in Vietnamese); Hoa Bang, op. cit., p. 115.

45 Fonds du Résident-Supérieur du Tonkin, National Archives Centre No. 1, Hanoi; file 58,644.

46 Fonds de la Mairie-Résidence, Service du Cadastre et des Domaines de Hanoi, National Archives Centre No. 1, Hanoi; files F.791, 783.

47 The Chua Bao An was known by various other names: Chua Quan Thuong or Chua Nguyen Dang Giai Pagoda after the extravagant Tong Doc who had built it in 1842. The French referred to it as the Pagode des Supplices (Pagoda of Torments).

48 Masson, op. cit., p. 75.

49 *Tonkin du sud. Hanoi* (Comité de l'Asie Française, Paris, 1907), p. 14.

50 Louis Bézacier, *Relevés de monuments anciens du Nord Viet Nam* (EFEO, Paris, 1959), p. iii.

51 Masson, op. cit., pp. 77, 81.

52 Paul Bonnetain, *Au Tonkin* (Charpentier, Paris, 1887), p. 221 (cited in Masson, op. cit., p. 79).

53 Fonds du Résident-Supérieur du Tonkin, National Archives Centre No. 1, Hanoi; file 5383.

54 Reinach, op. cit., p. 22.

55 Report on 'La colonisation française au Tonkin, 24 Septembre 1898' (quoted in *Les Grands Dossiers de L'Illustration. L'Indochine: Histoire d'un Siècle 1843–1944* (Le Livre de Paris, Paris, 1987), p. 91).

56 Fonds du Résident-Supérieur du Tonkin, National Archives Centre No. 1, Hanoi; file 56,728.

57 Dang Thai Hoang, op. cit., p. 21.

58 Fonds du Résident-Supérieur du Tonkin, National Archives Centre No. 1, Hanoi; files 56,735, 58,806.

59 The term 'Beaux-Arts' is used to identify a way of designing buildings that was usually associated with classical modes of architecture and characterised by a strict adherence to design rules, including symmetry, and the use of ornate decoration. It was also associated with the teaching of the École des Beaux-Arts founded in Paris in 1671 and frequently seen to oppose innovation in architectural design.

60 For example, Christian Pédélahore, 'Hanoi, miroir de l'architecture indochinoise', in Maurice Colet and Jean Marie Thiveaud (eds), *Architecture française outre-mer* (Mardaga, Liege, Belgium, 1992), pp. 292–321.

61 Paul Doumer, *L'Indo-Chine française (Souvenirs)* (Viubert et Nony Editeurs, Paris, 2nd edn, 1905), p. 139.

62 Augustin, op. cit., p. 20.

63 'École Française d'Extrême-Orient', *Exposition Coloniale International Paris, 1931. Indochine Française. Section des Arts.* L'Ecole Française d'Extrême-Orient, Hanoi (Imprimerie d'Extrême-Orient, Hanoi, 1930), pp. 11–12.

64 Fonds du Résident-Supérieur du Tonkin, National Archives Centre No. 1, Hanoi; file 38,438.

65 *Bulletin de l'Ecole Française d'Extrême-Orient* (Imprimerie d'Extrême-Orient, Hanoi, 1926), pp. 525, 546.

66 Ibid., pp. 552–69.

67 Ibid. Also Fonds de la Mairie-Résidence, Service du Cadastre et des Domaines de Hanoi,

National Archives Centre No. 1, Hanoi; files 791, 768. Ngo Huy Quynh, *Understanding Vietnamese Architecture* (Nha Xuat Ban Xay Dung, Hanoi, 1991, 2 vols), vol. 2, p. 44 (in Vietnamese).

68 Tran Ham Tan, 'Étude sur le Van-Mieu de Ha-Noi (Temple de Littérature)', *Journal Asiatique*, vol. 140, pp. 89–95.

69 Georges Maspéro, *L'Indochine. Un empire colonial français* (Les Editions G. van Oest, Paris and Brussels, 1929, 2 vols), vol. 1, p. 49.

70 Henri-Philippe, Duc d'Orléans, *Autour du Tonkin* (Calmann Levy, Paris, 1894), p. 70.

71 Pédélahore, op. cit., p. 296. Louis Hubert Gonzales Lyautey (1854–1934) was in Indochina from 1894 to 1897, commander of the troops and adjoint to Marshall Galliéni. He went with Galliéni to Madagascar in 1897. But his North African postings (Algeria, Morocco) in 1880–87 and 1903–18 saw his main involvement in urban development.

72 See Gwendolyn Wright, *The Politics of Design in French Colonial Urbanism* (University of Chicago Press, Chicago, 1991), for a discussion of Lyautey's role in French colonial planning.

73 See Claude Bourrin, *Le vieux Tonkin. Le théâtre. Le sport. La vie mondaine de 1890 à 1894* (Imprimerie de l'Extrême-Orient, Hanoi, 1941).

74 Meyer, op. cit., p. 211.

75 Christian Pédélahore, 'Constituent elements of Hanoi city (19th–20th centuries)', *Vietnamese Studies*, 12 (New Series), 1986, pp. 105–59.

76 Paul Doumer, *Situation de l'Indochine (1897–1901). Rapport au Conseil Supérieur de l'Indochine (Session extraordinaire de février 1902)* (F.-H. Schneider, Hanoi, 1902), p. 67.

77 *Tonkin du sud. Hanoi,* op. cit., p. 18. Also Pédélahore, op. cit., p. 296.

78 Eugène Brieux, *Voyages aux Indes et Indochine* (Delagrave, Paris, 1910); quoted in Wright, ibid., p. 162.

79 Dang Thai Hoang, op. cit., p. 22.

80 Virginia Thompson, *French Indochina* (Octagon Books, New York, 1968), p. 219. In the 1905 census there were 2,665 French civilians in Hanoi of whom 1,350 were men, 545 women and the remainder children (Andreas Augustin, *Sofitel Metropole Hanoi* (The Most Famous Hotels in the World Ltd, London, 1998), p. 46).

81 Harry Franck, *East of Siam: Ramblings in the Five Divisions of French Indochina* (The Century Company, New York, 1926), p. 210.

82 Ibid., p. 202.

83 Ibid., p. 203.

84 Exposition Internationale Paris 1931, L'Indochine française, Gouvernement Général de l'Indochine, Hanoi.

85 Vice-Amiral de Marolles, op. cit.; Avant Propos.

86 *Les Grands Dossiers de 'L'Illustration'. L'Indochine: Histoire d'un siècle 1843–1944*, pp. 127–28: 'Simples notes d'un touriste 16 juillet 1910'.

87 Henry G. Bryant, 'Travel notes on French Indochina', *Travel and Exploration*, vol. 2, no. 8, August 1909, pp. 65–77.

88 *Bulletin de l'Ecole Française d'Extrême-Orient*, op. cit., 1926, p. 526.

89 Raymond F. Betts, *Assimilation and Association in French Colonial Theory: 1890–1914* (Columbia University Press, New York, 1961), p. 1.

90 Christian Pédélahore, 'Hanoi, miroir de l'architecture indochinoise', in Maurice Colet and Jean Marie Thiveaud (eds), *Architecture française outre-mer* (Mardaga, Liege, Belgium, 1992), pp. 292–321.

91 Wright, op. cit., p. 190.

92 Betts, op. cit., p. 106.

93 Gwendolyn Wright, 'Tradition in the service of modernity: Architecture and urbanism in

French colonial policy, 1900–1930', *Journal of Modern History*, vol. 59, 1987, pp. 291–316; *The Politics of Design in French Colonial Urbanism*, op. cit., 1991. Also Gwendolyn Wright and Paul Rabinow, 'Savoir et pouvoir dans l'urbanisme moderne colonial d'Ernest Hébrard', *Cahiers de la recherche architecturale*, no. 9, January 1982, pp. 26–43.

94   Pédélahore, op. cit., p. 299.

95   Fonds du Résident-Supérieur du Tonkin, National Archives Centre No. 1, Hanoi; file H.3: 58,861.

96   Wright, 'Tradition in the service of modernity: ...', op. cit., p. 292.

97   Giuliano Gresleri and Dario Matteoni, *La Città Mondiale. Anderson, Hébrard, Otlet, Le Corbusier* (Polis/Marsilio Editori, Venice, 1982).

98   Eugène Teston and Maurice Percheron, *L'Indochine moderne. Encyclopédie administrative, touristique, artistique et économique* (Librarie de France, Paris, [c. 1931]), p. 215.

99   Dang Thai Hoang, op. cit., p. 27.

100 The final drawings are held in the Fonds d'Architecture (Kien Truc), box 523, document 13 in the National Archives Centre No. 1, Hanoi. The preliminary drawings are located in the Fonds du Résident-Supérieur; file 32,106 – also in the Hanoi Archives.

101 Pédélahore, op. cit., p. 304.

102 Wright, *The Politics of Design* ..., op. cit., p. 217.

103 Ibid., pp. 2069.

104 Pédélahore, op. cit., pp. 300, 304.

105 Ernest Hébrard, 'L'urbanisme en Indochine', *L'Architecture*, vol. 41, no. 2, 1928, pp. 33–48.

106 Ernest Hébrard, 'L'urbanisme en Indochine', in Jean Royer (ed), *L'Urbanisme aux colonies et dans les pays tropicaux. Communications et rapports du Congrès International de l'Urbanisme aux Colonies et dans les Pays de Latitude Intertropicale* (Delayance, La Charité-sur-Loire, 1932), vol. 1, pp. 278–89.

107 Wright and Rabinow, op. cit., p. 40.

108 Robert Home, *Of Planting and Planning: The Making of British Colonial Cities* (E & FN Spon, London, 1997), p. 135.

109 Hébrard, op. cit., pp. 278–79.

110 Irene Nordlund, 'The French empire, the colonial state in Vietnam and economic policy: 1885–1940', *Australian Economic History Review*, vol. 31, no. 1, 1991, pp. 72–89.

111 Hébrard, op. cit., p. 284.

112 Wright and Rabinow, op. cit., p. 32.

113 Fonds de la Mairie-Résidence, Service du Cadastre et des Domaines de Hanoi, National Archives Centre No. 1, Hanoi; file 4,172.

114 Fonds du Résident-Supérieur du Tonkin, National Archives Centre No. 1, Hanoi; file 79,013.

115 William S. Logan, *Hanoi Planning and Development Control Project Report 3. The Hai Ba Trung Structure Planning Area* (Melbourne, 1995), p. 32.

116 Mai Hang, 'Cultural, Economic, Political Background and Revolutionary Movements in Hanoi during the French Occupation', in Tran Huy Lieu (ed), *History of Hanoi* (Institute of History, Hanoi, 1960) (in Vietnamese).

117 A. Agard, *L'Union Indochinoise Française our Indochine Orientale. Régions naturelles et géographie économique* (Imprimerie d'Extrême-Orient, Hanoi, 1935), p. 265.

118 Greg Lockhart and Monique Lockhart (eds), *The Light of the Capital* (Oxford University Press, Kuala Lumpur, 1995).

119 R.A. O'Connor, *A Theory of Indigenous Southeast Asian Urbanism* (Institute of Southeast Asian Studies, Singapore, 1983), p. vi. See also his extension of the debate in 'Indigenous urbanism, class, city and society in Southeast Asia', *Journal of Southeast Asian Studies*, vol. 26, March 1995, pp. 30–45.

120 Nguyen Duc Nhuan, 'Do the urban and regional policies of socialist Vietnam reflect the

patterns of the ancient mandarin bureaucracy?', *International Journal of Urban and Regional Research*, vol. 8, 1984, pp. 78–89.

121 For example, Nigel Worden, 'Contesting Heritage in a South African City: Cape Town', in Brian J. Shaw and Roy Jones (eds), *Contested Urban Heritage: Voices from the Periphery* (Ashgate, Aldershot, UK, c. 1997). This is also reflected by the establishment in 1999 of a new ICOMOS International Scientific Committee on Shared Colonial Architecture and Town Planning. The ISC is chaired by Frits van Voorden who, like Worden, has a research and practitioner interest in the landscapes shared today by South Africans of many racial and ethnic backgrounds.

122 Gail Ching-Liang Low, 'White Skins/Black Masks', in Erica Carter, Donald James and Judith Squires (eds), *Space and Place: Theories of Identity and Location* (Lawrence and Wishart, London, 1993), p. 243.

123 Truong Buu Lam and Mai Van Lam, *Resistance, Rebellion, Revolution: Popular Movements in Vietnamese History* (Institute of Southeast Asian Studies, Singapore, c. 1984), p. 26.

124 Pierre-Richard Feray, *Le Viet Nam au xxe siècle* (Presses Universitaires de Paris, Paris, 1979), p. 74.

Chapter 4 The Japanese interlude: Vietnamese resistance, French collaboration and collapse

1 David Marr, *Vietnam 1945: The Quest for Power* (University of California Press, Berkeley, Calif., 1995), p. 1.

2 Hanoi Cultural Service, *The Revolutionary Vestiges of Hanoi* (So Van Hoa Hanoi, Hanoi, 1962), p. 4 (in Vietnamese). See also Nguyen Vinh Phuc, *Hanoi Past and Present* (The Gioi Publishers, Hanoi, 1995), pp. 197–98.

3 Huynh Kim Khanh, *Vietnamese Communism, 1925–1945* (Cornell University Press, Ithaca, NY, 1982).

4 Truong Buu Lam, *Resistance, Rebellion, Revolution: Popular Movements in Vietnamese History* (Institute for Southeast Asian Studies, Singapore, 1984), p. 27.

5 Joseph Buttinger, *Vietnam: A Dragon Embattled* (Frederick A. Praeger, New York, 1967), p. vii.

6 Ralph B. Smith, *Viet-Nam and the West* (Heinemann, London, 1968), p. 37.

7 Ibid., p. 99.

8 Hanoi Cultural Service, op. cit., p. 10.

9 Smith, op. cit., p. 106. See also B.B. Fall, *The Two Viet-Nams: A Political and Military Analysis* (Frederick A. Praeger, New York, 1964), p. 61.

10 Sachiko Murakami, *Japan's Thrust into French Indochina: 1940–1945,* unpublished PhD thesis, Department of History, New York University, 1981, p. 96.

11 Ibid., p. 99.

12 Ibid., p. 100.

13 Minami Yoshizawa, 'The Nishihara Mission in Hanoi, July 1940', in Takashi Shiraishi and Motoo Furata (eds), *Indochina in the 1940s and 1950s* (Southeast Asia Program, Cornell University, Ithaca, NY, 1992), vol. 2, pp. 9–54.

14 Masay Shiaishi and Motoo Furuta, 'Two Features of Japan's Indochina Policy during the Pacific War', in Shiraishi and Furata (eds), op. cit., pp. 55–86.

15 Vu Duong Ninh, 'Hanoi – Les journées de 9 mars à 19 août 1945', Paper presented to the International Euroviet Colloquium, University of Provence, France, May 1995, p. 2.

16 Murakami, op. cit., pp. 371, 373.

17 Ibid., p. 378.

18 Yukichika Tabuchi, 'Indochina's Role in Japan's Greater East Asia Co-Prosperity Sphere: A Food-procurement Strategy', in Shiraishi and Furata, op. cit., p. 89.

19 Murakami, op. cit., p. 388.

20 Quoted in Yoshizawa, op. cit., pp. 45–46.

21 Ibid.

22 Interview, Hanoi, 6 June 1992.

23 Murakami, op. cit., p. 384.

24 Fall, op. cit., p. 48.

25 Unlike in Seoul, for instance, the Japanese in Hanoi did not construct major buildings, demolish old ones, or redesign street patterns and historic precincts. See Hae Un Rii, 'Foreign Influences upon the Townscape of Seoul, Korea', in Brian J. Shaw and Roy Jones (eds), *Contested Urban Heritage: Voices from the Periphery* (Ashgate Publishing Ltd, Aldershot, UK, 1997), pp. 156–68.

26 Amiral Decoux, *A la Barre de l'Indochine: Histoire de mon Gouvernement Général (1940–1945)* (Librairie Plon, Paris, 1949), pp. 458–62.

27 H. Guirec, 'Les réalisations dans le plus grand Hanoi', *Indochine. Hebdomadaire illustré*, nos 164–65, 28 October 1942, pp. 47–50.

28 [Henri Cérutti-Maori], 'Les plans de villes et l'aménagement des villes indochinoises', *Indochine, Hebdomadaire Illustré*, nos 164–65, 28 October 1942, pp. 34–35.

29 'L'Indochine du Nord', *Indochine, Hebdomadaire Illustré*, no. 155, 19 August 1943, pp. xxxi–xlvi.

30 Fonds du Résident-Supérieur du Tonkin, National Archives Centre No. 1, Hanoi; file 58,955. Fonds de la Mairie de Hanoi, National Archives Centre No. 1, Hanoi; files 4170, 4171.

31 [Louis-Georges] Pineau, 'Le plus grand Hanoi', *Indochine. Hebdomadaire illustré*, no. 108, 24 September 1942, pp. 5–8.

32 Fonds de la Mairie de Hanoi, op. cit.; file H.35 4,171.

33 Nguyen Quoc Thong, 'Morphological changes in the spatial planning of Hanoi under French colonialism', *Kien Truc*, vol. 31, no. 2, 1988, pp. 40–49 (in Vietnamese).

34 Ngo Huy Quynh, *Understanding the History of Vietnamese Architecture* (Hanoi, Nha Xuat Ban Xay Dung, 1991), p. 157 (in Vietnamese).

35 De Gaulle's 3 December 1942 claim is quoted in *Indochine, terre française* (Ministère de la Guerre, Paris, [1945]).

36 Marr, op. cit., p. 43. See also Ralph B. Smith, 'The Japanese period in Indochina and the coup of 9 March 1945', in *Journal of Southeast Asian Studies*, vol. 9, no. 2, September 1978, pp. 268–301.

37 Marr, op. cit., p. 69.

38 Murakami, op. cit., pp. 512, 535–38.

39 Ibid., p. 539.

40 Vu Duong Ninh, op. cit., p. 1.

41 Marr, op. cit., p. 121. Since the government represented non-communist elitist Vietnamese groups, many of the names they chose were later changed again by Ho's government.

42 Ibid. See also 'Seminar on Vietnam's August 1945 Revolution', Australia Vietnam Science-Technology Link posting, 9 October 1996. Vo Nguyen Giap was honorary president of the Vietnamese Historical Sciences Association at the time of the revolution versus insurrection debate that Marr reports in the posting.

43 Archimedes L.A. Patti, *Why Viet Nam? Prelude to America's Albatross* (University of California Press, Berkeley, Calif., 1980), p. 167.

44 Ibid., p. 164.

45 David G. Marr, 'Ho Chi Minh's Independence Declaration', in K.W. Taylor and J.K.

Whitmore (eds), *Essays into Vietnamese Pasts* (Southeast Asia Program, Cornell University, Ithaca, NY, 1995), pp. 221–31.

46   Philippe Richer incorrectly has Ho delivering his Proclamation of Independence at a meeting in front of the municipal theatre (*Hanoï 1975: Un diplomate et la réunification du Viet-nam* (L'Harmattan, Paris, 1993), p. 58).

47   Marr, op. cit.

48   Ibid., p. 221.

49   *La Guerre en Indochine 1945–1954. Textes et documents* (Service Historique de l'Armée de Terre, Paris, 1987, 2 vols), vol. 1, p. 14. See also Harvey H. Smith et al. (eds), *Area Handbook for North Vietnam* (Department of the Army, Washington, DC, 1967), p. 57.

50   Thomas Hodgkin, *Vietnam: The Revolutionary Path* (St Martin's Press, New York, 1981), p. 2.

51   Murakami, op. cit., p. 483.

52   Fonds de la Mairie de Hanoi, op. cit.; file 3,499. These figures are cited by Vu Duong Ninh (op. cit., p. 5) who says they are incomplete.

53   *La Guerre en Indochine ...*, op. cit., p. 17.

54   Smith et al. (eds), op. cit., p. 58.

55   Fall, op. cit., p. 77.

56   Phuong Anh, 'Glimpses of old Hanoi', *Vietnam Courier*, no. 10, 1982, pp. 13–17.

57   Fonds de la Mairie-Résidence, Service du Cadastre et des Domaines de Hanoi, National Archives Centre No. 1, Hanoi; file M.3/803.

58   Letter from Tham Hoang Tin, Hanoi Mayor, to Résident Supérieur, dated 5 January 1952, in Fonds de la Mairie-Résidence ..., op. cit.; file M.3/801.

59   Suzanne de Saint-Exupéry, 'Où bat le coeur de Hanoï'?, *Indochine Sud-Est Asiatique*, no. 12, November 1952, pp. 19–24.

60   Laurent Weill, 'Travaux publics et colonisation: l'Entreprise Eiffel et la mise en valeur du Vietnam (1889–1965)', Paper presented to the Euroviet International Colloquium 'Vietnam: Sources and Approaches', University of Provence, 1995, p. 5.

61   Dang Thai Hoang, *Hanoi's Architecture in the Nineteenth and Twentieth Centuries* (Nha Xuat Ban Xay Dung, Hanoi, 1985, 2 vols), p. 32 (in Vietnamese).

62   William S. Turley, 'Urbanization in war: Hanoi, 1946–1973', *Pacific Affairs*, vol. 48, pp. 370–97.

63   Ibid., pp. 372, 379.

64   Letter from Tham Hoang Tin, Hanoi Mayor, to Résident Supérieur, dated 5 January 1952, in Fonds de la Mairie-Résidence ..., op. cit; file M.3/801.

65   A. Franck, 'En flânant autour de Hanoi et dans quelques problèmes d'urbanisme', *L'Entente*, 3 March 1953, p. 3.

66   Letter from Tham Hoang Tin, Hanoi Mayor, to Résident Supérieur, dated 5 January 1952, in Fonds de la Marie-Résidence ..., op. cit.; file M.3/801. Agence France Presse also reported on 6 November 1951 that American aid had funded the construction of 140 small houses in Hanoi with electricity and running water, and that a further 200 were to be built 'nearby'. No location is specified. ('Construction des cités populaires au Vietnam', in Fonds Ministériels, Agence Economique de la France d'Outre-Mer, box 236, file 294, *Indochine. Urbanisme: Villes 1918–1954*, Centre des Archives d'Outre-Mer, Aix-en-Provence.)

67   I.M. Shchedrov, *Hanoi* (State Publishing House, Geographic Literature, Moscow, 1961), pp. 51–52.

68   The Indochina Community Party had been voluntarily dissolved in 1945 to placate China supporters and the non-communist Viet Minh alliance partners. Ho was, of course, able to maintain communist dominance through the formation of front organisations.

69   Hanoi Cultural Service, op. cit., pp. 5, 11, 17, 22, 25. Mrs Hai Ve's house in Hanoi's

northern outskirts at Phu Gia hamlet, Tu Liem district, was also memorialised in this way. It was here that the Central Committee operated from 1941 to 1945 and it was last dwelling place of the revolutionary martyr Hoang Van Thu.

70   Tim Larimer, 'Decadence restored in Hanoi', Time Asia, vol. 150, no. 18, 3 November 1997, via http://www.pathfinder.com./asia,decadence_res.html

71   Phil Melling and Jon Roper (eds), America, France and Vietnam: Cultural History and Ideas of Conflict (Avebury, Aldershot, UK, 1991), p. 3.

72   Pham Sy Liem, 'Conservation du patrimoine architectural dans le développement des cités du Vietnam, en particulier des cités riches en patrimoine (Hanoi, Hue ...)', Paper presented to the UNESCO International Seminar 'Urban Policy and the Protection of the Architectural Heritage of Vietnam', Hanoi and Hue, 29 March–2 April 1994, p. 10.

73   Dang Thai Hoang, op. cit., p. 18.

74   Ibid., p. 31.

75   Nguyen Quoc Thong, op. cit., pp. 46, 49.

76   Michael Schudson, 'Dynamics of Distortion in Collective Memory', in Daniel L. Schacter (ed), Memory Distortion: How Minds, Brains, and Societies Construct the Past (Harvard University Press, Cambridge, Mass., 1995), pp. 346–64; p. 349. See also Paul Ricoeur, Contribution to Colloquium 'Mémoire et histoire: pourquoi se souvenir?' (Académie Universelle des Cultures, Paris, 25–26 March 1998).

77   Annabel Biles, Kate Lloyd and William S. Logan, '"Tiger on a bicycle": The growth, character and dilemmas of international tourism in Vietnam', Pacific Tourism Review, vol. 3, no. 1, 1999, pp. 11–23. The number of international visitors (excluding overseas Vietnamese, or Viet kieu) in 1990 was 181,175. This grew to an estimated 1.5 million by 1997. This number includes business travellers as well as tourists.

78   Raymond F. Betts, Assimilation and Association in French Colonial Theory: 1890–1914 (Columbia University Press, New York, 1961), p. 1.

79   Norindr Panivong, Phantasmatic Indochina: French Colonial Ideology in Architecture, Film and Literature (Duke University Press, Durham, NC, 1996), p. 1.

80   Annabel Biles, Kate Lloyd and William S. Logan, 'Romancing Vietnam: The Formation and Function of Tourist Images of Vietnam', in J. Forshee and C. Fink (eds), Converging Interests: Traders, Travelers, and Tourists in Southeast Asia (University of California Press, Berkeley, Calif., 1999), pp. 207–34.

81   Biles, Lloyd and Logan, '"Tiger on a bicycle"...', op. cit. The 'backpacker' or lower end of the tourist market was discouraged because they tended to wander off the usual tourist trails and mix with the local people.

82   Andreas Augustin, Sofitel Metropole Hanoi (The Most Famous Hotels in the World Ltd, London, 1998). See also Denis D. Gray, 'Colonial past turns to gloss', The Age, 31 October 1992.

83   Quoted in Doan Duc Thanh, 'The Metropole Hotel', Kien Truc, vol. 41, no. 3, 1993, pp. 11–12 (in Vietnamese).

84   Fergus T. Maclaren, 'Building Transformation in Hanoi's French Colonial Quarter', unpublished paper, [1993], p. 6.

Chapter 5: Under American bombs: Hanoi during the Vietnam War

1   F. de Quirielle, À Hanoi sous les bombes américaines. Journal d'un diplomate français (1966–1969) (Tallendier, Paris, 1992), p. 124.

2   The various efforts made by Ho Chi Minh to win the United States to its side were discounted by President Harry S. Truman who was more concerned to enlist France's support for the reconstruction of Europe and for the development of a strong NATO to

contain the Soviet Union. See Richard Dean Burns and Milton Leitenberg, *The Wars in Vietnam, Cambodia and Laos, 1945–1982: A Bibliographic Guide* (ABC-Clio Information Services, Santa Barbara, Calif., 1984), p. xx.

3   *Nam: l'histoire vécue de la Guerre du Vietnam. L'engagement* (Éditions Atlas, Paris, 1988), pp. 80–81.

4   Mark Clodfelter, *The Limits of Air Power: The American Bombing of North Vietnam* (The Free Press, New York, 1989), pp. 84–85.

5   De Quirielle, op. cit., pp. 94–96, 98.

6   J.F. Cairns, *The Eagle and the Lotus. Western Intervention in Vietnam 1847–1968* (Lansdowne Press, Melbourne, 1969), p. 150.

7   Quoted in de Quirielle, op. cit., p. 103.

8   John Gerassi, *North Vietnam: A Documentary* (Allen & Unwin, London, 1968), pp. 45, 56. See also Harrison E. Salisbury, *Behind the Lines — Hanoi December 23–January 7* (Secker & Warburg, London, 1967), pp. 66–67.

9   Clodfelter, op. cit., p. 103.

10   Edward Doyle, Samuel Lipsman and Terence Maitland (eds), *The North* (Boston Publishing Co., Boston, Mass., 1986), p. 68. Gerassi, op. cit., pp. 45, 48, 55. Salisbury, op. cit., p. 66.

11   De Quirielle, op. cit., p. 110.

12   The North Vietnamese official statistics are given in Gerassi, op. cit., pp. 40, 48, 55.

13   Salisbury, op. cit., pp. 61–63.

14   Ibid., pp. 64, 209.

15   Ibid., pp. 210, 215.

16   Clodfelter, op. cit., p. 103.

17   De Quirielle, op. cit., p. 114.

18   For details, see Clodfelter, op. cit., pp. 104–6; Doyle et al., op. cit., p. 82; Gerassi, op. cit., p. 44; Zalin Grant, *Over the Beach: The Air War in Vietnam* (W.W. Norton, New York, 1986), pp. 182–87; de Quirielle, op. cit., pp. 119–21; John Morrocco (ed), *Thunder from Above: Air War, 1941–1968* (Boston Publishing Co., Boston, Mass., 1984), pp. 151–57; *Vietnam: Destruction, War Damage* (Foreign Languages Publishing House, Hanoi, 1977).

19   Grant, op. cit., pp. 186–87. The Truc Bach Lake, like the West Lake, was heavily fortified with anti-aircraft guns. It was the Truch Bach battery that shot down the plane piloted by John McCain on 26 October 1967 (Gemma Cruz Araneta, *Hanoi Diary* (self-published, Manila, 1968), p. 15). McCain, now a US senator and unsuccessful contender for the Republic presidential nomination in 2000, was held in the Hoa Lo Prison for five years.

20   Malcolm Salmon, *North Vietnam: First-hand Account of the Blitz* (*Tribune*, Sydney, n.d. [c. 1967]), pp. 4, 6. Salmon had spent the three years 1958–60 in Hanoi, and returned for a short visit in 1967.

21   Clotfelder, op. cit., pp. 112–13. See also de Quirielle, op. cit., p. 125.

22   Mary McCarthy, *Hanoi* (Weidenfeld & Nicolson, London, 1968), pp. 47–48.

23   This is historian Michael Maclear's '1000 days'. See M. Maclear, *Vietnam. The Thousand Day War* (Thames Methuen, London, 1981).

24   *Pentagon Papers*, quoted by Maclear, op. cit., p. 326.

25   Maclear, op. cit., p. 361.

26   William S. Turley, 'Urbanisation in war: Hanoi, 1946–1973', *Pacific Affairs*, vol. 48, 1975, pp. 370–96.

27   This section is an edited version of the longer paper 'Hanoi after the Bombs: Post-war Reconstruction of a Vietnamese City under Socialism', in Sultan Barakat, Jon Calame and Esther Charlesworth (eds), *Urban Triumph or Urban Disaster? Dilemmas of Contemporary Post-War Reconstruction. Report of the Symposium hosted by the Aga Khan Program at MIT,*

Cambridge, Massachusetts, USA, 27–29 September 1996 (The Post-war Reconstruction and Development Unit, The University of York, UK, 1998), pp. 23–40.

28 Kenneth Hewitt, 'Place annihilation: Area bombing and the fate of urban places', *Annals of the Association of American Geographers,* vol. 73, no. 2, 1983, pp. 257–84.

29 Jeffry M. Diefendorf (ed), *Rebuilding Europe's Bombed Cities* (Macmillan, London, 1990), pp. 1–2.

30 Ly Thu Ho, *Au milieu du carrefour (In the Middle of the Crossroads)* (J. Peyronnet et Cie, Paris, 1969).

31 Salmon, op. cit., p. 4.

32 McCarthy, op. cit., p. 48.

33 Maclear, op. cit., p. 325.

34 *Thu Do Ha Noi (Hanoi, Capital City)* (Culture & Information Service, Hanoi, 1984) (in Vietnamese).

35 Harvey H. Smith et al., *Area Handbook for North Vietnam* (Government Printing Office, Washington, DC, 1967), p. 393. The Labour Youth Union had, in turn, been founded in 1931 as the Indochinese Communist Youth League.

36 *Thu Do Ha Noi,* op. cit., p. 48.

37 Kim Anh hamlet was awarded the title of 'Heroes of the People's Military Forces'. Thanh Tri District was the first district whose members were awarded the title 'Heroes of agricultural production' (ibid., pp. 31, 35).

38 McCarthy, op. cit., p. 47.

39 Fonds d'Archives de la Mairie-Résidence, Service du Cadastre et des Domaines de Hanoi; file M.3/804, letter dated 16 May 1952. In addition, the municipal service had approved 785 new low-cost public housing units and major repairs to six police stations, four markets, six schools, the public baths and 120 kilometres of damaged streets.

40 The Vietnamese Communist Party by this stage had developed its decision-making structure down to the local level in both rural and urban areas. The administration of Hanoi took place (and still does) through a hierarchy of Hanoi's People's Committee and lower committees in the *quan* (districts), *phuong* (wards) and *cum* (ward subdivisions). The four districts – Hoan Kiem, Ba Dinh, Hai Ba Trung and Dong Da – were postcolonial in origin, whereas the *phuong* are traditional units, pre-dating the French and originally set up to ensure that the dyke protection and fire-fighting systems were properly maintained. The *phuong* are also the lowest political level in which there are elections for a representative people's committee. At a more local level, people relate to the *cum*, a group of up to about 200 houses, and, finally, to the *to* which comprises about 30 houses. The *to* operate informally as grass-roots entities through which information is passed up to and down from the *phuong* level.

41 Taken from *President Ho Chi Minh's Testament,* dated 10 May 1969 (Central Committee of the Communist Party of Viet Nam, Hanoi, 1995), p. 53.

42 See J. Raffaelli, *Hanoi, capitale de la survie* (Éditions Bernard Grasset, Paris, 1967), pp. 43–44.

43 Smith et al., op. cit., p. 115. Also N.J. Thrift and D.J. Forbes, 'Cities, socialism and war: Hanoi, Saigon and the Vietnamese experience of urbanisation', *Environment and Planning D: Society and Space,* vol. 3, 1985, pp. 279–308; p. 293. Thrift and Forbes, relying heavily on Turley (op. cit.), maintain that the order was given to evacuate Hanoi's children and old residents on 28 February 1965 after major air strikes on other centres in the Democratic Republic of Vietnam earlier in the month. Martin F. Herz ('What Really Happened', in M.F. Herz et al. (eds), *The Prestige Press and the Christmas Bombing: 1972, Images and Reality in Vietnam* (Ethics & Public Policy Centre, Washington, DC, 1980), pp. 54–63) says that two-thirds of the population were evacuated.

44 Smith et al., op. cit., p. 127. Also de Quirielle, op. cit., p. 103.

45 Ibid., p.104. Doyle et al. (op. cit., p. 71) refer to people trying to evade evacuation, but the urban authorities conducted street-by-street censuses and marked each person's record as 'essential' or 'non-essential'. Only the 'essential' were to stay in Hanoi and to receive food; those who did not comply starved.

46 Smith et al., op. cit., pp. 126–27.

47 Ibid., p. 119.

48 Bao Ninh, *The Sorrow of War* (Secker & Warburg, London, 1993), p. 62.

49 Araneta, op. cit., p. 13.

50 Bao Ninh, op. cit., p. 149.

51 Smith et al., op cit., p. 124.

52 De Quirielle, op. cit., p. 84.

53 McCarthy, op. cit., p. 47.

54 Maclear, op. cit., p. 330.

55 Wilfred G. Burchett, *North Vietnam* (Lawrence & Wishart, London, 1966), p. 91. Bao Ninh (op. cit., p. 121) points out that the harshest of these 'frenzied campaigns' was the 'Three Don'ts' that forbade sex, love or marriage among young people.

56 This occurred from June 1966, according to de Quirielle (op. cit., pp. 99–100). He witnessed 50 or so prisoners being marched through Hanoi on 6 July.

57 De Quirielle, op. cit., p. 106. See also the views given by observers Wilfred Burchett (in Maclear, op. cit., p. 329) and Felix Greene (*North Vietnam: A Personal Report*).

58 To Hoai, *Cat Bui Chan Ai (Dust and Sand upon Somebody's Feet)* (Hong Linh Publisher, [Los Angeles], Calif., 1993) (in Vietnamese).

59 Martha Hess, *Then the Americans Came: Voice from Vietnam* (Rutgers University Press, New Brunswick, NJ, 1994), p. 53.

60 Raffaelli, op. cit., p. 41.

61 De Quirielle, op. cit., pp. 78–84.

62 Philippe Richer, *Hanoi 1975: Un diplomate et la réunification du Viet-nam* (L'Harmattan, Paris, 1993), p. 5.

63 De Quirielle, op. cit., pp. 87–88.

64 Ibid., p. 91.

65 McCarthy, op. cit., p. 46.

66 Abraham L. Feinberg, *Rabbi Feinberg's Hanoi Diary* (Longman's Canada, Don Mills, Ont., 1968), p. 229.

67 Araneta, op. cit., p. 21. Araneta was then a Filipino television journalist, was formerly Miss Philippines and Maryknoll BA graduate, and is now Secretary, Department of Tourism, in the current Estrada government of the Philippines.

68 Nguyen Vinh Phuc, *Hanoi Past and Present* (The Gioi Publishers, Hanoi, 1996), p. 195.

69 Herbert Aptheker, *Mission to Hanoi* (International Publishers, New York, 1966), p. 55.

70 McCarthy, op. cit., p. 50.

71 Gerassi, op. cit., p. 55.

72 Daniel Berrigan, *Night Flight to Hanoi. War Diary with 11 Poems* (Collier-Macmillan, New York, 1968), p. 61.

73 *The Economist*, reprinted in *The Australian*, 10 June 1996.

74 Ibid., p. 163.

75 John Morrocco, *Rain of Fire: Air War, 1941–1968* (Boston Publishing Co., Boston, Mass., 1985), p. 138.

76 Ibid., p. 157.

77 Neil Sheehan, *Two Cities: Hanoi and Saigon* (Jonathon Cape, London, 1992), pp. 38–39.

78 Morrocco, op. cit., p. 154.

79 Clotfelder, op. cit., pp. 186–87.

80 'Photos detail heavy damage to North Vietnamese targets by USAF bombing', *Aviation Week and Space Technology*, vol. 98, no. 7, 23 April 1973, pp. 17–24.
81 Turley, op. cit., pp. 386–87. See also *Aviation Week and Space Technology*, op. cit., pp. 17, 21.
82 *Newsweek*, 8 January 1973, p. 9.
83 Hess, op. cit., p. 63.
84 Ibid., p. 67.
85 Sheehan, op. cit., p. 38.
86 Ibid., p. 37. Also Kathleen Gough, *Ten Times More Beautiful: The Rebuilding of Vietnam* (Monthly Review Press, New York and London, 1978), pp. 217–18. Other variations of the 'historic record' include Sheehan's description of the nearby airfield as a helicopter base. John Morrocco (op. cit., p. 157) reconnaissance photos later confirmed that the hospital damage had been caused by a single B-52 that had released its load prematurely. He notes that it was very close to a POL storage facility. Martin F. Herz (op. cit., p. 59) adds that photos show the airfield had been hit as well, the runway being cut in two points and ten support buildings and ten barracks destroyed. De Quirielle (op. cit., p. 124) gives 17 November 1967 as the date the Bach Mai Hospital was bombed. It is unclear whether the hospital was also attacked then or whether de Quirielle's memoirs are incorrect.
87 Hesse, op. cit., p. 74.
88 Morrocco, op. cit., p. 157.
89 Clodfelter, op. cit., p 177.
90 Sheehan, op. cit., p. 40.
91 Robert Hotz, 'B-52s over Hanoi', *Aviation Week and Space Technology*, vol. 98, 12 February 1973, p. 7.
92 Wilfred G. Burchett, *Vietnam. Inside Story of the Guerilla War* (International Publishers, New York, 1965), p. xii. Burchett was accused of acting against Australia's national interests during the Vietnam War and had his passport confiscated. The story of his support for the communist Vietnamese and his fight with the Australian government is told in the film *Public Enemy Number One* (Australian Film Corporation, 1980).
93 Turley, op. cit., p. 387. John Morrocco (op. cit., p. 160) quoted official North Vietnamese sources as putting civilian deaths at 1,318 during Linebacker II. This source (Hanoi's mayor) was also cited by Mark Clodfelter (op. cit., p. 195). These tally with Turley's description of the first report of civilian casualties, figures that were later increased as more complete information came to hand.
94 Hewitt (op. cit., p. 263) lists civilian deaths during World War 2 in Britain, Italy, Germany and Japan as 60,595, 59,796, c. 600,000 and more than 900,000, respectively. The urban areas in these countries destroyed by area bombing were c. 15, c. 100, 333 and 425 square kilometres, respectively, and the number of people rendered homeless ranged from c. 500,000 in Britain to 8.3 million in Japan.
95 Fred Kaplan, 'Vietnam: Stalemate', in F. Kaplan (ed), *The Wizards of Armageddon* (Simon & Schuster, New York, 1984), p. 329.
96 These following figures were made some time after the event – by Nguyen Duc Hanh, head of the War Crimes Investigation Commission in Hanoi, in the late 1980s. They are quoted in Hess, op. cit., p. 60.
97 Turley, op. cit., pp. 388–89.
98 *Hanoi Moi*, 17 January 1973.
99 Thrift and Forbes, op. cit., pp. 287, 291, 293.
100 Turley, op. cit., pp. 377–38.
101 *Vietnam Courier*, no. 10, 1982, p. 18. Much of the increase in the rural population was due to an extension of the municipal boundaries.
102 Thrift and Forbes, op. cit., pp. 293–94.

103 Bao Ninh, op. cit., p. 216.

104 Phil Melling and Jon Roper (eds), *America, France and Vietnam: Cultural History and Ideas of Conflict* (Avebury, Aldershot, UK, 1991), p. 6.

105 Quirielle, op. cit., pp. 9–10.

106 Ibid., pp. 94–95.

107 Martin F. Herz and Leslie Ridler, 'Reporting by the Prestige Press', in Martin F. Herz et al. (eds), *The Prestige Press and the Christmas Bombing: 1972, Images and Reality in Vietnam* (Ethics and Public Policy Centre, Washington, DC, 1980), pp. 15–43; p. 26.

108 Joseph Kraft, 'Letter from Hanoi', *The New Yorker*, 12 August 1972, pp. 58–72; p. 58.

109 *Nam. L'Histoire vécue ...*, op. cit., p. 86.

110 Herz and Ridler, op. cit., p. 22.

111 Gerassi, op. cit., p. 44. Cf. Salisbury, op. cit., p. 65.

112 For example, Daniel Berrigan, S.J., who wrote of a 'monstruous and intentionally genocidal air war' (op. cit., p. 65).

113 Susan Sontag, *Trip to Hanoi* (Farrar, Straus and Giroux, New York, [1968]), p. 58.

114 Robert Hotz, 'Fumbling the facts', *Aviation Week and Space Technology*, vol. 98, 23 April 1973, p. 9.

115 Quoted in M. Clodfelter, op. cit., p. 195, and Herz and Rider, op. cit., p. 58.

116 Melling and Roper (eds), op. cit., p. 4.

117 Maclear, op. cit., p. 427.

118 Bao Ninh, op. cit., p. 138.

Chapter 6: Red River, red city: Creating Hanoi's socialist face

1 Quoted in Irina Chepnukova, 'The history of Soviet architecture', *Soviet Architecture: 1917–1987* (exhibition catalogue) (Art Unlimited Books, Amsterdam, 1989), pp. 5–8. Modern Constructivism gave way to more classical buildings in the 1930s and 1940s, before experiencing a revival in the late 1950s and early 1960s to become the dominant style at the time the Soviet architects were working in Vietnam. See also Alexei Trakhanov and Sergei Kavtaradze, *Stalinist Architecture* (Lawrence King Publishing, London, 1992), p. 16.

2 E. Melnikov, 'Trade Union Cultural Palace in Hanoi', *Arkhitektura SSSR*, no. 2, March–April 1986, pp. 104–7; p. 104 (in Russian).

3 Under the 1955 agreement, the Soviet Union assisted with repairs to thermo-power stations and the railway line from Hanoi towards Moscow, as well as geological surveys in preparation for natural gas, coal and iron ore exploration (Buu Hoan, 'Soviet economic aid to Vietnam', *Contemporary Southeast Asia*, vol. 12, 1991, pp. 360–76).

4 Under the 1958 agreement the port of Haiphong was enlarged, particularly to strengthen the Vietnam–Vladivostock trade route. The agreement required all of Vietnam's foreign trade with the Soviet Union to be carried out on Soviet or Soviet-chartered ships. Many state farms and factories were also established under this agreement (ibid., p. 362).

5 Ibid., p. 364.

6 Ibid., p. 367.

7 A. Kudriavtsev. and A. Krivov, 'Pursuit of Continuity', in C. Cooke and A. Kudriavtsev (eds), *Uses of Tradition in Russian and Soviet Architecture* (London, St Martin's Press, 1987), pp. 46–76.

8 R. Antony French, *Plans, Pragmatism & People: The Legacy of Soviet Planning for Today's Cities* (UCL Press, London, 1995), p. 195.

9 Gérard Tongas, *J'ai vécu dans l'enfer communiste au Nord Viet-Nam* (Nouvelles Éditions Debresse, Paris, 1960), p. 258 (in French).

10 Bui Tam Trung, 'Hanoi today and tomorrow', *Kien Truc*, no. 3, 1984, pp. 9–10.

11 I.M. Shchedrov, *Hanoi* (Geographic Literature, State Publishing House, Moscow, 1961), pp. 32–33.

12 Anthony King has written many works on this theme, but see particularly his chapter, 'Architecture, Capital and the Globalisation of Culture', in Mike Featherstone (ed), *Global Culture: Nationalism, Globalization and Modernity. A Theory, Culture and Society Special Issue* (Sage, London, 1990), vol. 7, pp. 397–411.

13 See, for instance, Roland Robertson, 'Glocalisation: Time-space and Homogeneity-heterogeneity', in M. Featherstone, S. Lash and R. Robertson (eds), *Global Modernities* (Sage, London, 1995), pp. 25–41.

14 King, op. cit., p. 410.

15 See, for instance, Robert Freestone (ed), *Twentieth Century Urban Planning Experience: Proceedings of the International Planning History Conference, University of New South Wales, 15–18 July 1998* (UNSW, Sydney, 1998).

16 Stephen V. Ward, 'Re-examining the International Diffusion of Planning', in Freestone (ed), op. cit., pp. 935–40.

17 Jeffrey W. Cody, 'Private Hands and Public Gloves: Options for Globalising US Planners, 1945–75', in Freestone (ed), op. cit., pp. 95–100.

18 A.T. Polyansky, 'The role of architects in the U.S.S.R.', *Process Architecture*, no. 54, January 1985, special issue on 'Contemporary Soviet architecture', p. 5.

19 Ngo Huy Quynh, *Understanding the History of Vietnamese Architecture* (Nha Xuat Ban Xay Dung, Hanoi, 1991), p. 167 (in Vietnamese).

20 Ibid., p. 160.

21 Dang Thai Hoang, *Hanoi's Architecture in the Nineteenth and Twentieth Centuries* (Nha Xuat Ban Xay Dung, Hanoi, 1985), pp. 33–34 (in Vietnamese).

22 Hoang Ni Tiep, 'The architecture of Hanoi today and tomorrow', *Arkhitektura CCCP* (*Architecture of the USSR*), nos 7–8, 1982, pp. 34–36; p. 36 (in Russian).

23 P. Prikhodko, 'Progressive features in the architecture of Vietnam', *Stroitelstvo i arkhitektura* (Kiev), no. 7, 1965, pp. 35–50 (in Russian).

24 Interview with Dr Arch. Hoang Dao Kinh, Hanoi, 4 December 1995.

25 North Vietnamese development planning began with two three-year plans — 1955–57 and 1957–59 — and continued with the first five-year plan in 1960. The second five-year plan started in 1965 but was abandoned because of the United States' bombing in 1966. Until the ceasefire in 1974, the country followed a series of one-year plans. The two-year plan of 1974 was replaced in 1975 by a new series of five-year plans. See A.D. Cao, 'Development planning in Vietnam: A problem of postwar transition', *Asia Quarterly*, vol. 4, 1978, pp. 265–76.

26 'The Polytechnical Institute in Hanoi City, DRV', *Gyporovuz*, no. 2, 1967.

27 Mary McCarthy, *Hanoi* (Weidenfeld & Nicolson, London, 1968), p. 47.

28 *Far Eastern Economic Review*, 'Vietnam — North', *Asia 1976 Yearbook* (FEER, Hong Kong, 1976), pp. 315–20.

29 Ibid., p. 318.

30 Bogdan Szajkowski, *Marxist Governments: A World Survey* (Macmillan, London, 1981),vol. 3, p. 721.

31 Dao Van Tap, 'On the transformation and new distribution of population centres in the socialist republic of Vietnam', *International Journal of Urban and Regional Research*, vol. 4, 1980, pp. 503–15.

32 Dang Thai Hoang, op. cit., p. 34.

33 Anatoli A. Sokolov ('Comintern and Vietnam: The Training of Vietnamese Political Cadres in the Soviet Communist Universities, 1920s–1930s' (Historical and Political Essay), Institute of Oriental Studies, Russian Academy of Sciences, Moscow, 1998 (in Russian)

outlines the early educational contacts that took place between Vietnam and the Soviet Union. These were within the framework of Comintern and were related to the training of revolutionary youth. The graduates, who included Ho Chi Minh, formed the basis of the political elite that introduced and implemented communist ideas in Vietnam.

34 Buu Hoan, op. cit., pp. 367–68.

35 R.A. Longmire, *Soviet Relations with Southeast Asia: An Historical Survey* (London, Kegan Paul International, 1989), p. 131.

36 P. Prikhodko, 'The first brigade of young Vietnamese architects', *Stroitelstvo i arkhitektura* (Kiev), no. 8, 1966, pp. 36–40 (in Russian); Dang Thai Hoang, op. cit., part 3.

37 Ibid., p. 49.

38 Prikhodko, op. cit.

39 Anatoli A. Sokolov, *Curriculum Vitae, Garold Grigorievich Isakovich* (unpublished document, Moscow, 1997). Sometimes Isakovich is given the first name of Garony.

40 The information about these architects was obtained during interviews conducted in Moscow by Anatoli A. Sokolov and myself in September–November 1996 (N.D. Sulimova, I.G. Zabolotskaya, S.I. Sokolov, K.S. Shehoian) and from written questionnaires administered by A. Sokolov in June–November 1996 (V.I. Reviakin, A.A. Kanyghin).

41 Interview with Natalia Dmitrievna Sulimova, Moscow, 9 October 1996.

42 Interview with Dr Arch. Hoang Dao Kinh, Hanoi, 4 December 1995.

43 Interview with Dr Hoang Dao Kinh, Hanoi, 4 December 1995.

44 Dang Thai Hoang, op. cit., pp. 35–36.

45 Sokolov, op. cit.

46 The term 'mausoleum', meaning an elaborate funerary monument having the dimensions of a building and usually erected for a person of distinction, is derived from the tomb of Mausolus, King of Caria, erected in the mid-fourth century at Halicarnassus by his wife Artemisia (*Oxford English Dictionary*).

47 Dang Thai Hoang, op. cit., p. 66.

48 The following story of the negotiations between the Russian and Vietnamese architects is given in Nguyen Ngoc Chan, 'The process of designing the Ho Chi Minh mausoleum', *Kien Truc*, vol. 27, no. 1, 1990, pp. 13–23 (in Vietnamese).

49 Interview with Mr Vladimir Ivanovich Reviakin, Moscow, December 1995.

50 Nguyen Truc Luyen, 'The Ho Chi Minh Museum in Ba Dinh Square', *Kien Truc*, vol. 27, no. 1, 1990, pp. 19–23 (in Vietnamese).

51 Interview with Mr Vladimir Ivanovich Reviakin, Moscow, December 1995.

52 F. Guilbert, 'Viet Nam and perestroika', *The Pacific Review*, vol. 3, 1990, pp. 272–74.

53 Other members included L. Krikuov, E. Lech and G. Sulimova (Melnikov, op. cit., p. 104).

54 Ibid., p. 107.

55 A.V. Ryabushin, 'Soviet architecture of the seventies and eighties', *Process Architecture*, no. 54, January 1985, pp. 9–28.

56 Kudriavtsev and Krikov, op. cit.

57 *Process Architecture*, no. 54, January 1985, p. 4; Polyansky, op. cit., p. 6.

58 Ryabushin, op. cit., p. 13.

59 Dang Thai Hoang, op. cit., p. 46.

60 Ibid., p. 37.

61 Ibid., p. 42.

62 Ibid., p. 38.

63 Nguyen The Ba, 'Urban residential quarters', *Kien Truc*, nos 3–4, 1988, pp. 21–24 (in Vietnamese); Tran Hung, 'Residential quarters and streets', *Kien Truc*, no. 3, 1989, pp. 26–27 (in Vietnamese).

64 Han Tat Ngan, 'The residential quarter reconsidered', *Kien Truc*, no. 2, 1994, pp. 22–23 (in Vietnamese).

65 Ibid., p. 22.

66 M. Beresford, 'Issues in Economic Unification: Overcoming the Legacy of Separation', in D.G. Marr and C.P. White (eds), *Postwar Vietnam: Dilemmas in Socialist Development* (Cornell South East Asia Program, Ithaca, NY, 1988), p. 101.

67 Editorial comment, *Vietnam Courier*, vol. 18, no. 10, 1982, p. 2.

68 Dang Thai Hoang, op. cit., p. 40.

69 A. Kopp, *L'architecture de la période stalinienne* (Presses Universitaires de Grenoble, Grenoble, 1985), p. 151. Earlier the Soviet planners had called on Le Corbusier to design the new socialist Moscow, but his 1930 proposal was rejected (ibid., p. 146).

70 Ryabushin, op. cit., p. 12.

71 N. Agafonov et al., 'The Course of Development of Socio-economic Geography in the USSR', in N. Agofonov et al. (eds), *Soviet Geography Today. Social and Economic Geography* (Progress Publishers, Moscow, 1984), pp. 5–15.

72 Lam Quang Cuong, 'Hanoi. Forty Years of Planning' (unpublished paper, n.d.), p. 1.

73 Dang Thai Hoang, op. cit., p. 47; Hoang Huu Phe and Y. Nishimura, *The Historical Environment and Housing Conditions in the '36 Old Streets' Quarter of Hanoi. A Conservation Study* (Division of Human Settlements Development, Asian Institute of Technology, Bangkok, HSD Research Report No. 23, 1990), p. 5.

74 Literally the Leningrad Scientific Research Centre for Town Planning and Construction. The Institute appears to no longer exist. For details of this plan, see S.I. Sokolov, 'Town on the Red River: In Leningrad a general plan has been formulated for the development of the capital of Vietnam', *Leningradskaya Panorama*, no. 8, August 1983, pp. 26–29 (in Russian). Also published as 'General plan of Hanoi', *Architecture of the USSR*, no. 3, May–June 1984, pp. 106–9 (in Russian). The team included M.G. Vasilyeva, N.V. Romniuk, A. Shelekhov, L.I. Syrnikov and S.N. Samonina (A. Kucher, 'Hanoi horizons, according to our project', *Leningradskaya Pravda,* 15 July 1980 (in Russian)).

75 Ibid.

76 The Noi Bai Airport terminal was constructed in the 1980s. In 1990, when the author first visited Hanoi, it was still little more than a dingy shed, with conveyor belts unable to handle the suitcases from a single plane, and customs declaration forms in Vietnamese and Russian only.

77 Hoang Huu Phe and Nishimura, op. cit., p. 5.

78 Kudriavtsev and Krivov, op. cit., p. 71.

79 Ngo Huy Quynh, op. cit., vol. 2, p. 160.

80 David G. Marr, *Vietnamese Anticolonialism, 1885–1925* (University of California Press, Berkeley, Calif., 1971), p. 3.

81 Longmire, op. cit., p. 132.

82 Guilbert, op. cit., pp. 272–74.

83 Longmire, op. cit., p. 136.

84 Than, Gabriel Thien, 'Vietnam: vivre en ville aujourd'hui', *Habitat. Revue de l'habitat social,* no. 97, June 1984, pp. 75–85.

85 Palazzoli, op. cit., p. 17.

86 J. le Boutillier, *Vietnam Now: A Case for Normalising Relations with Hanoi* (Praeger, Westport, Conn., 1989), p. 2.

87 W. Shawcross, 'The people of the two Vietnams', *New Society*, 8 October 1981, pp. 56–59. This was corroborated by Pike, who found that many Vietnamese regarded the Soviet presence with a malicious disdain, referring to them as 'our latest barbarians' (D.F. Pike, *Vietnam and the Soviet Union: Anatomy of an Alliance* (Westview Press, Boulder, Colo., 1987), p. 246).

88 M. Yeong, 'New thinking in Vietnamese foreign policy', *Contemporary Southeast Asia*, vol. 14, 1992, pp. 257–68.

89   R. Thakur and C.A. Thayer, *Soviet Relations with India and Vietnam* (Macmillan, London, 1992), p. 24.

Chapter 7: Doi moi and the return of capitalism: Hanoi in the 1990s

1   See W.S. Logan, 'The Angel of Dien Bien Phu: Making the Australia–Vietnam Relationship 1955–1995', in M. McGillivray and G. Smith (eds), *Australia and Asia* (Oxford University Press, Melbourne, 1997), pp. 178–202.

2   Vietnamese Architects' Association, 'Residential architecture and construction by individual resident investors', *Kien Truc*, vol. 32, no. 2, 1991, pp. 17–22 (in Vietnamese).

3   K. Huus, 'Boom and busted', *Far Eastern Economic Review*, 13 April 1995, p. 48.

4   *The Economist*, 7 January 1995.

5   René Parenteau, 'Impacts de la privatisation du logement public dans certains îlots du Quartier colonial français', in René Parenteau and Luc Champagne (eds), *La Conservation des quartiers historiques en Indochine. Actes du Séminaire Régional (Viet-nam, Laos, Cambodge) tenu à Hanoi, Viet-nam, du 23 au 27 mai 1994* (Éditions Karthala, Paris, 1997), p. 112.

6   Trinh Duy Luan, 'Hanoi: Balancing Market and Ideology', in Won Bae Kim et al. (eds), *Culture and the City in East Asia* (Clarendon Press, Oxford, 1997), pp. 167–84.

7   As reported by Agence France Presse, 8 September 1993.

8   *Viet Nam News*, 29 June 1998, via *vnforum* http://home.vnd.net/english/news/news.html.

9   Dang Thai Hoang, 'Socially-oriented building projects for Hanoi', *Nhan Dan* (newspaper), 7 October 1994, p. 3 (in Vietnamese).

10   Quoted in Do Quang Hanh, 'Meeting with Nguyen Vinh Phuc, an expert in Hanoi studies', *Lao Dong* (newspaper), 6 October 1994 (in Vietnamese).

11   In 1992, the decision by the United States to end its veto on loans to Vietnam by the World Bank, Asian Development Bank and International Monetary Fund was followed by the withdrawal of the American government's prohibition of American firms tendering for non-governmental contracts in Vietnam and, finally, to the complete abandonment of the embargo on 3 February 1994.

12   For example, see Han Tat Ngan, 'Dialectical structures in urban planning', *Kien Truc*, nos 3–4, 1988, pp. 25–30 (in Vietnamese); also Nguyen Tha Ba, 'Urban residential quarters', *Kien truc*, nos 3–4, pp. 21–24 (in Vietnamese).

13   Dang Thai Hoang, 'The construction of office buildings in Hanoi', *Kien Truc*, no. 37, 1992, pp. 21–22 (in Vietnamese).

14   Nguyen Truc Luyen, 'The Ho Chi Minh Museum on Ba Dinh Square', *Kien Truc*, vol. 27, no. 1, 1990, pp. 19–23 (in Vietnamese).

15   W.S. Logan, 'Hanoi Townscape: Symbolic Imagery in Vietnam's Capital', in M. Askew and W.S. Logan (eds), *Cultural Identity and Urban Change in Southeast Asia: Interpretative Essays* (Deakin University Press, Geelong, Vic., 1994), pp. 43–69.

16   Nguyen Ngoc Khoi, 'Building management in Hanoi', *Kien Truc*, vol. 35, no. 1, 1992, pp. 17–18 (in Vietnamese).

17   The Chief Architect is the senior planner for the city responsible for the preparation and implementation of Hanoi's master plan and detailed plans. Before 1993 the NIURP was in charge of master planning for the capital and other major cities.

18   Nguyen Ngoc Khoi, op. cit. Nguyen Lan, 'On improving urban planning', *Kien Truc*, vol. 30, no. 4, 1990, pp. 29–30 (in Vietnamese).

19   Phan Ham, 'Is this the way to build Hanoi?, *Kien Truc*, vol. 34, no. 4, 1991, p. 29 (in Vietnamese).

20 See also Vietnamese Architects' Association, 'Residential architecture and construction by individual resident investors', *Kien Truc*, vol. 32, no. 2, 1991, 17–22 (in Vietnamese).

21 P. Prikhodko, 'Progressive features in the architecture of Vietnam', *Stroitelstvo i arkhitektura* (Kiev), no. 7, 1965, pp. 35–50 (in Russian).

22 C. Palazzoli, *Le Viet Nam entre deux mythes* (Economica, Paris, 1981), p. 4.

23 Tran Hung, 'Residential quarters and streets', *Kien Truc*, no. 3, 1989, pp. 26–27.

24 I.M. Shchedrov, *Hanoi* (Geographic Literature, State Publishing House, Moscow, 1961), p. 35 (in Russian).

25 Ngo The Thi, 'Tranforming hazardous enterprises and sectors in the Thuong Dinh industrial area', *Kien Truc*, no. 1, 1991, pp. 26–32.

26 Nguyen Ba Dang, 'Preservation of the French colonial quarter in Hanoi', *Kien Truc Viet Nam*, no. 1, 1994, pp. 16–20.

27 Annabel Biles, Kate Lloyd and William S. Logan, 'Romancing Vietnam: The Formation and Function of Tourist Images of Vietnam', in J. Forshee and C. Fink (eds), *Converging Interests: Traders, Travelers, and Tourists in Southeast Asia* (University of California Press, Berkeley, Calif., 1999), pp. 207–34.

28 Annabel Biles, Kate Lloyd and William S. Logan, '"Tiger on a bicycle": The growth, character and dilemmas of international tourism in Vietnam', *Pacific Tourism Review*, vol. 3, no. 1, 1999, pp. 11–23.

29 Quoted in 'Building blocks. Where is the Vietnamese identity in the new architecture?', *Heritage*, Vietnam Airlines in-flight magazine, January/February 1996, pp. 27–30.

30 The 15,000 apartments in 350 four- or five-storey blocks made of cement-panels are still fully occupied, but their foundations are subsiding seriously (Hanh Dung, op. cit., p. 23).

31 *Vietnam News* on-line, 25 February 1998.

32 *vnforum* on-line, 12 March 1999.

33 Interview with Dr Hoang Dao Kinh, Hanoi, 4 December 1995.

34 James Button, 'Battle for the streets', *Time*, 18 April 1994, pp. 32–33.

35 Russell Agle, 'Wait for it: Foreign contractors have been losing the battle to meet construction deadlines', *Vietnam Economic Times*, January 1998, pp. 24–25.

36 *Xua vang Nay* (*Past and Present*), February 1997, pp. 18–19; *Vietnam Courier*, 18–24 August 1996.

37 Ibid.

38 Nguyen Manh Hung, 'Grand opera', *Vietnam Economic Times*, January 1999, pp. 22–23.

39 Ngo Quang Nam, 'The Issue of the Space Environment', Paper presented to the 'Developing Whilst Preserving Hanoi' Workshop, Friends of Hanoi, Hanoi, November 1993, p. 2.

40 Quoted in Murray Hiebert, 'Going down the tubes. Will new money destroy buildings the bombers spared?', *Far Eastern Economic Review*, 8 August 1991, pp. 44–45.

41 Nguyen Huy Bay, 'L'Arrondissement Hoan Kiem avec ses "rues antiques"', Paper presented to the UNESCO/Governments of France and Vietnam symposium 'Politique urbaine et protection du patrimoine architectural du Vietnam', Hanoi and Hue, March–April 1994.

42 Quoted in F. Gibney, 'Saving Hanoi from itself', *Time*, 16 April 1995.

43 Quoted in Denis D. Gray, 'Saving old Hanoi', *Kien Truc*, no. 6, 1993, pp. 21–22.

44 Hoan Van Nghien built up Vietnam's biggest electronics conglomerate, Hanel.

45 Nguyen Lan, 'Interview given by Mr Nguyen Lan, Chief Architect of Hanoi City', *Kien Truc*, vol. 41, 1993, pp. 21–22.

46 Fergus T. Maclaren, *The French Colonial Quarter in Hanoi, Vietnam: A Preservation Approach*, unpublished Master of Environmental Design (Planning) thesis, University of Calgary, 1995, p. 66.

47 Giang Minh, 'Ha Noi sees red as its "green lungs" are choked by squatters', *Viet Nam News*, 11 January 2000, p. 5.

48 Pham Sy Liem, 'Conservation du Patrimoine Architectural dans le Développement des Cités du Vietnam, en particulier des Cités Riches en Patrimonie', Paper presented to the UNESCO International Seminar 'Urban Policy and the Protection of the Architectural Heritage of Vietnam', Hanoi and Hue, 29 March–2 April 1994.

49 'Mr Vo Van Kiet's meeting with the cultural-artistic associations', *Kien Truc*, no. 3, 1992, pp. 16–17.

50 David Lamb, 'Vietnam's open door now exit for investors', *Los Angeles Times*, 25 December 1998.

51 John Mant, 'Commentary', Paper presented to the 'Developing Whilst Preserving Hanoi' Workshop, Friends of Hanoi, Hanoi, November 1993, p. 1.

52 W.S. Logan, *Planning for the Protection of the Old Sector of Hanoi City, Socialist Republic of Vietnam. Report to UNESCO and National Institute of Urban and Rural Planning, Ministry of Construction, Socialist Republic of Vietnam* (UNESCO, Paris, 1990).

53 The AusAID project is discussed in W.S. Logan, 'Protecting "historical Hanoi" in a context of heritage contestation', *International Journal of Heritage Studies*, vol. 2, nos 1–2, Spring 1996, pp. 76–92.

54 Nguyen Ngoc Khoi, 'Plan for Protecting, Preserving and Developing the Ancient Quarter of Hanoi', Paper presented to the 'Developing Whilst Preserving Hanoi' Workshop, Friends of Hanoi, Hanoi, November 1993.

55 Quoted in Dam Hai Van, 'Scraping the sky', *The Saigon Times Weekly*, 16 January 1999, p. 31.

56 Ibid.

57 Official Dispatch 690/CP-KTN. See *Vietnam News*, 22 and 30 June 1998.

58 Quoted in Adam Schwarz, 'Permission slips', *Far Eastern Economic Review*, 13 April 1995, pp. 46–48.

59 Ibid.

60 Promulgated in conjunction with Decision No. 3234 QD/UB issued by the Hanoi Municipal People's Committee on 30 August 1993. See Gillespie and Logan, op. cit., for discussion.

61 Nguyen Lan, 'Conservation and Management of the Architectural Heritage in Hanoi', Paper presented to the 'Developing Whilst Preserving Hanoi' Workshop, Friends of Hanoi, Hanoi, November 1993, p. 3.

62 Thanh Ha, 'Tougher measures to save Old Hanoi', *Vietnam Investment Review*, no. 15, 1995, p. 21.

63 'Building blocks. Where is the Vietnamese identity in the new architecture?', *Heritage*, Vietnam Airlines in-flight magazine, January/February 1996, pp. 27–30.

64 Interview with Dr Nguyen Ba Dang, Director of the Architectural Research Institute, Hanoi, 18 April 1995.

65 'Adjustment for Ha Noi's master plan', *Vietnam News*, 22 December 1998, p. 3.

66 Decision 45/1999/QD-UB, 4 June 1999.

67 'New regulation to preserve old quarter of Ha Noi', *vnforum* on-line, 21 June 1999.

68 Trinh Duy Luan, op. cit., pp. 178–79.

69 Quoted in Don Pathan, 'No consensus in Hanoi's new look', *The Australian*, 28 July 1997.

70 Ibid.

71 Ibid.

72 Interviews with Dr Nguyen Ba Dang, Director of the National Architectural Research Institute, Hanoi, 18 and 19 April 1995.

73 For example, see the highly critical speech by Deputy Prime Minister Ngo Xuan Loc (via *vnforum* on-line, 15 March 1999).

74 'Plans to mark 1,000 years of Thang Long', *vnforum* on-line, 29 June 1999.

Chapter 8: Creeping pluralism: Hanoi faces the new millennium

1   New land laws were enacted in 1988 and 1989, housing laws in 1991, and town planning laws in 1992. While the State remains owner of all lands in Vietnam, the occupants of land have been given a 'land-use right' which can be bought and sold, bequeathed and inherited, and used as the basis of raising mortgages. See John Gillespie and William S. Logan, 'Heritage planning in Hanoi', *The Australian Planner*, vol. 32, no. 2, 1995, pp. 96-108.

2   For example, see the 1992 survey reported by Trinh Duy Luan, 'Hanoi: Balancing Market and Ideology', in Won Bae Kim et al. (eds), *Culture and the City in East Asia* (Clarendon Press, Oxford, 1997), pp. 167-84.

3   Significant steps towards democratisation include the possibility of independent candidates standing for national and municipal elections and the symbolic downgrading of the Vietnamese Communist Party in the new Constitution of 1992. See Carlyle A. Thayer, 'Recent Political Development: Constitutional Change and the 1992 Elections', in C.A. Thayer and D.G. Marr (eds), *Vietnam and the Rule of Law* (Research School of Pacific Studies, Australian National University, Canberra, Political and Social Change Monograph No. 19, 1993), pp. 50-80.

4   'Hanoi struggles to fill void left by foreign investors', *VNA*, 10 February 2000, via vnforum@saigon.com.

5   Stephanie Fahey, 'Vietnam: "Pivotal Year"?', in D. Singh (ed), *Southeast Asian Affairs 1994* (Institute of Southeast Asian Studies, Singapore, 1994), pp. 337-50. The Vice-Prime Minister, Nguyen Khanh, revealed the government's very considerable concern at the perceived loss of human values − that is, the growing Western impact on the local culture − in his opening address to the UNESCO seminar in Hanoi, 29 March 1994.

6   See Huw Watkin, 'Vice war in high places', *The Australian*, 6 July 1999.

7   Adam Schwarz, 'Bonfire of vanities', *Far Eastern Economic Review*, 7 March 1996.

8   See *Our Creative Diversity. Report of the World Commission on Culture and Development* (UNESCO, Paris, 1995).

9   Doreen Massey, 'A global sense of place', *Marxism Today*, June 1991, pp. 24-29.

10 Erica Carter, James Donald and Judith Squires, *Space and Place: Theories of Identity and Location* (Lawrence & Wishart, London, 1993), p. viii.

11 Roland Robertson, *Globalisation: Social Theory and Global Culture* (Sage, London, 1992).

12 Carlyle Thayer, quoted in Huw Watkin, 'Trying La Vida Loca', *The Australian*, 22 July 1999.

13 H. Tran and Q.T. Nguyen, *Thang Long — Hanoi: Ten Centuries of Urbanisation* (Construction Publishing House, Hanoi, 1995), p. 167.

14 This apparent re-entry of the State into housing provision recognises that public tolerance of current housing conditions is wearing thin. Currently, one-third of Hanoi's population live in an area of three square metres per person (Hanh Dung, 'Flat plan: Investors aren't interested in the government's housing initiatives', *Vietnam Economic Times*, September 1998, p. 23). It has been decided to aim at increasing per capita residential floor space in Hanoi to an average eight square metres by 2010 by creating up to two million square metres of new housing (*Viet Nam News*, 14 and 29 May 1998, via *vnforum* http://home.vnd.net/english/news/news.html).

15 On the need for closer links between urban planning practice and heritage protection, see William S. Logan, 'Sustainable cultural heritage tourism in Vietnamese cities: The case of Hanoi', *Journal of Viet Nam Studies*, vol. 1, no. 1, 1998, pp. 32-40.

16 The best local statement of the key elements of the Hanoi heritage is the paper given to a 1994 conference by Dao Quoc Hung, Hoang Dao Kinh, Dang Thai Hoang and Tran Hung, 'Le patrimoine architectural de Hanoi'. This may be found in René Parenteau and Luc Champagne (eds), *La Conservation des quartiers historiques en Indochine. Actes du Séminaire Régional (Viet-nam, Laos, Cambodge) tenu à Hanoi, Viet-nam, du 23 au 27 mai 1994* (Éditions Karthala, Paris, 1997), pp. 75–79.

17 Information provided by the Australian Embassy, Hanoi, 27 January 2000.

18 Van Quan – Duc Dung, 'Can we allow a great national spirit to fade away? Ho Guon [Hoan Kiem] is under threat of destruction', *The Saigon Times*, 13–19 July 1996, p. 30.

19 Interview with Ha Van Que, Hanoi, 17 January 2000.

20 Quoted in 'Building blocks. Where is the Vietnamese identity in the new architecture?', *Heritage*, Vietnam Airlines in-flight magazine, January/February 1996, pp. 27–30.

21 Susan Balderstone, *Hanoi. Conservation of the Ancient Quarter* (unpublished AusAID/OPCV Report, November 1994), p. 4.

22 Hanoi People's Committee, 'Recommendation on Recognition of Hanoi City as Heritage of World Culture', Paper presented to the UNESCO International Seminar 'Urban Policy and the Protection of the Architectural Heritage of Vietnam', Hanoi and Hue, 29 March–2 April 1994.

23 Hoang Dao Kinh, 'Les valeurs de l'héritage urbain et architectural de Hanoi', Paper presented to the UNESCO International Seminar 'Urban Policy and the Protection of the Architectural Heritage of Vietnam', Hanoi and Hue, 29 March–2 April 1994.

INDEX

Page numbers in *italics* refer to photographs and other illustrations.